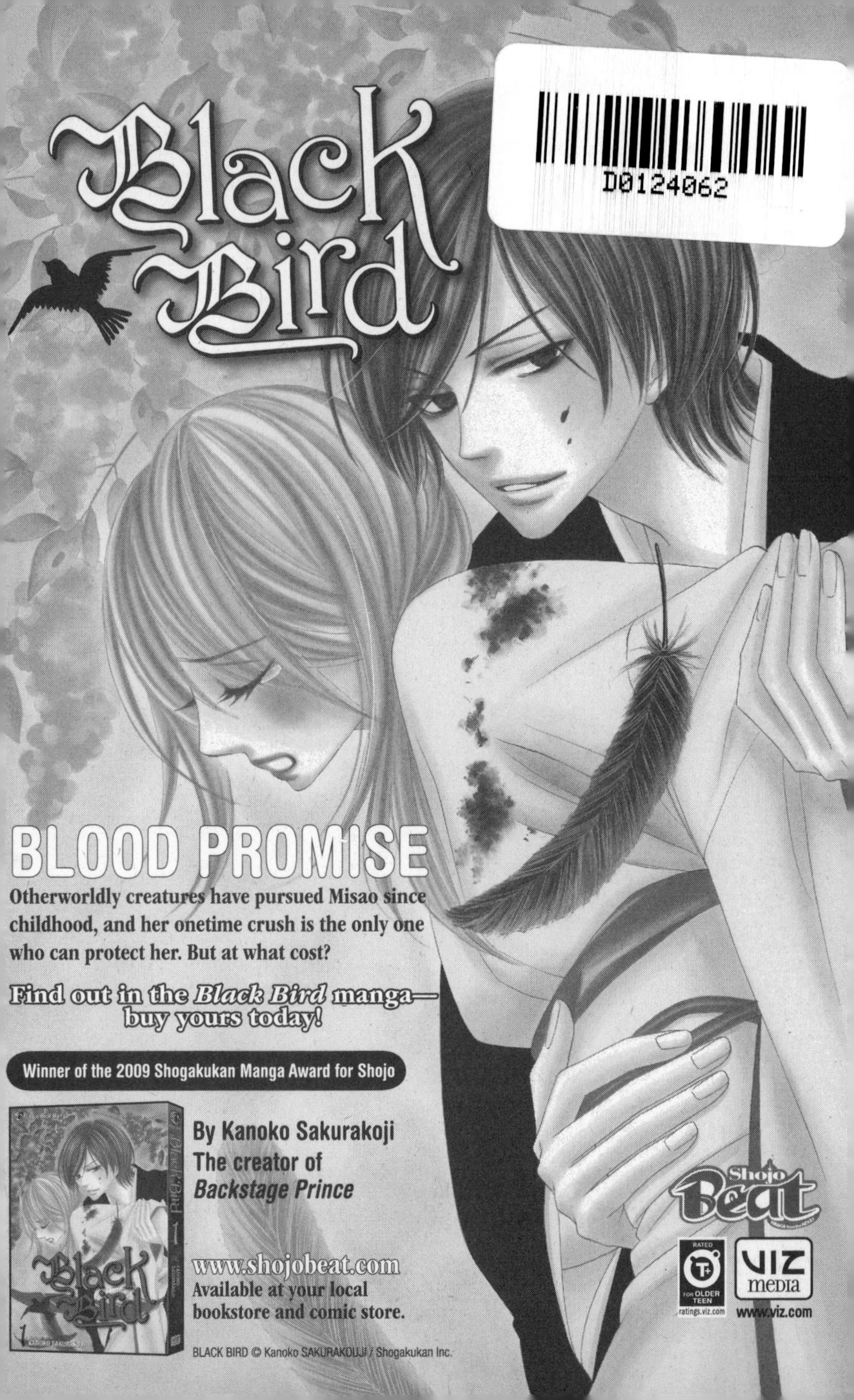
D0124062
Black Bird
BLOOD PROMISE
Otherworldly creatures have pursued Misao since childhood, and her onetime crush is the only one who can protect her. But at what cost?
Find out in the Black Bird manga—buy yours today!
Winner of the 2009 Shogakukan Manga Award for Shojo
By Kanoko Sakurakoji
The creator of Backstage Prince
www.shojobeat.com
Available at your local bookstore and comic store.
Shojo Beat
RATED T+ FOR OLDER TEEN
ratings.viz.com
VIZ media
www.viz.com
BLACK BIRD © Kanoko SAKURAKOUJI / Shogakukan Inc.

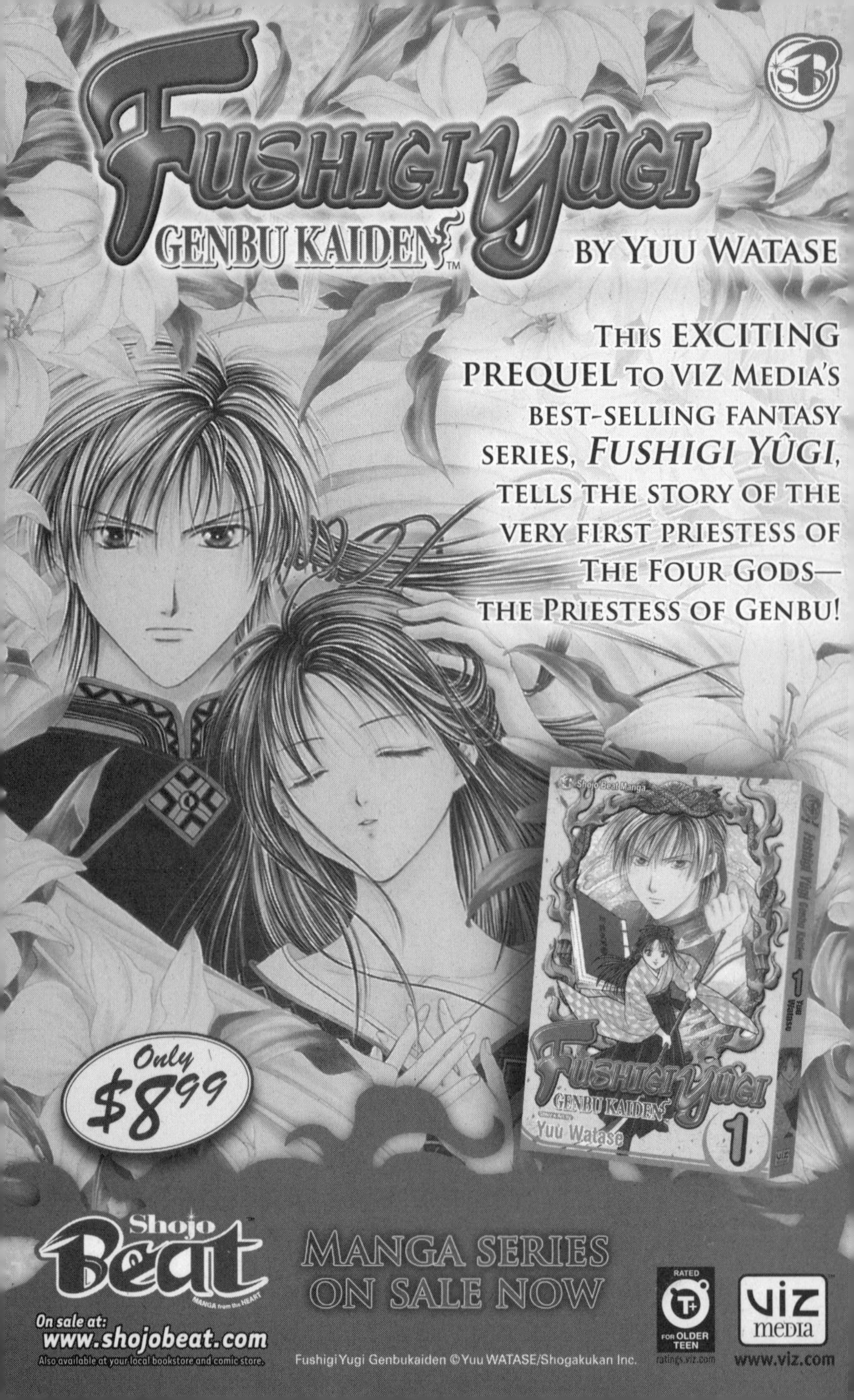
Fushigi Yûgi
Genbu Kaiden™
By Yuu Watase
This EXCITING PREQUEL to VIZ Media's best-selling fantasy series, Fushigi Yûgi, tells the story of the very first priestess of The Four Gods—the Priestess of Genbu!
Only $8.99
Shojo Beat Manga
Fushigi Yûgi
Genbu Kaiden
Yuu Watase
1
Shojo Beat
MANGA from the HEART
Manga Series On Sale Now
On sale at:
www.shojobeat.com
Also available at your local bookstore and comic store.
Fushigi Yugi Genbukaiden ©Yuu WATASE/Shogakukan Inc.
RATED T+ FOR OLDER TEEN
ratings.viz.com
VIZ media
www.viz.com

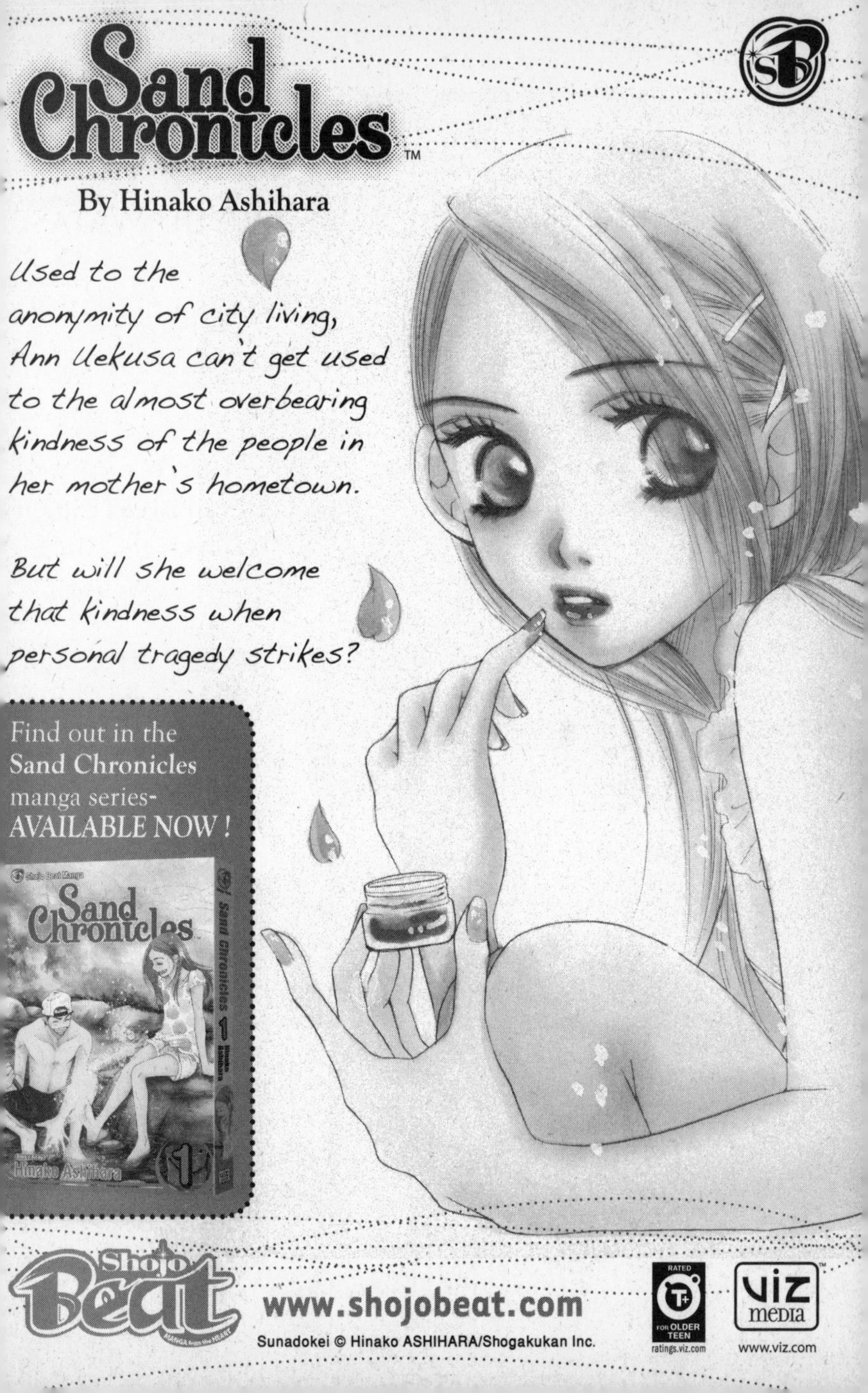

Sand Chronicles™
By Hinako Ashihara
Used to the anonymity of city living, Ann Uekusa can't get used to the almost overbearing kindness of the people in her mother's hometown.
But will she welcome that kindness when personal tragedy strikes?
Find out in the Sand Chronicles manga series- AVAILABLE NOW !
Shojo Beat Manga
Sand Chronicles
1
Hinako Ashihara
Shojo Beat
www.shojobeat.com
Sunadokei © Hinako ASHIHARA/Shogakukan Inc.
RATED T+ FOR OLDER TEEN
ratings.viz.com
VIZ media
www.viz.com

WE WERE THERE
Vol. 13
Shojo Beat Edition

STORY & ART BY
YUUKI OBATA

© 2002 Yuuki OBATA/Shogakukan
All rights reserved.
Original Japanese edition "BOKURA GA ITA"
published by SHOGAKUKAN Inc.

Adaptation/Nancy Thistlethwaite
Translation/Tetsuichiro Miyaki
Touch-up Art & Lettering/Inori Fukuda Trant
Design/Courtney Utt
Editor/Nancy Thistlethwaite

The stories, characters and incidents mentioned
in this publication are entirely fictional.

Printed in Canada

Published by VIZ Media, LLC
P.O. Box 77010
San Francisco, CA 94107

10 9 8 7 6 5 4 3 2 1
First printing, November 2011

Sorry to have kept you all waiting. Here is volume 13. It's been more than two years since volume 12 was published in Japan. I cannot thank you enough for buying volume 13 after so much time has passed. I appreciate it. There was a year and a half gap between chapter 51 and chapter 52, so I'm not sure how you will react. There may be those who think, "I've had enough," and let go of this series. But if there are some who still feel up to following this series... I am a very happy person. I'll see you all in volume 14.

—Yuuki Obata

Yuuki Obata's birthday is January 9. Her debut manga, *Raindrops*, won the Shogakukan Shinjin Comics Taisho Kasaku Award in 1998. Her current series, *We Were There* (*Bokura ga Ita*), won the 50th Shogakukan Manga Award and was adapted into an animated television series. She likes sweets, coffee, drinking with friends, and scary stories. Her hobby is browsing in bookshops.

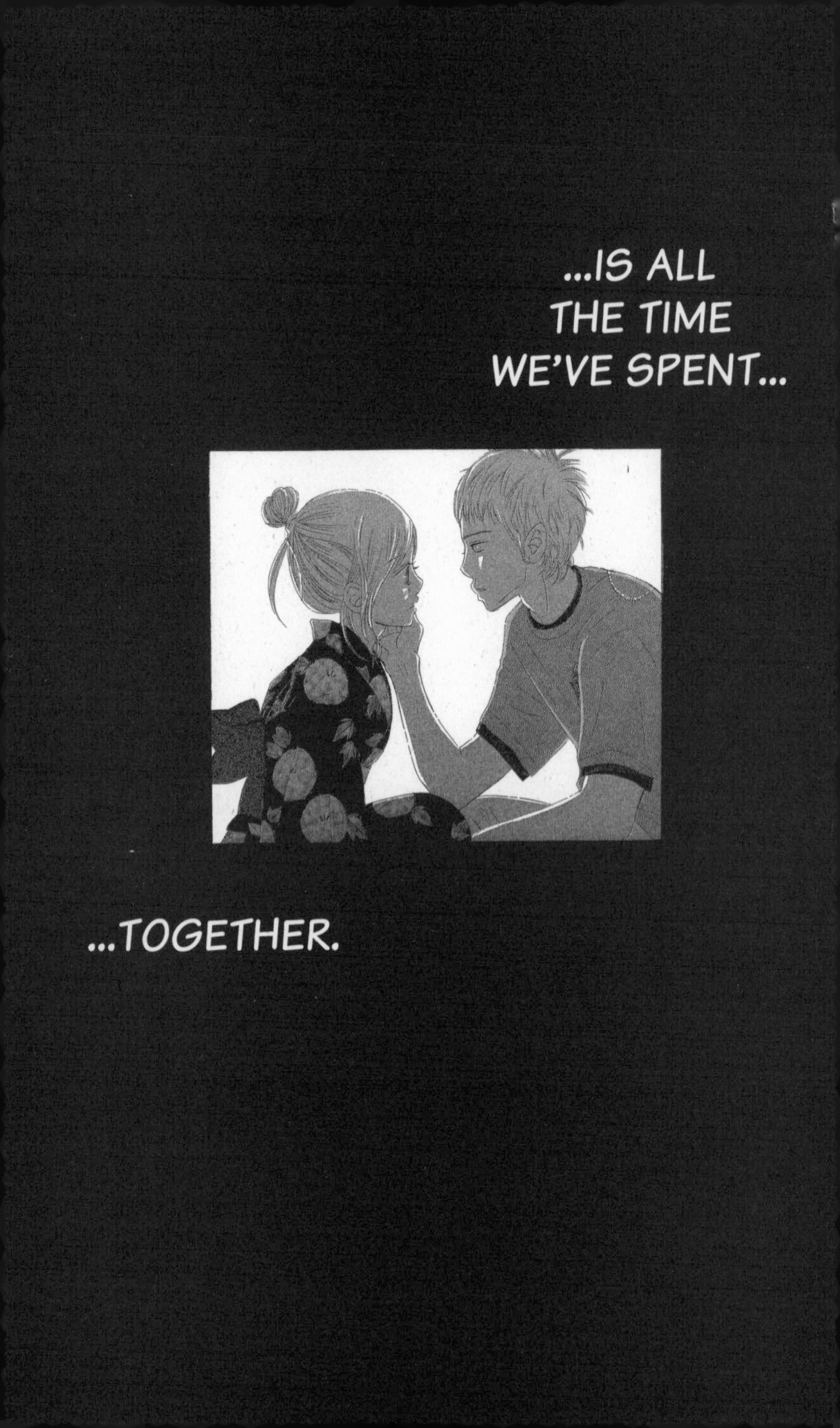
...IS ALL THE TIME WE'VE SPENT...
...TOGETHER.

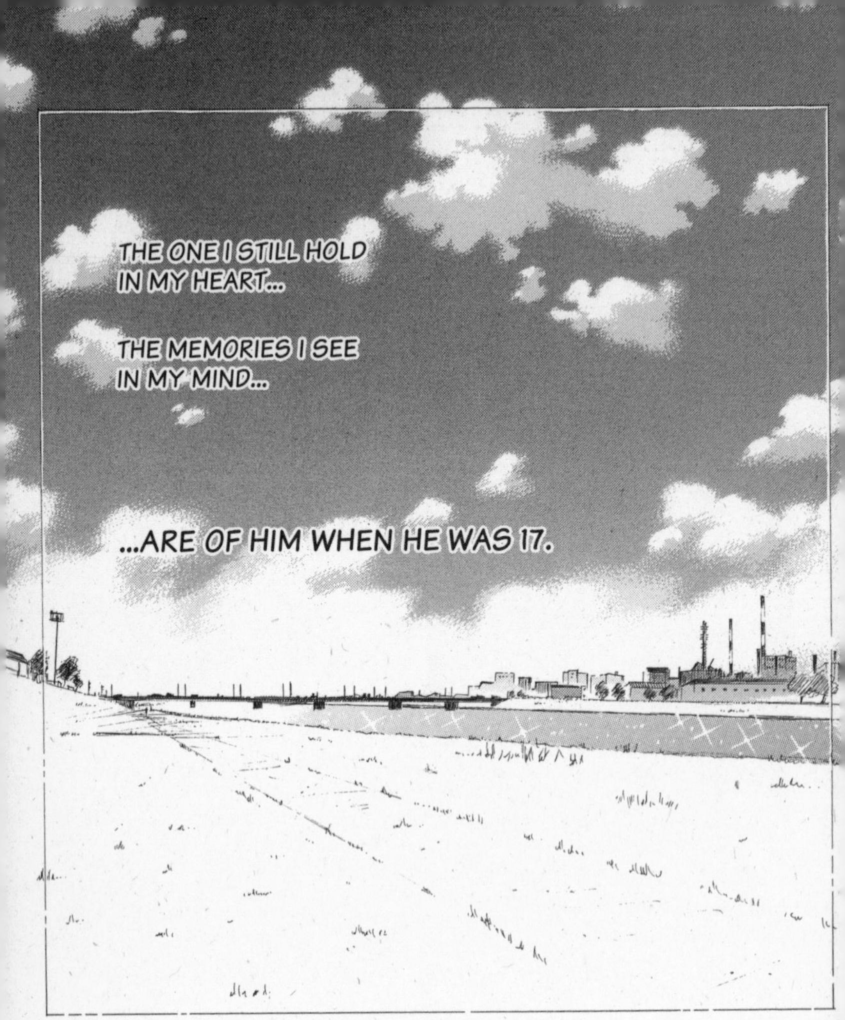
THE ONE I STILL HOLD IN MY HEART...
THE MEMORIES I SEE IN MY MIND...
...ARE OF HIM WHEN HE WAS 17.

Chapter 50

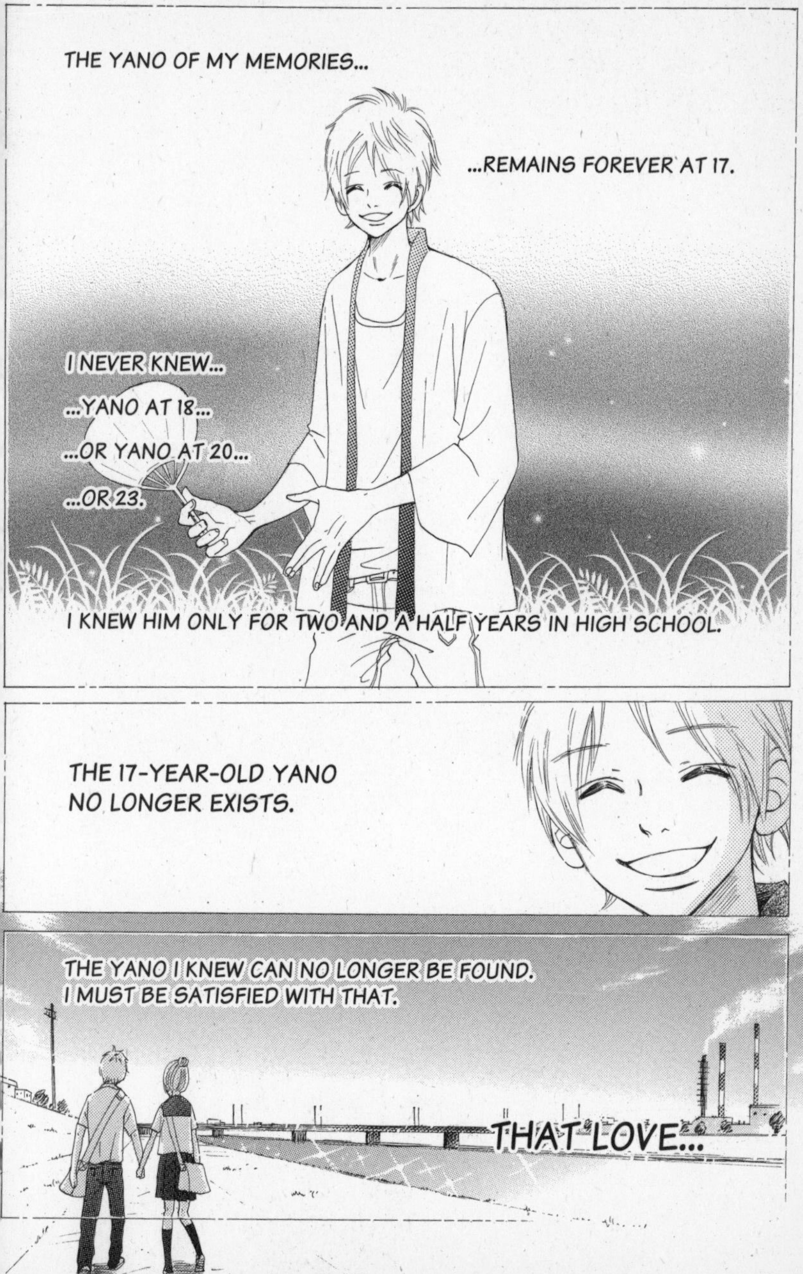
THE YANO OF MY MEMORIES...
...REMAINS FOREVER AT 17.
I NEVER KNEW...
...YANO AT 18...
...OR YANO AT 20...
...OR 23.
I KNEW HIM ONLY FOR TWO AND A HALF YEARS IN HIGH SCHOOL.
THE 17-YEAR-OLD YANO NO LONGER EXISTS.
THE YANO I KNEW CAN NO LONGER BE FOUND. I MUST BE SATISFIED WITH THAT.
THAT LOVE...

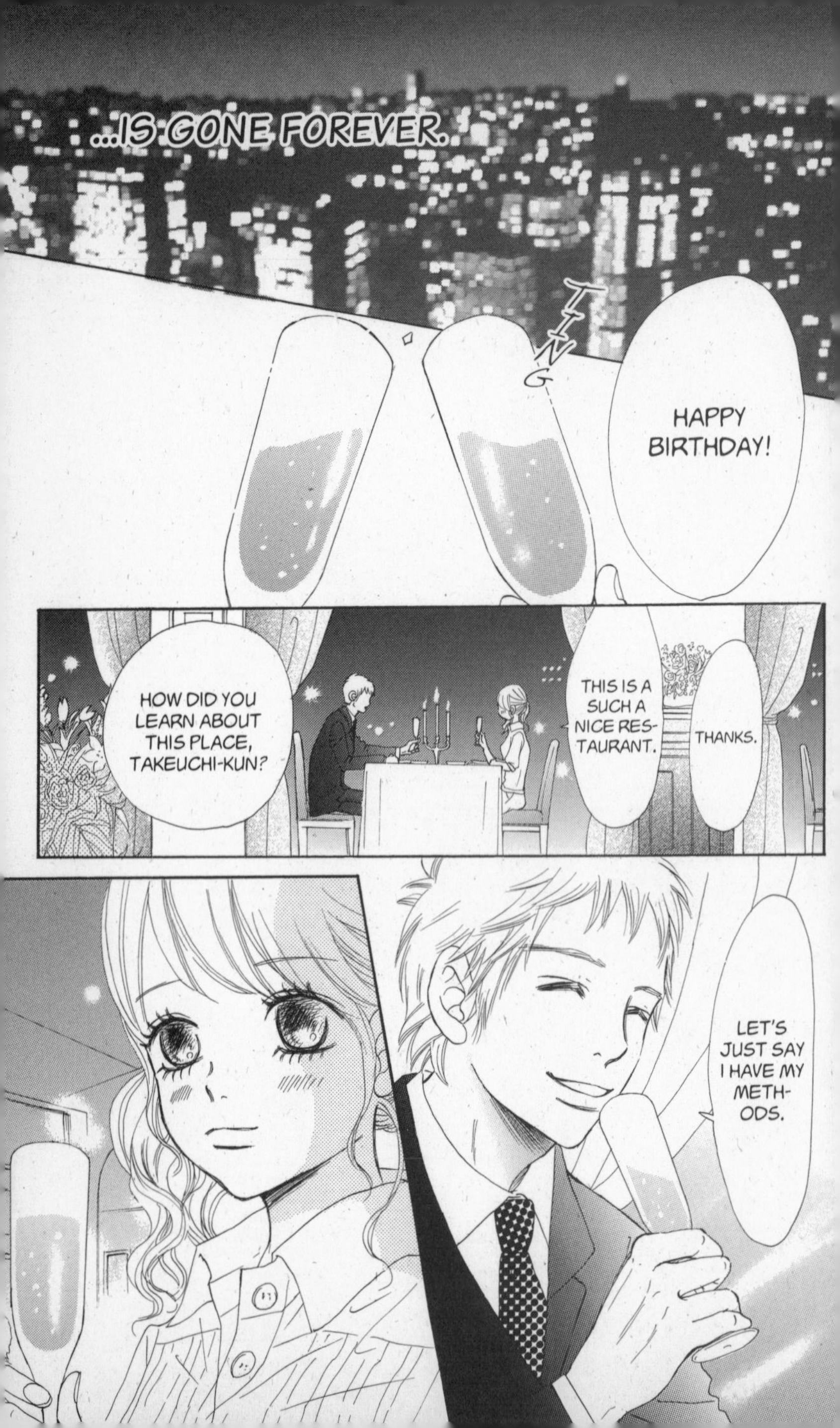
...IS GONE FOREVER.
TING
HAPPY BIRTHDAY!
THANKS.
THIS IS A SUCH A NICE RES-TAURANT.
HOW DID YOU LEARN ABOUT THIS PLACE, TAKEUCHI-KUN?
LET'S JUST SAY I HAVE MY METH-ODS.

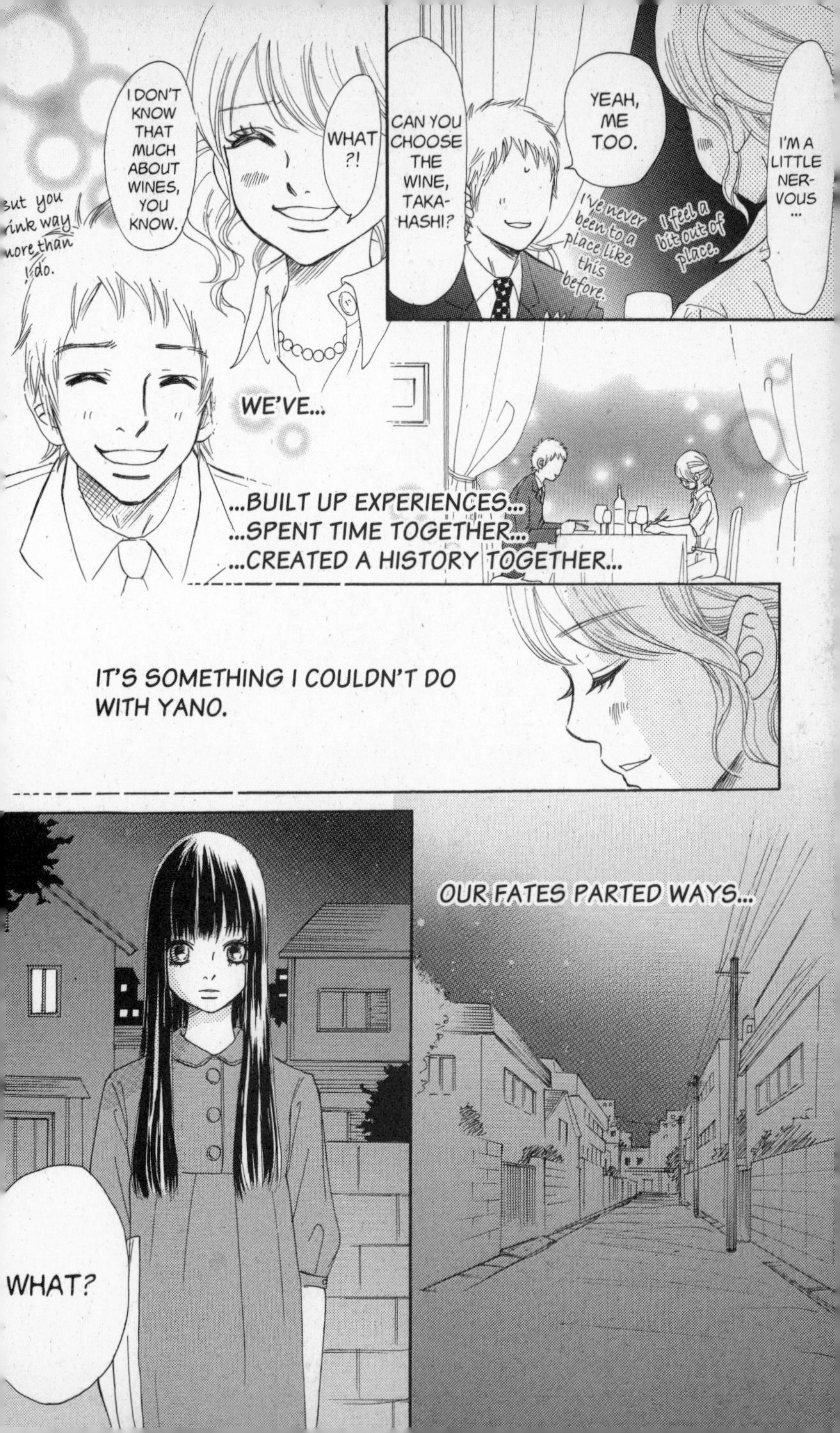
I'M A LITTLE NER-VOUS...
YEAH, ME TOO.
I feel a bit out of place.
I've never been to a place like this before.
CAN YOU CHOOSE THE WINE, TAKA-HASHI?
WHAT?!
I DON'T KNOW THAT MUCH ABOUT WINES, YOU KNOW.
ut you rink way ore than I do.
WE'VE...
...BUILT UP EXPERIENCES...
...SPENT TIME TOGETHER...
...CREATED A HISTORY TOGETHER...
IT'S SOMETHING I COULDN'T DO WITH YANO.
OUR FATES PARTED WAYS...
WHAT?

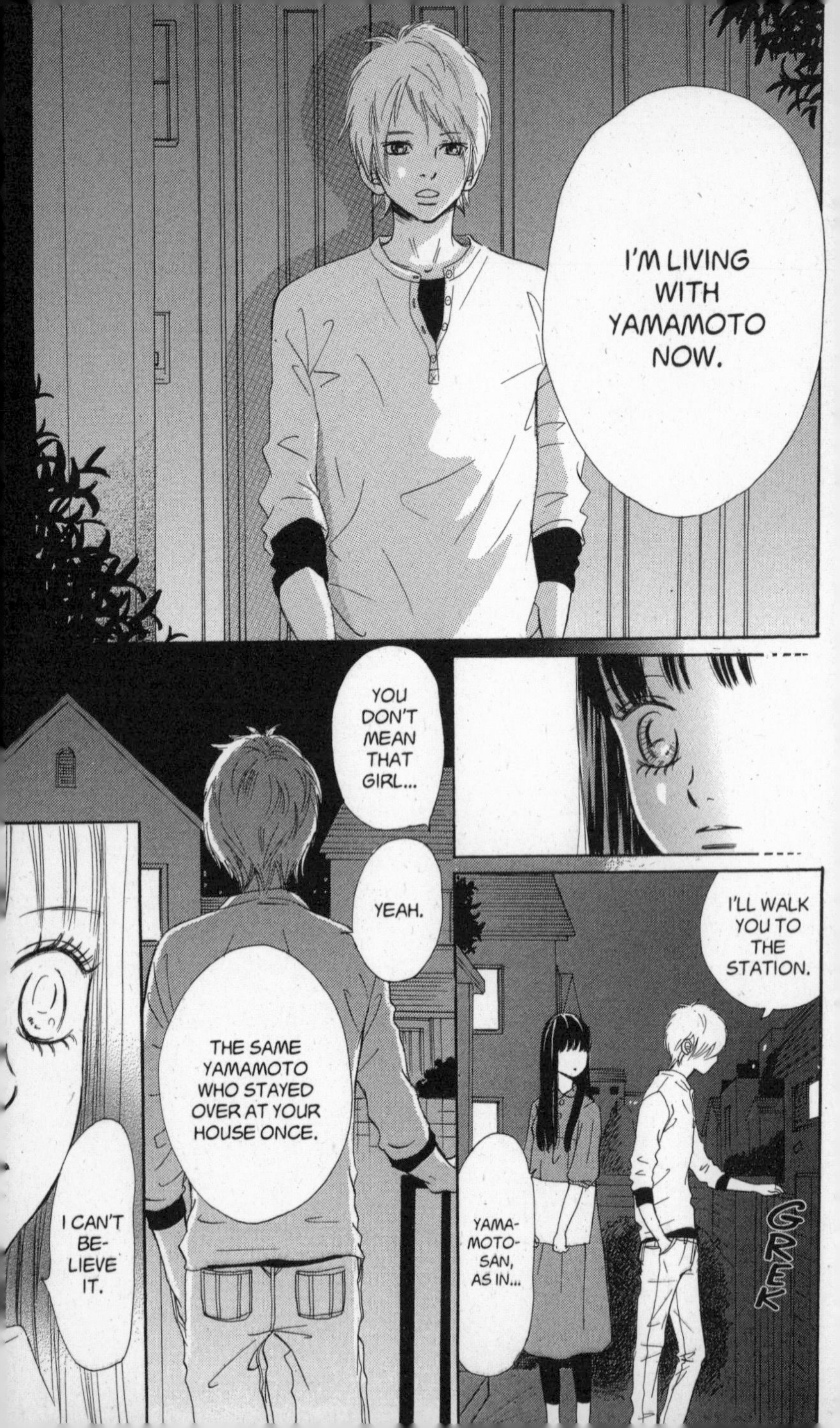
I'M LIVING WITH YAMAMOTO NOW.
I'LL WALK YOU TO THE STATION.
GREK
YAMA-MOTO-SAN, AS IN...
YOU DON'T MEAN THAT GIRL...
YEAH.
THE SAME YAMAMOTO WHO STAYED OVER AT YOUR HOUSE ONCE.
I CAN'T BE-LIEVE IT.

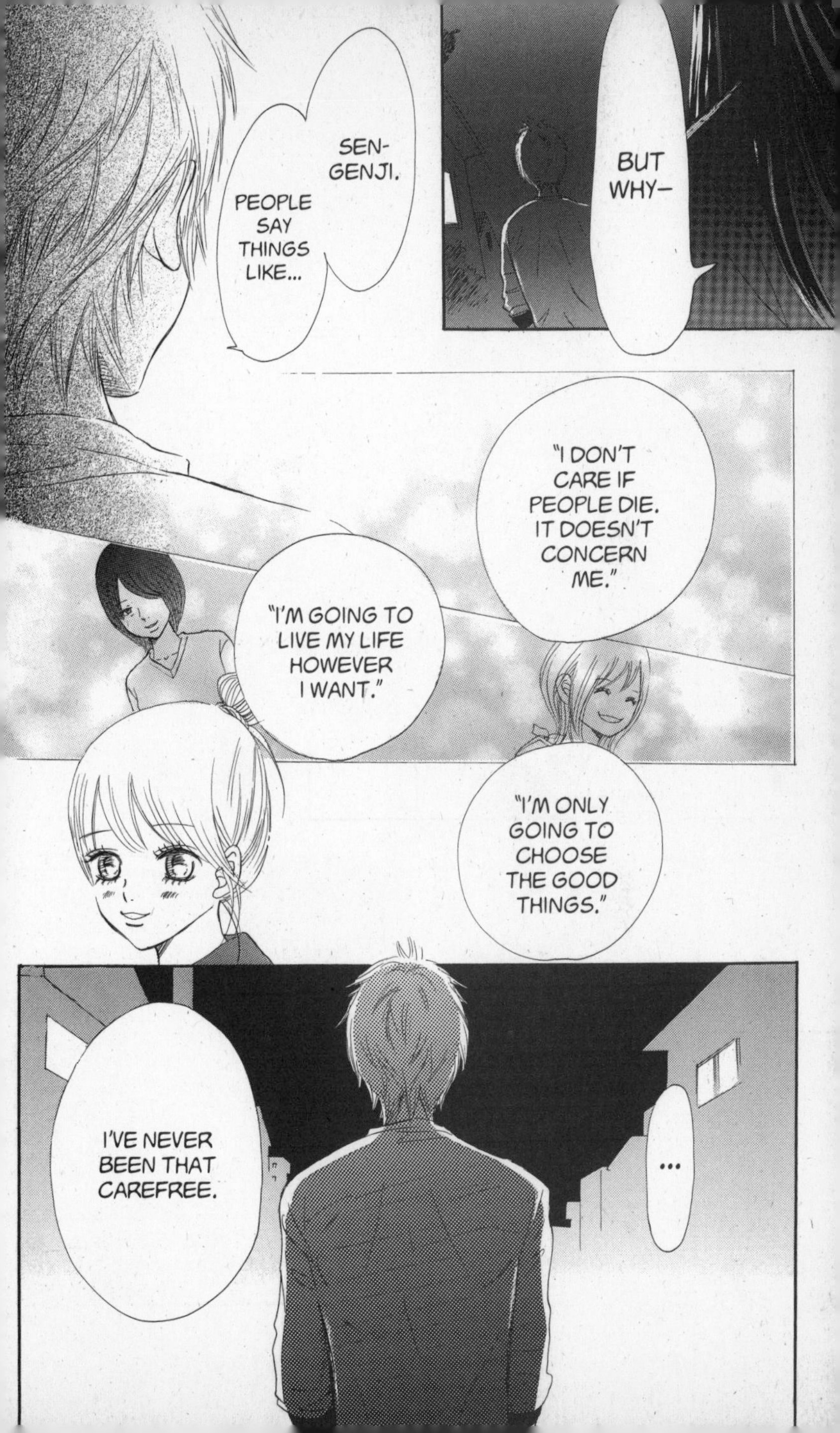
BUT WHY–
SEN-GENJI.
PEOPLE SAY THINGS LIKE...
"I DON'T CARE IF PEOPLE DIE. IT DOESN'T CONCERN ME."
"I'M GOING TO LIVE MY LIFE HOWEVER I WANT."
"I'M ONLY GOING TO CHOOSE THE GOOD THINGS."
...
I'VE NEVER BEEN THAT CAREFREE.

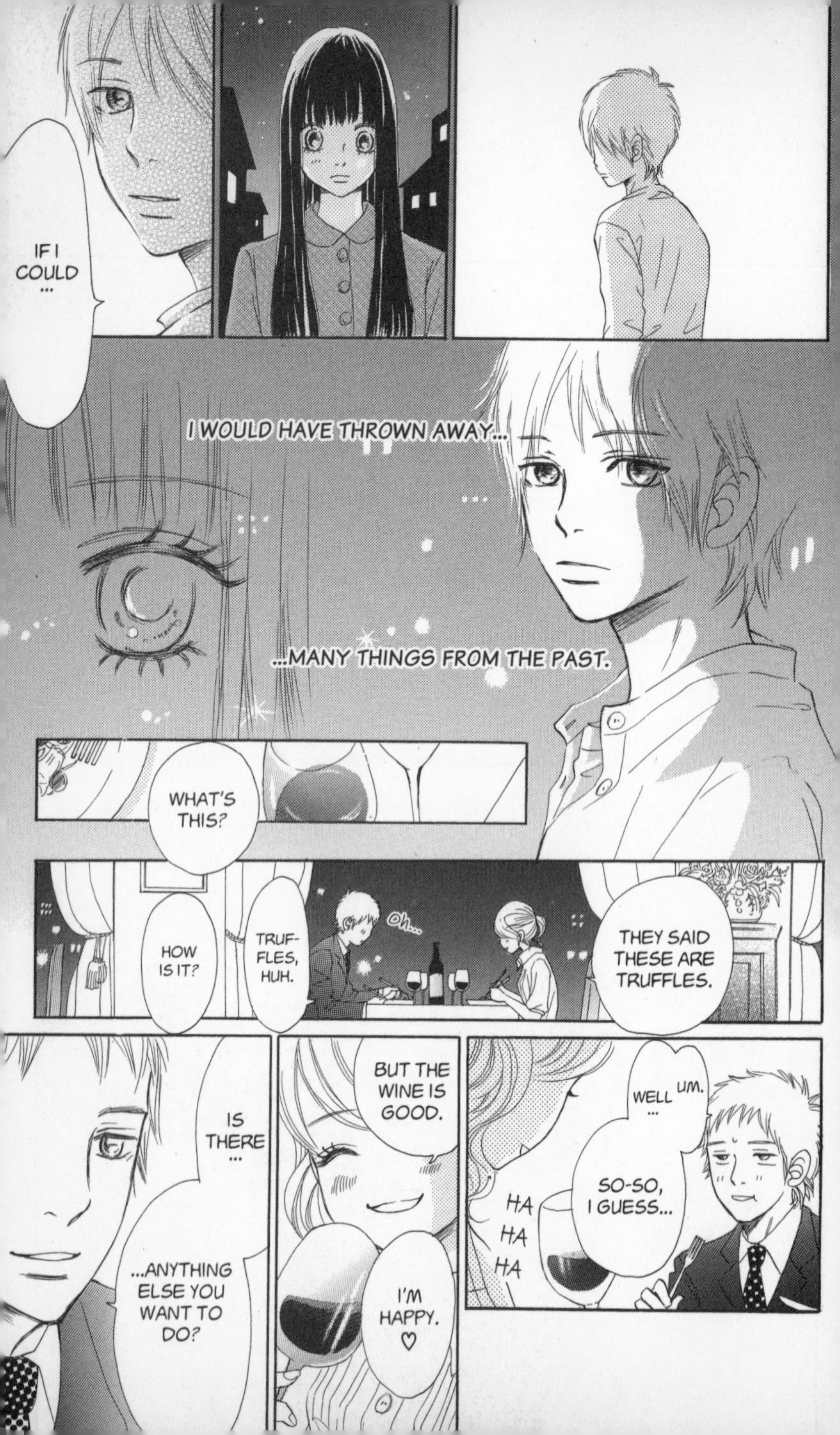
IF I COULD ...
I WOULD HAVE THROWN AWAY...
...MANY THINGS FROM THE PAST.
WHAT'S THIS?
THEY SAID THESE ARE TRUFFLES.
Oh...
TRUF-FLES, HUH.
HOW IS IT?
UM.
WELL ...
SO-SO, I GUESS...
HA HA HA
BUT THE WINE IS GOOD.
I'M HAPPY. ♡
IS THERE ...
...ANYTHING ELSE YOU WANT TO DO?

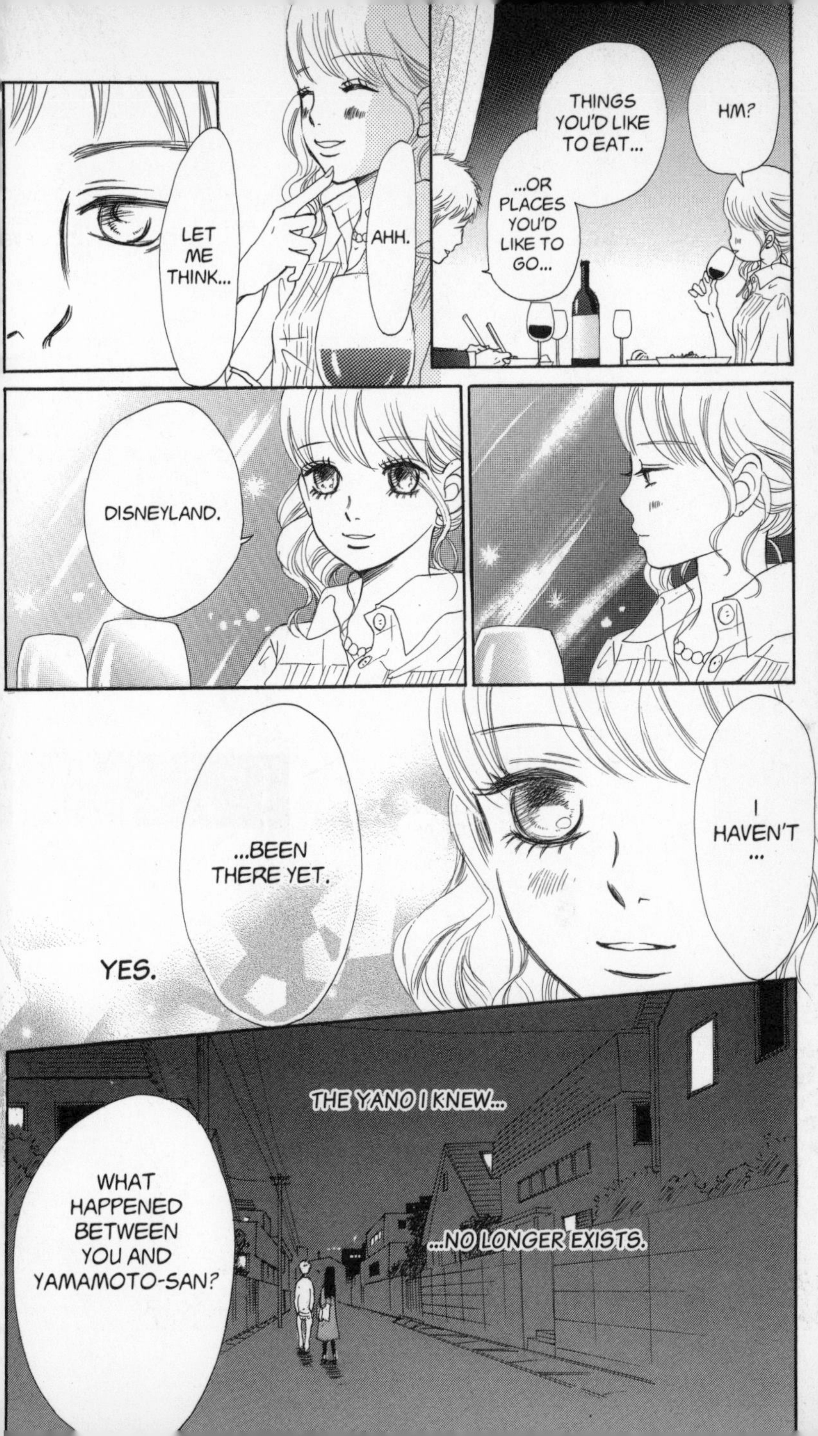
HM?
THINGS YOU'D LIKE TO EAT...
...OR PLACES YOU'D LIKE TO GO...
AHH.
LET ME THINK...
DISNEYLAND.
I HAVEN'T ...
...BEEN THERE YET.
YES.
THE YANO I KNEW...
...NO LONGER EXISTS.
WHAT HAPPENED BETWEEN YOU AND YAMAMOTO-SAN?

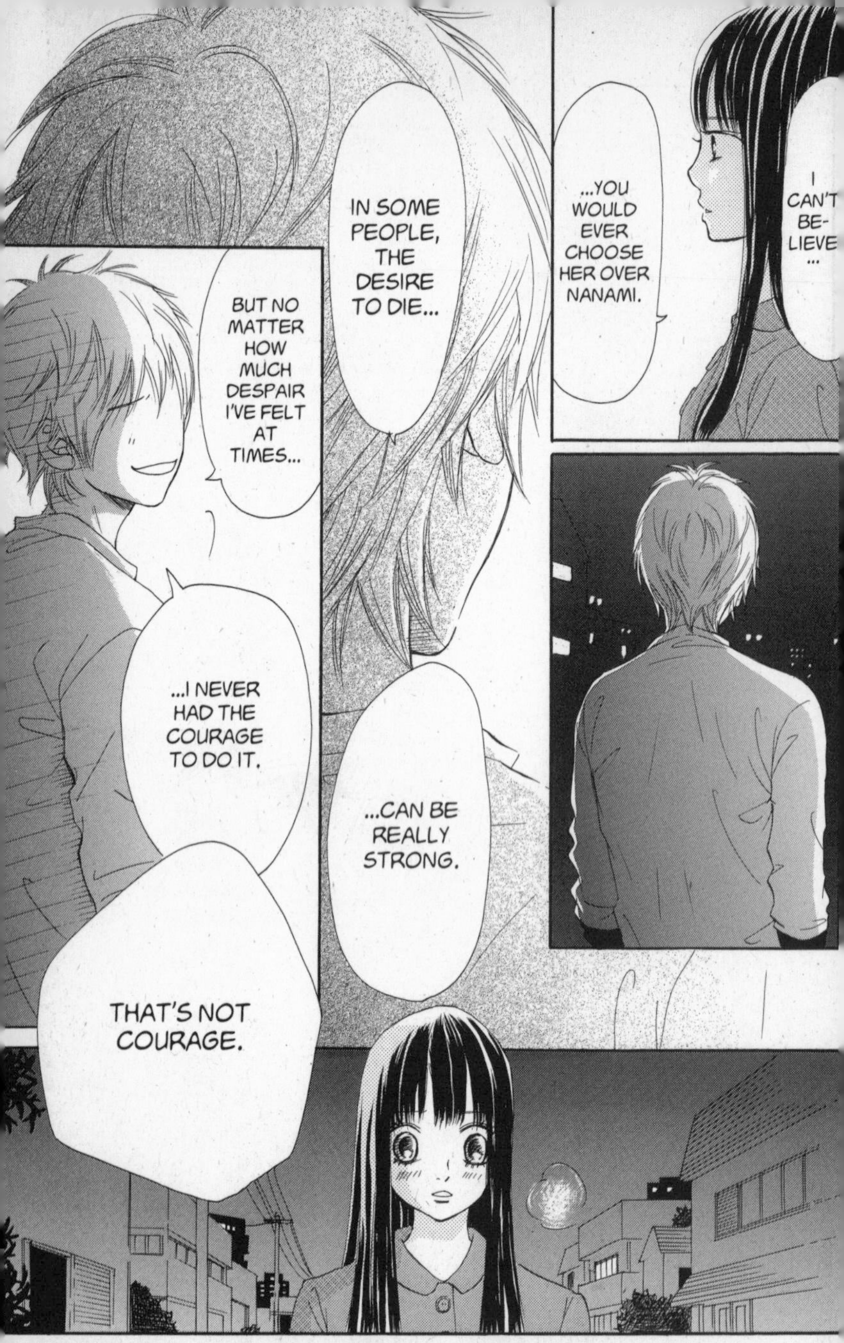
I CAN'T BE-LIEVE...
...YOU WOULD EVER CHOOSE HER OVER NANAMI.
IN SOME PEOPLE, THE DESIRE TO DIE...
...CAN BE REALLY STRONG.
BUT NO MATTER HOW MUCH DESPAIR I'VE FELT AT TIMES...
...I NEVER HAD THE COURAGE TO DO IT.
THAT'S NOT COURAGE.

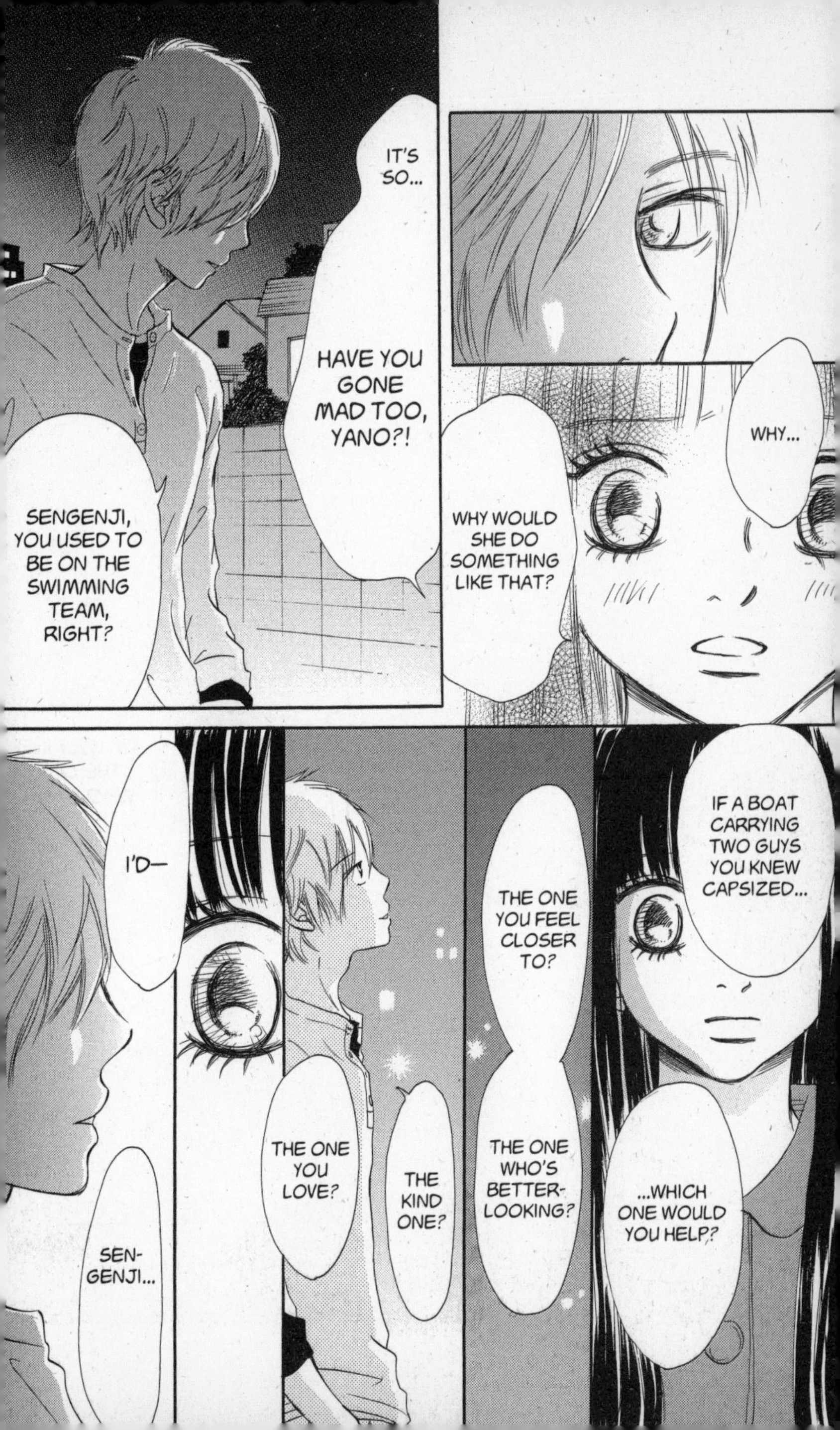
WHY...
WHY WOULD SHE DO SOMETHING LIKE THAT?
IT'S SO...
HAVE YOU GONE MAD TOO, YANO?!
SENGENJI, YOU USED TO BE ON THE SWIMMING TEAM, RIGHT?
IF A BOAT CARRYING TWO GUYS YOU KNEW CAPSIZED...
...WHICH ONE WOULD YOU HELP?
THE ONE YOU FEEL CLOSER TO?
THE ONE WHO'S BETTER-LOOKING?
THE KIND ONE?
THE ONE YOU LOVE?
I'D—
SEN-GENJI...

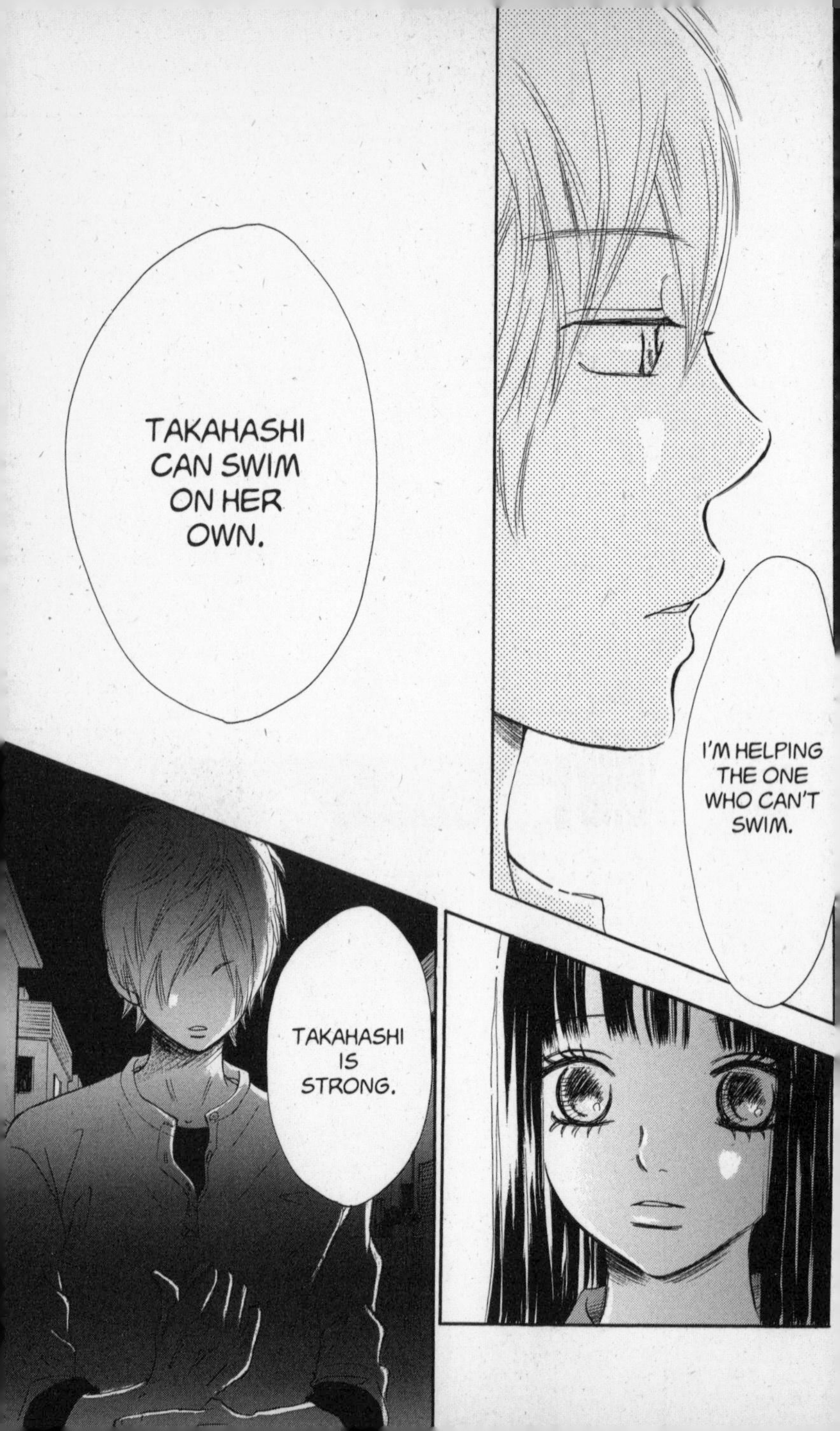
TAKAHASHI CAN SWIM ON HER OWN.
I'M HELPING THE ONE WHO CAN'T SWIM.
TAKAHASHI IS STRONG.

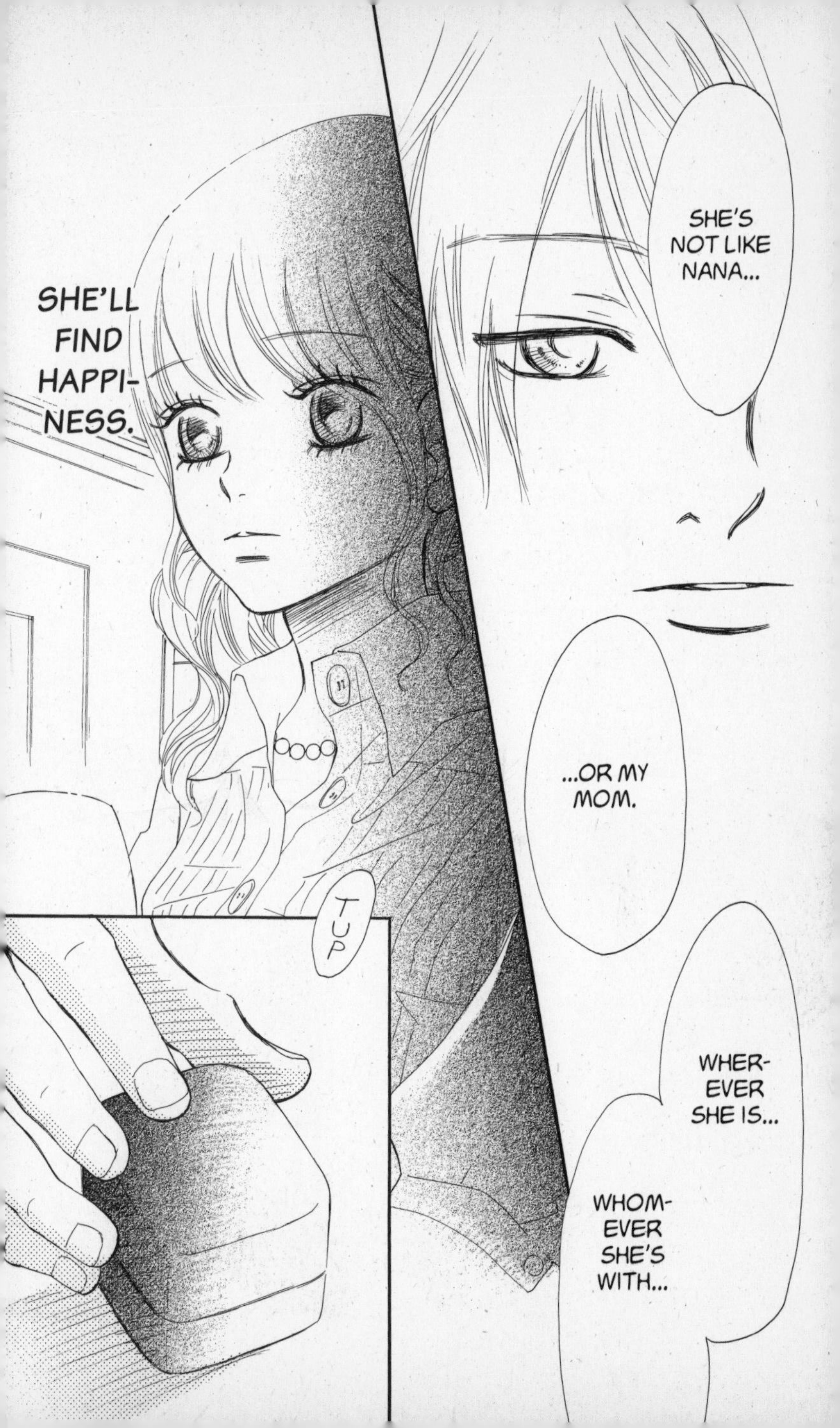
SHE'S NOT LIKE NANA...
...OR MY MOM.
WHER-EVER SHE IS...
WHOM-EVER SHE'S WITH...
SHE'LL FIND HAPPI-NESS.
TUP

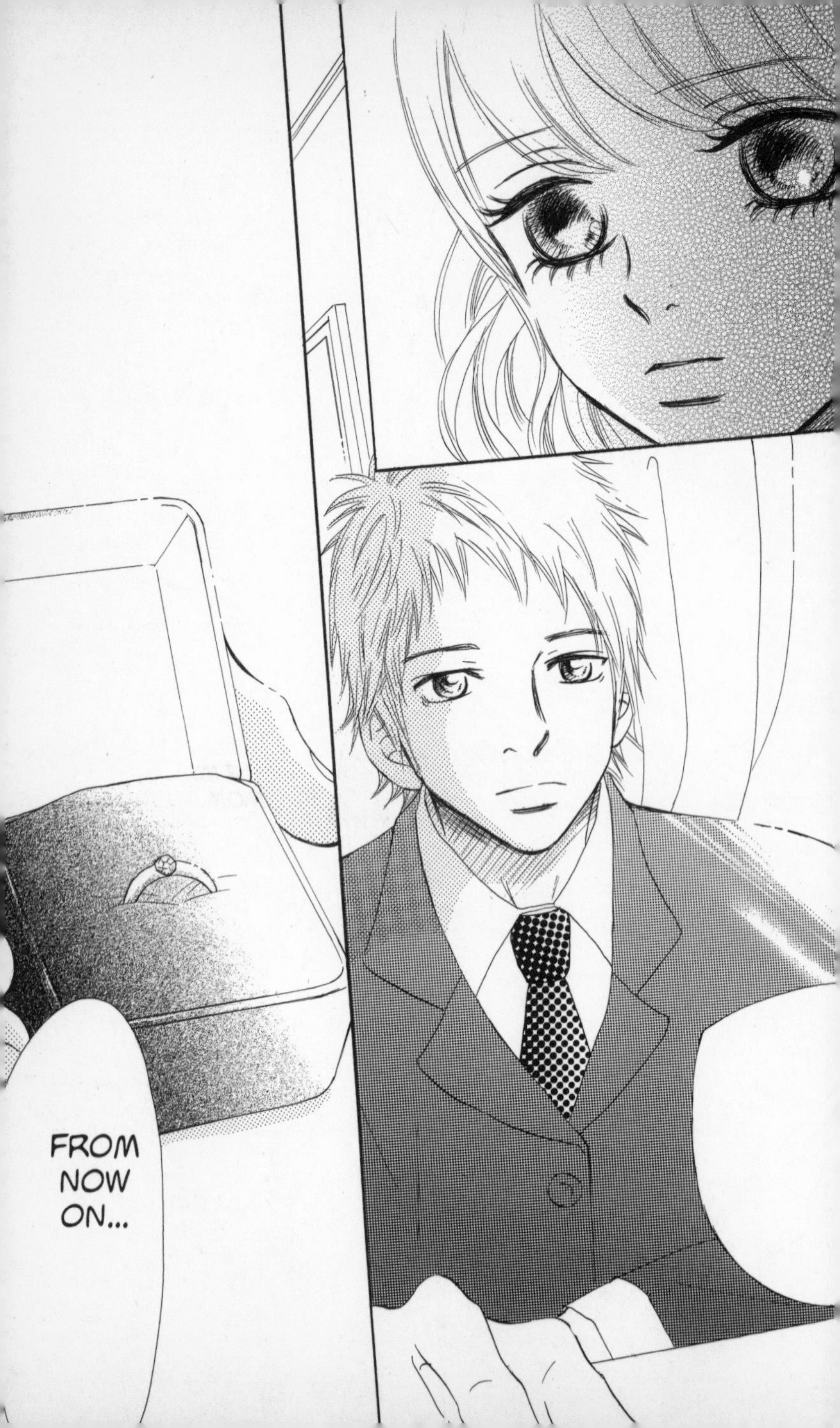
FROM NOW ON...

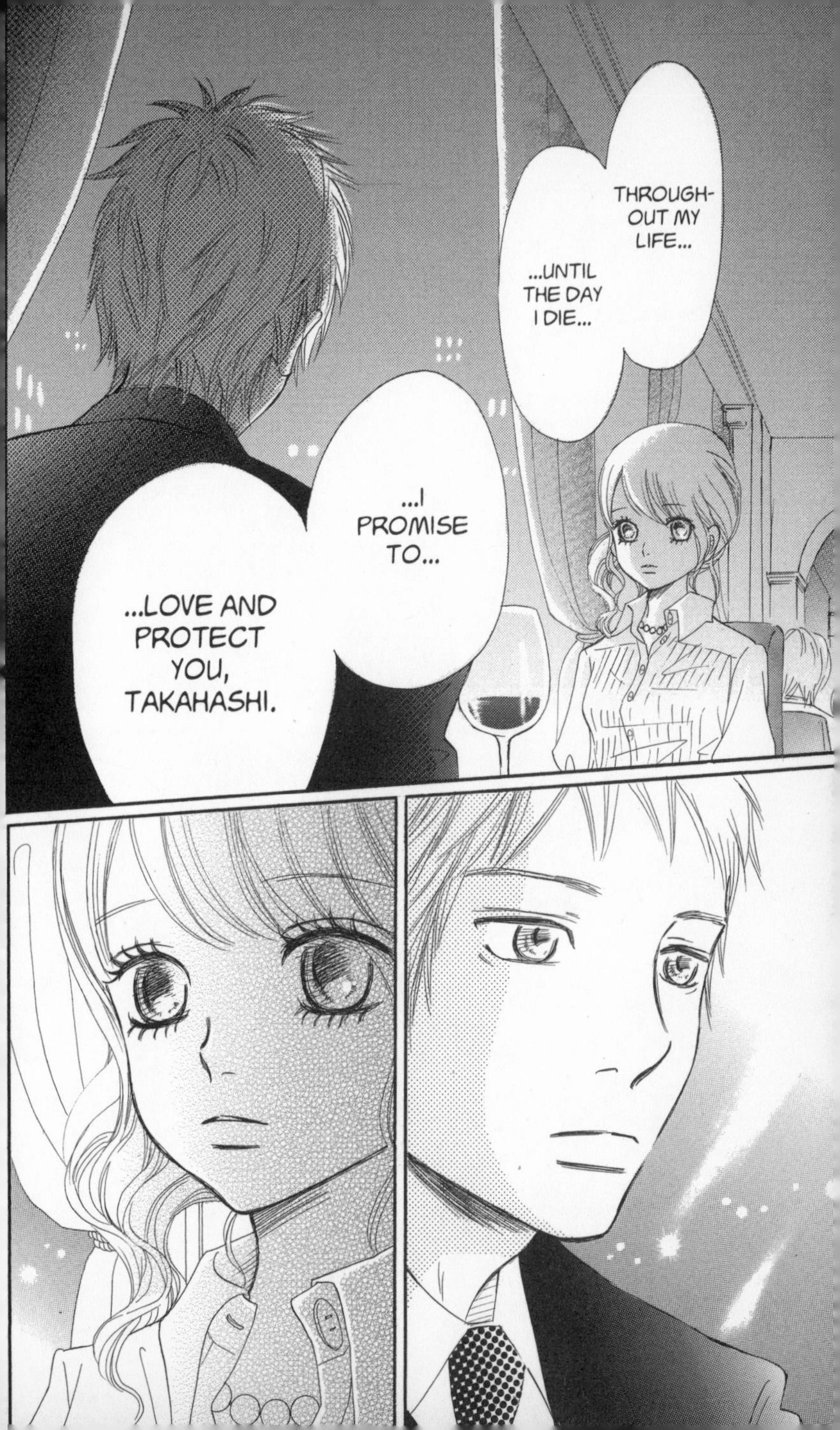
THROUGH-OUT MY LIFE...
...UNTIL THE DAY I DIE...
...I PROMISE TO...
...LOVE AND PROTECT YOU, TAKAHASHI.

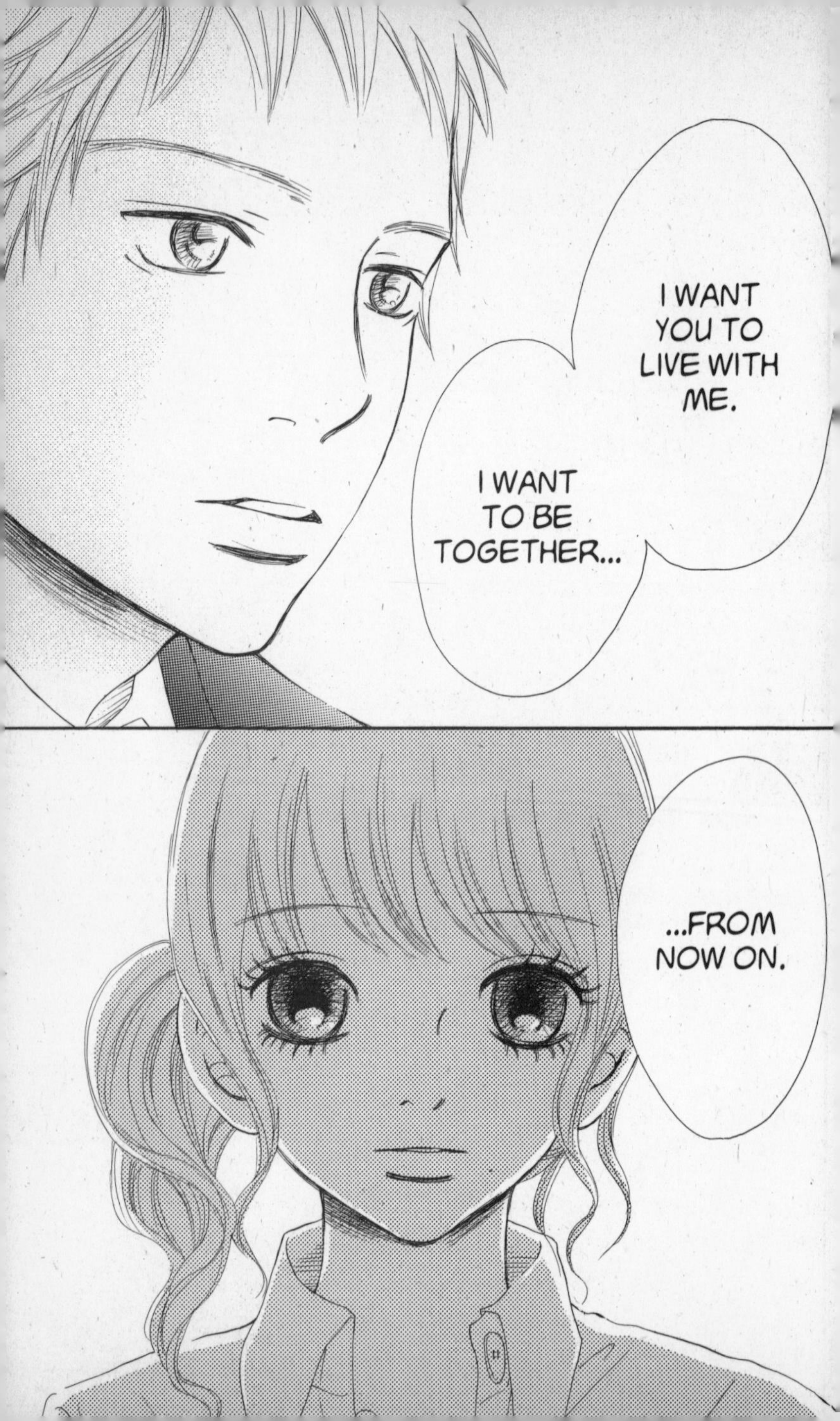
I WANT YOU TO LIVE WITH ME.
I WANT TO BE TOGETHER...
...FROM NOW ON.

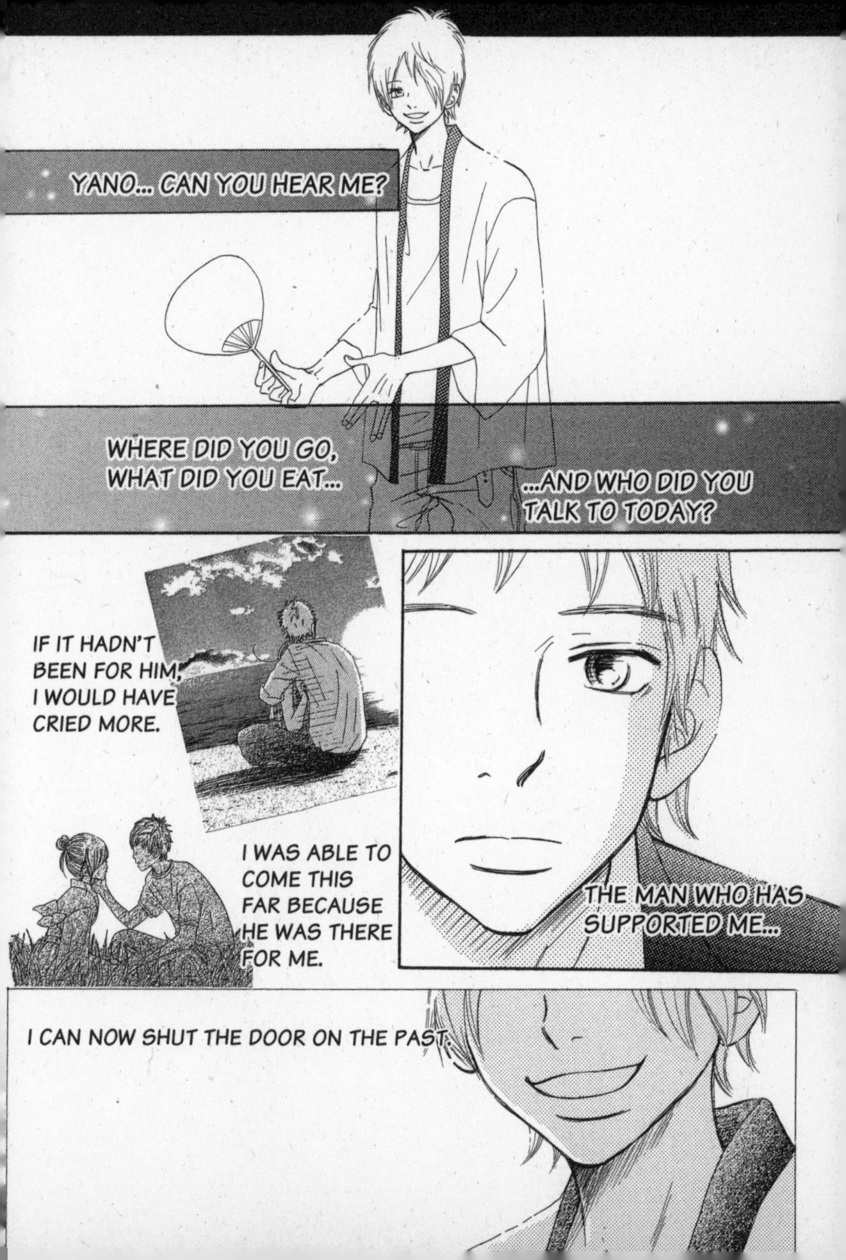
YANO... CAN YOU HEAR ME?
WHERE DID YOU GO, WHAT DID YOU EAT...
...AND WHO DID YOU TALK TO TODAY?
THE MAN WHO HAS SUPPORTED ME...
IF IT HADN'T BEEN FOR HIM, I WOULD HAVE CRIED MORE.
I WAS ABLE TO COME THIS FAR BECAUSE HE WAS THERE FOR ME.
I CAN NOW SHUT THE DOOR ON THE PAST.

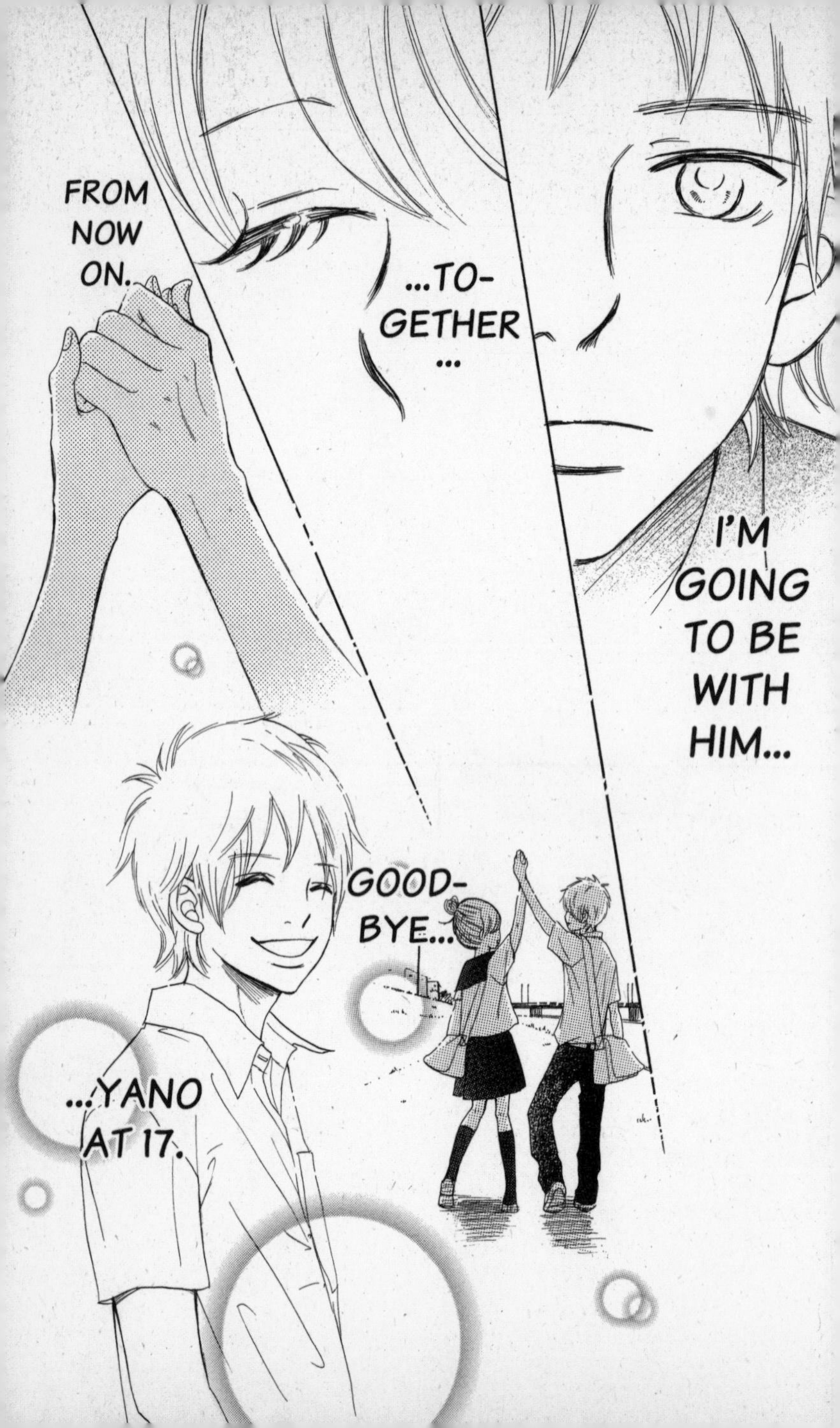
I'M GOING TO BE WITH HIM...
...TO-GETHER...
FROM NOW ON...
GOOD-BYE...
...YANO AT 17.

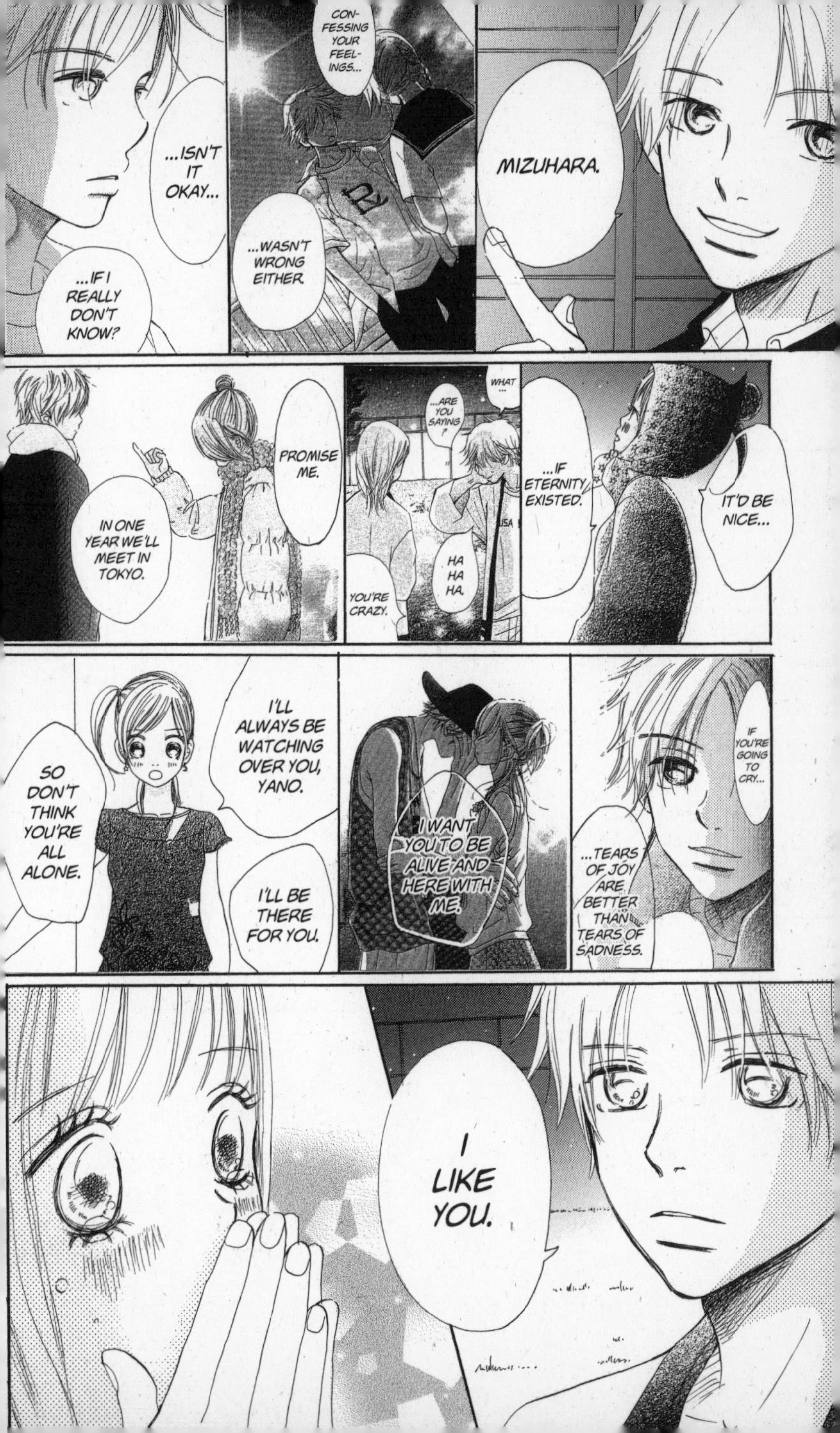
MIZUHARA.
CONFESSING YOUR FEELINGS...
...WASN'T WRONG EITHER
...ISN'T IT OKAY...
...IF I REALLY DON'T KNOW?
IT'D BE NICE...
...IF ETERNITY EXISTED.
WHAT...
...ARE YOU SAYING?
HA HA HA.
YOU'RE CRAZY.
PROMISE ME.
IN ONE YEAR WE'LL MEET IN TOKYO.
IF YOU'RE GOING TO CRY...
...TEARS OF JOY ARE BETTER THAN TEARS OF SADNESS.
I WANT YOU TO BE ALIVE AND HERE WITH ME.
I'LL ALWAYS BE WATCHING OVER YOU, YANO.
I'LL BE THERE FOR YOU.
SO DON'T THINK YOU'RE ALL ALONE.
I LIKE YOU.

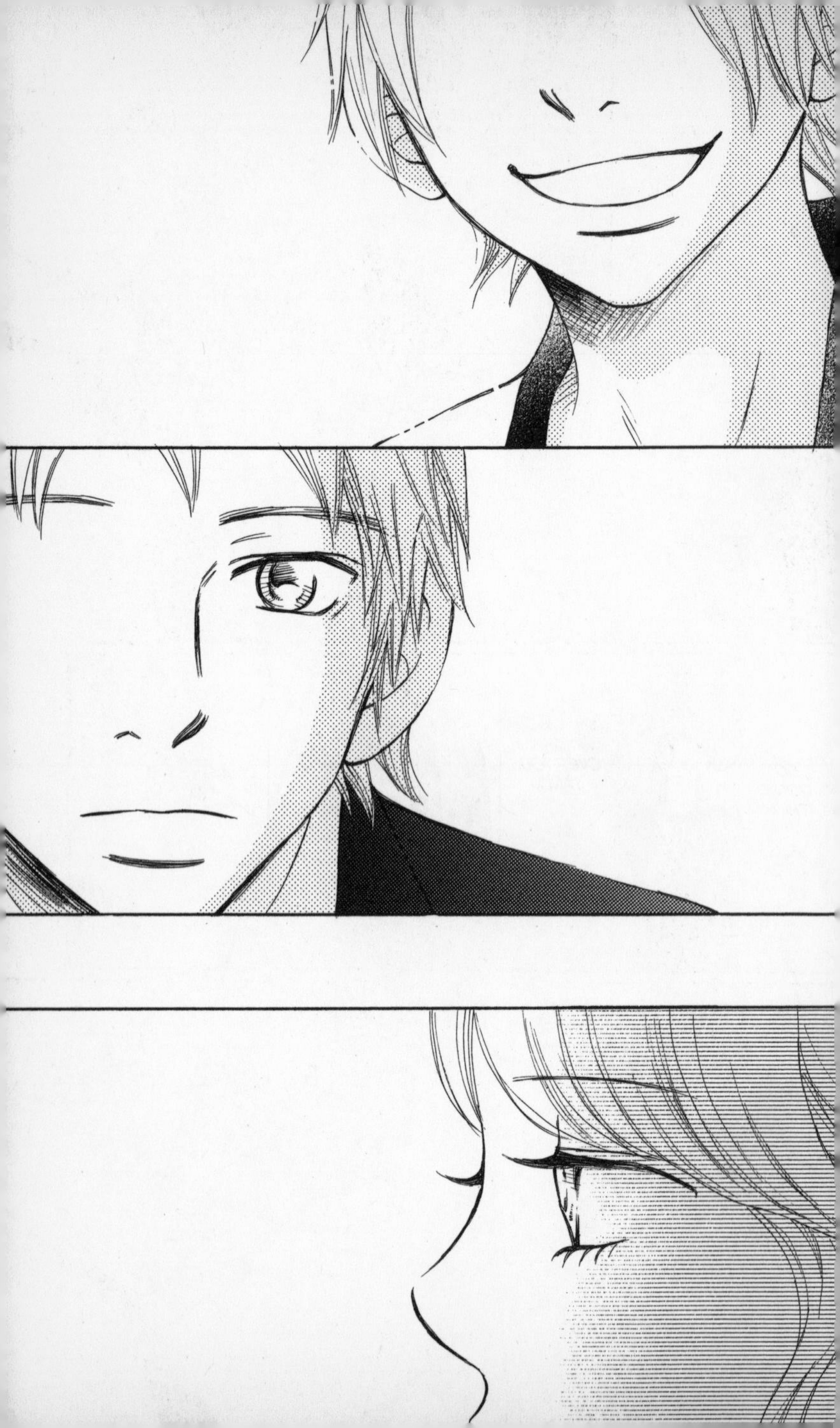

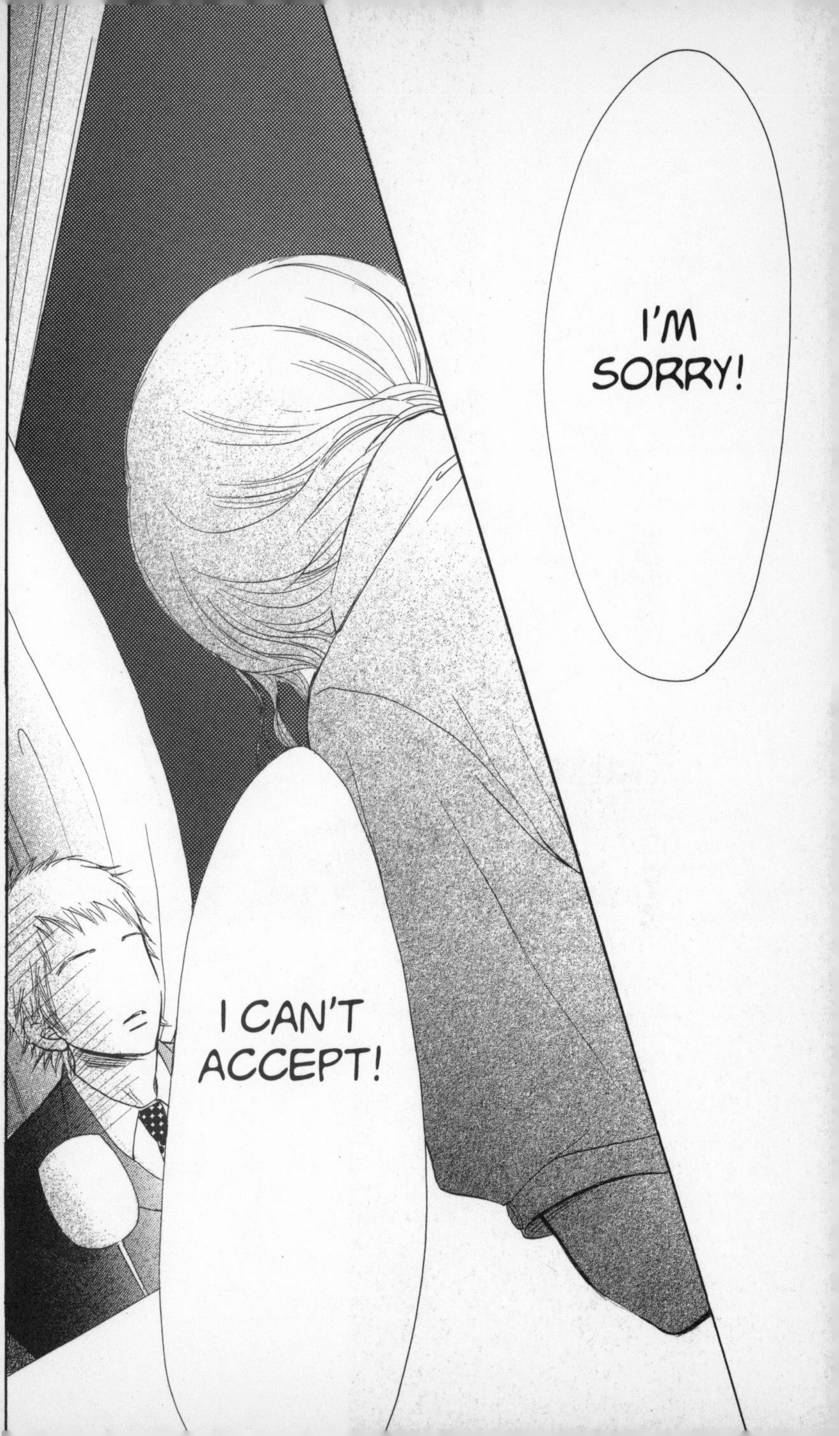
I'M SORRY!
I CAN'T ACCEPT!

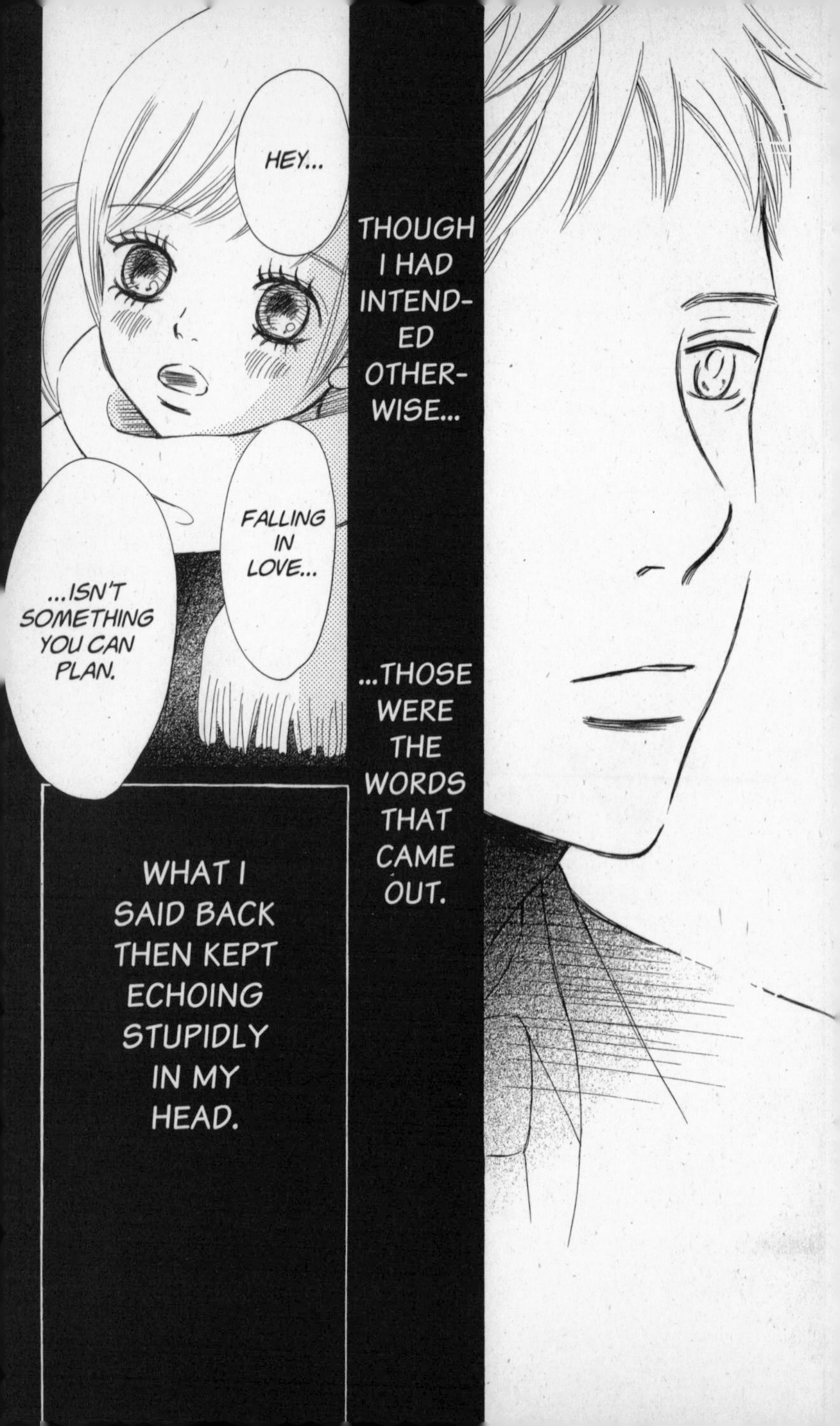
THOUGH I HAD INTENDED-ED OTHERWISE...
...THOSE WERE THE WORDS THAT CAME OUT.
HEY...
FALLING IN LOVE...
...ISN'T SOMETHING YOU CAN PLAN.
WHAT I SAID BACK THEN KEPT ECHOING STUPIDLY IN MY HEAD.

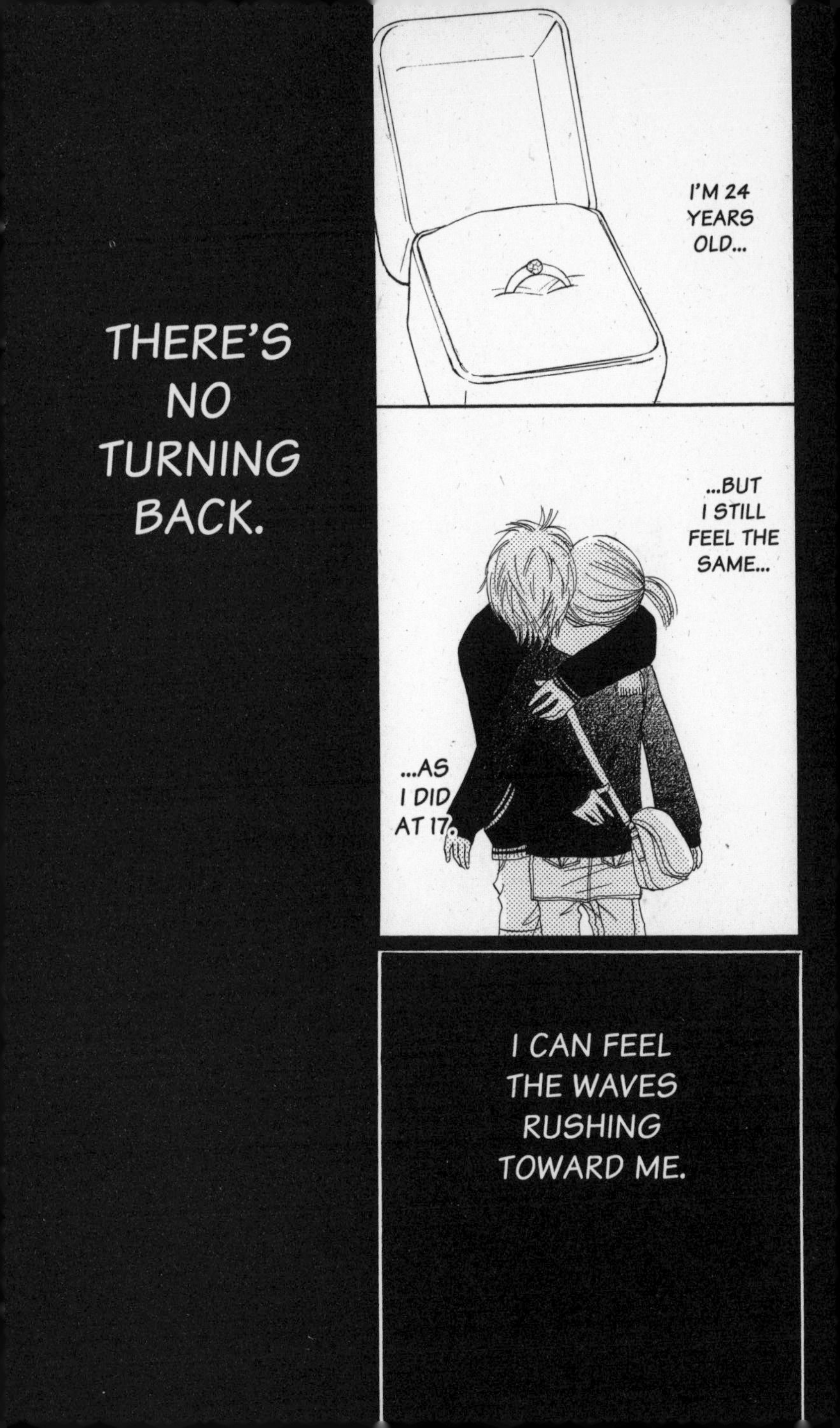
I'M 24 YEARS OLD...
...BUT I STILL FEEL THE SAME...
...AS I DID AT 17.
I CAN FEEL THE WAVES RUSHING TOWARD ME.
THERE'S NO TURNING BACK.

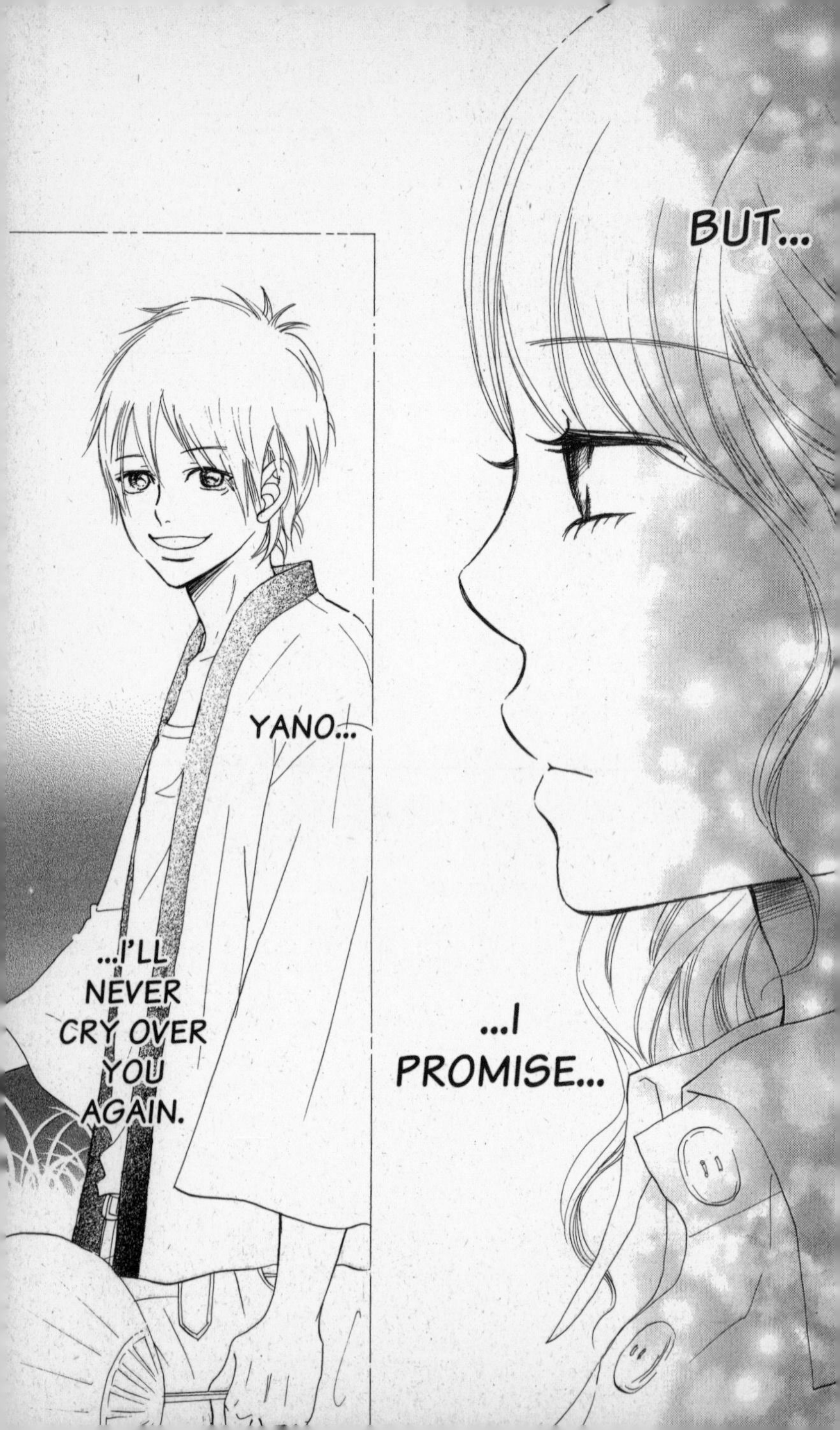
BUT...
...I PROMISE...
YANO...
...I'LL NEVER CRY OVER YOU AGAIN.

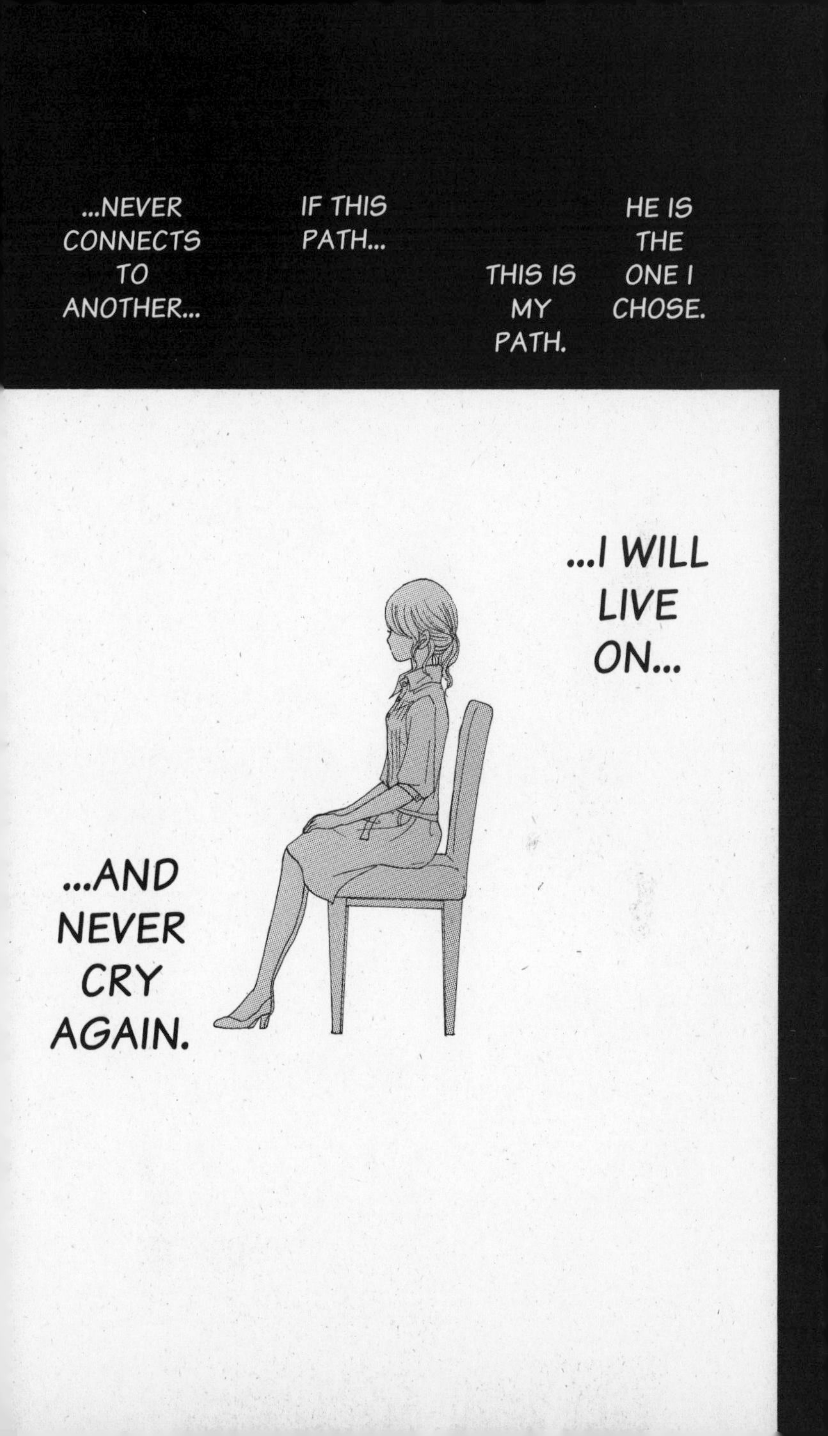
HE IS THE ONE I CHOSE.
THIS IS MY PATH.
IF THIS PATH...
...NEVER CONNECTS TO ANOTHER...
...I WILL LIVE ON...
...AND NEVER CRY AGAIN.

Chapter 51

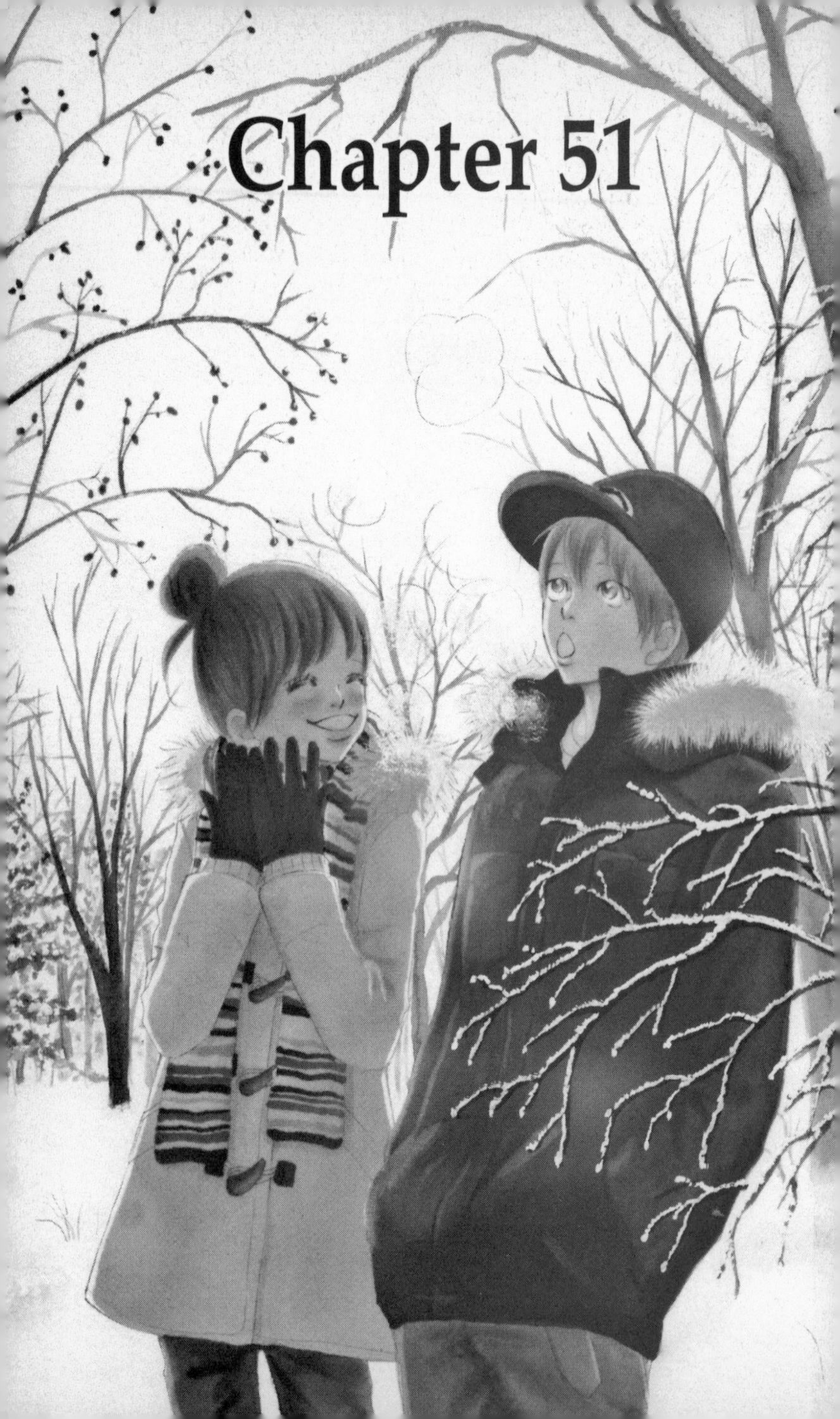

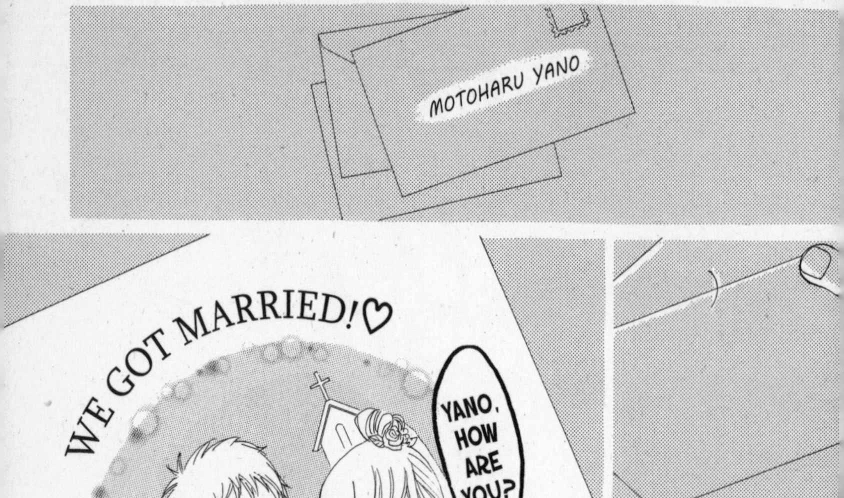
MOTOHARU YANO
WE GOT MARRIED!♡
YANO, HOW ARE YOU?
COME VISIT US SOMEDAY !!

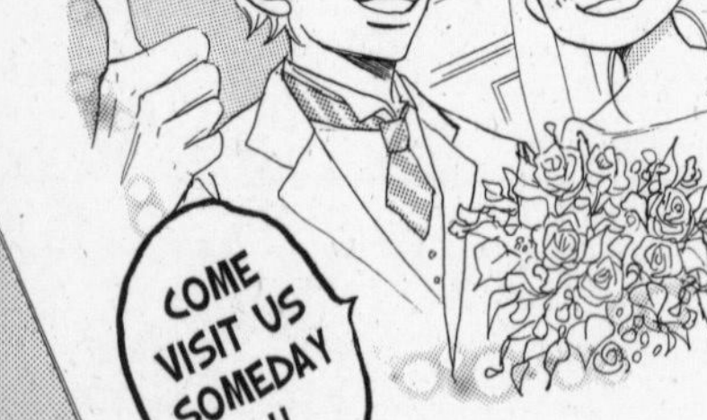
FWAK
HIYAH!
ACK!
FWAK
FWAK
FWAK

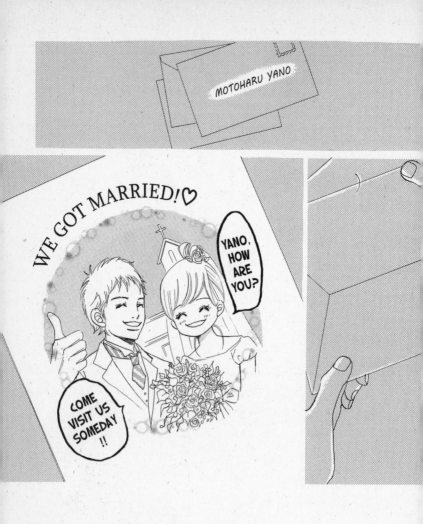

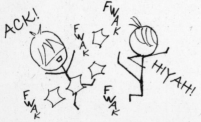

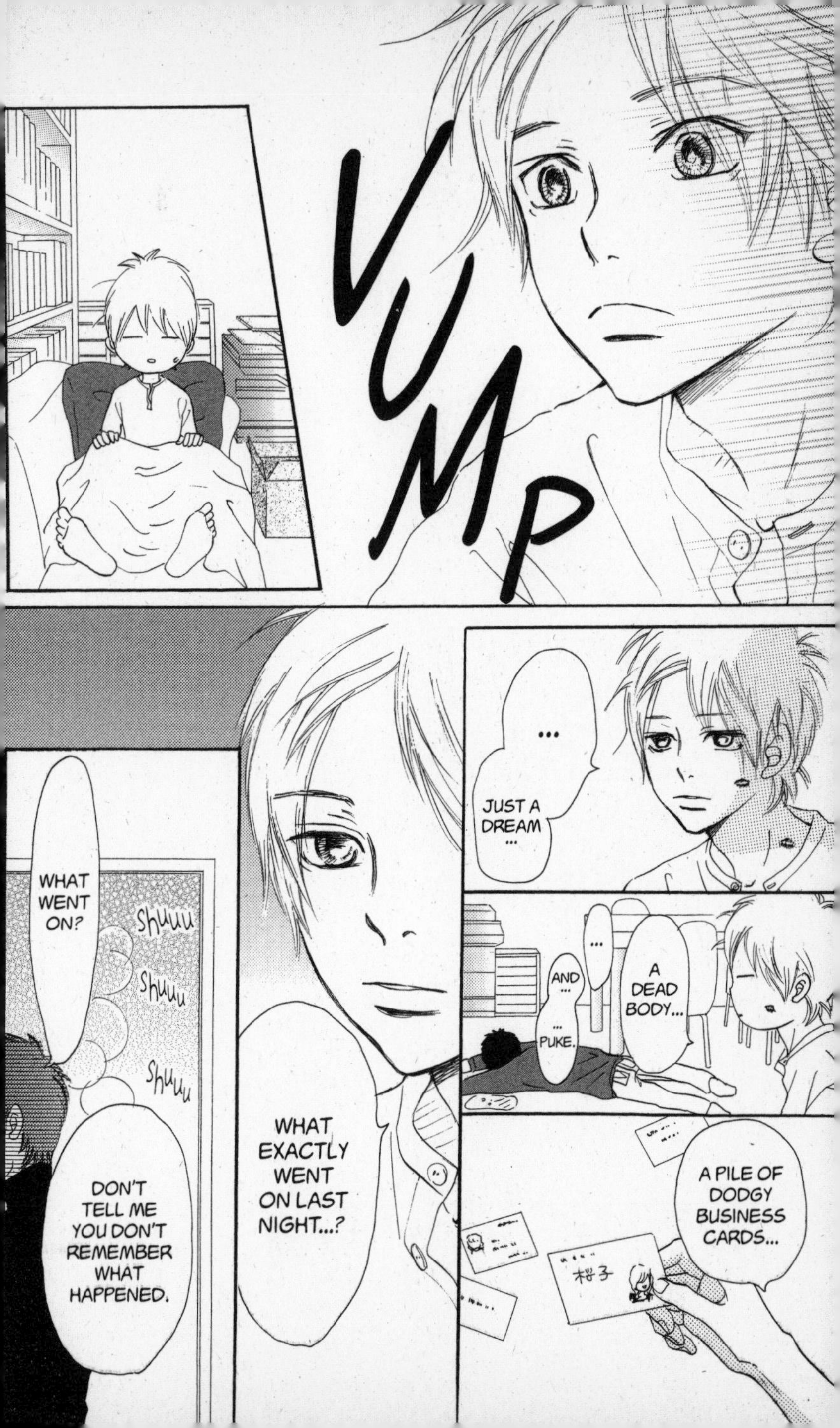
VUMP
...
JUST A DREAM ...
A DEAD BODY...
...
AND ...
... PUKE.
A PILE OF DODGY BUSINESS CARDS...
桜子
WHAT EXACTLY WENT ON LAST NIGHT...?
WHAT WENT ON?
Shuuu
Shuuu
Shuuu
DON'T TELL ME YOU DON'T REMEMBER WHAT HAPPENED.

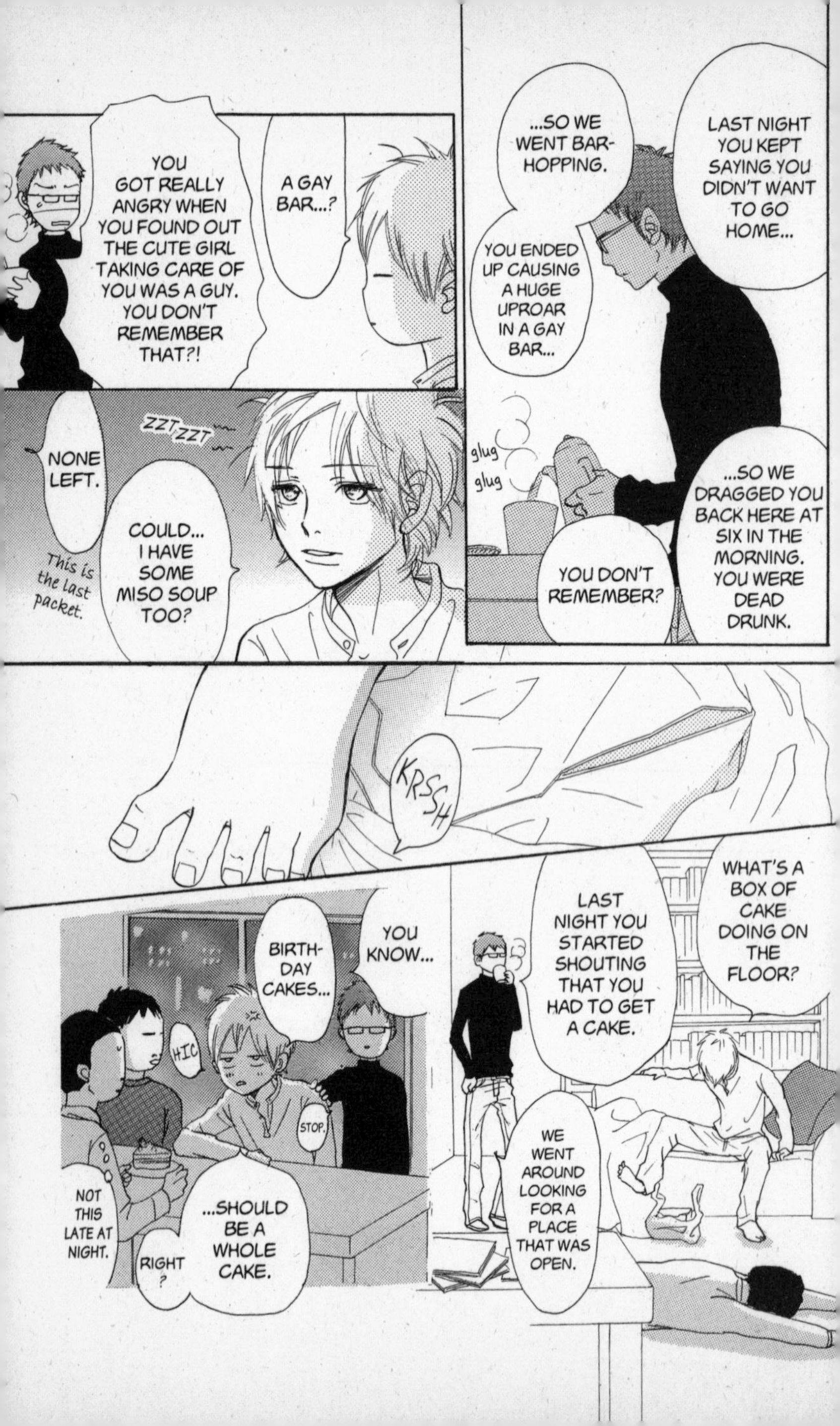
LAST NIGHT YOU KEPT SAYING YOU DIDN'T WANT TO GO HOME...
...SO WE WENT BAR-HOPPING.
YOU ENDED UP CAUSING A HUGE UPROAR IN A GAY BAR...
glug glug
...SO WE DRAGGED YOU BACK HERE AT SIX IN THE MORNING. YOU WERE DEAD DRUNK.
YOU DON'T REMEMBER?
A GAY BAR...?
YOU GOT REALLY ANGRY WHEN YOU FOUND OUT THE CUTE GIRL TAKING CARE OF YOU WAS A GUY. YOU DON'T REMEMBER THAT?!
ZZT ZZT
COULD... I HAVE SOME MISO SOUP TOO?
NONE LEFT.
This is the last packet.
KRSSH
WHAT'S A BOX OF CAKE DOING ON THE FLOOR?
LAST NIGHT YOU STARTED SHOUTING THAT YOU HAD TO GET A CAKE.
WE WENT AROUND LOOKING FOR A PLACE THAT WAS OPEN.
YOU KNOW...
BIRTH-DAY CAKES...
HIC
STOP.
...SHOULD BE A WHOLE CAKE.
RIGHT?
NOT THIS LATE AT NIGHT.

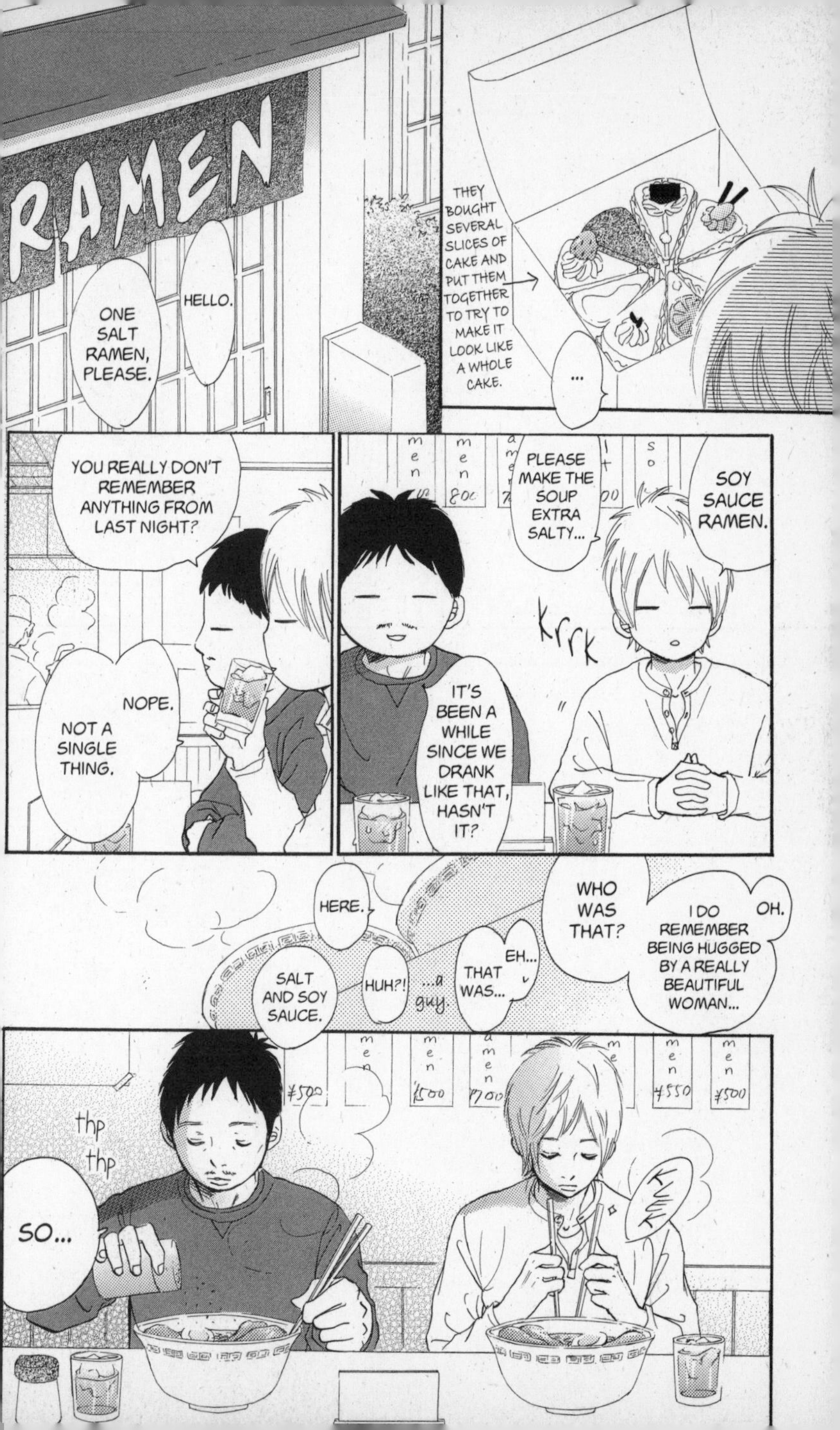
THEY BOUGHT SEVERAL SLICES OF CAKE AND PUT THEM TOGETHER TO TRY TO MAKE IT LOOK LIKE A WHOLE CAKE.
...
RAMEN
HELLO.
ONE SALT RAMEN, PLEASE.
SOY SAUCE RAMEN.
PLEASE MAKE THE SOUP EXTRA SALTY...
krrk
IT'S BEEN A WHILE SINCE WE DRANK LIKE THAT, HASN'T IT?
YOU REALLY DON'T REMEMBER ANYTHING FROM LAST NIGHT?
NOPE. NOT A SINGLE THING.
OH. I DO REMEMBER BEING HUGGED BY A REALLY BEAUTIFUL WOMAN...
WHO WAS THAT?
EH... THAT WAS...
...a guy.
HUH?!
HERE.
SALT AND SOY SAUCE.
thp thp
SO...

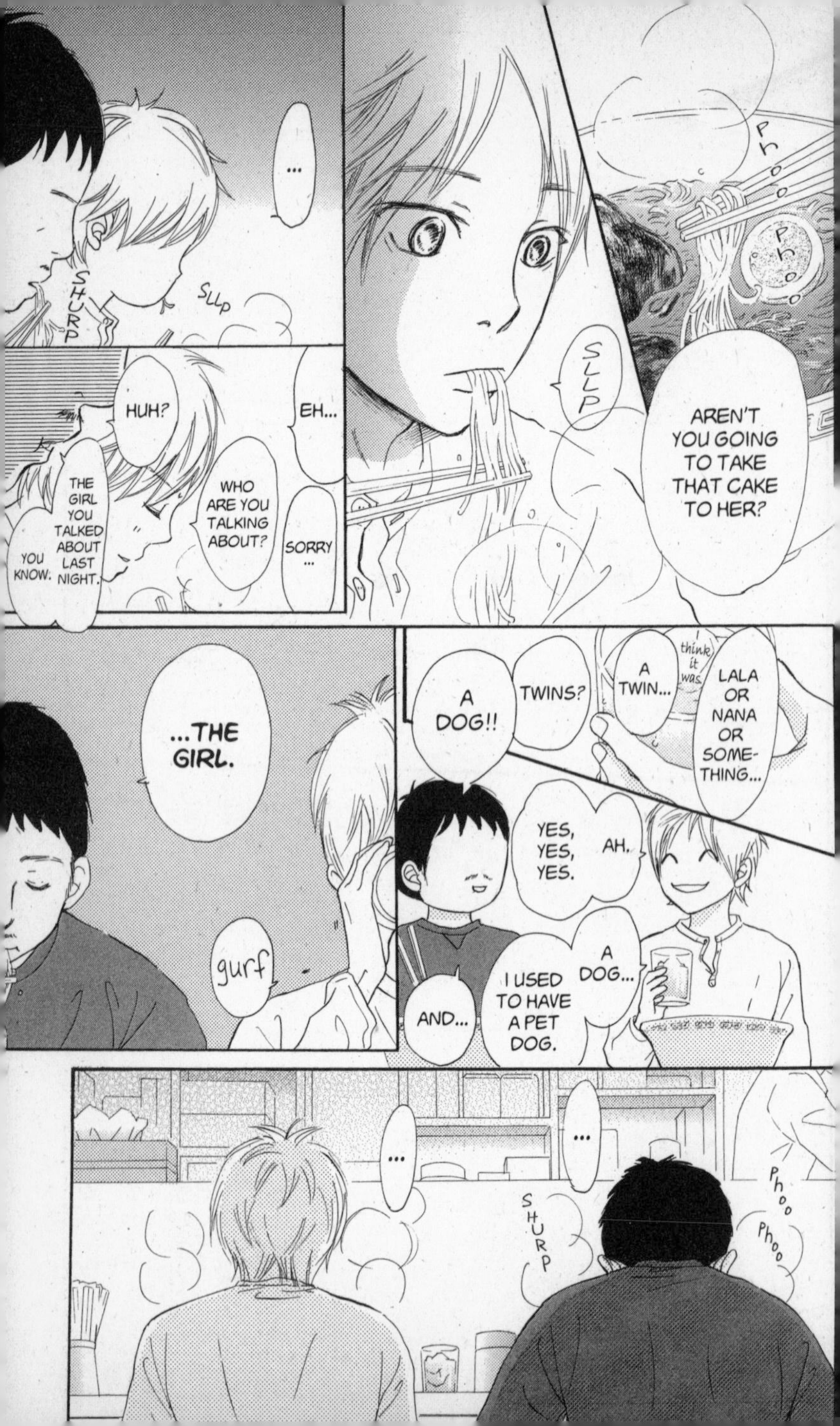
Phooo
Phooo
AREN'T YOU GOING TO TAKE THAT CAKE TO HER?
SLLP
...
SLLP
SHURP
EH...
SORRY...
WHO ARE YOU TALKING ABOUT?
HUH?
THE GIRL YOU TALKED ABOUT LAST NIGHT.
YOU KNOW.
LALA OR NANA OR SOME-THING...
I think it was.
A TWIN...
TWINS?
A DOG!!
AH.
YES, YES, YES.
A DOG...
I USED TO HAVE A PET DOG.
AND...
...THE GIRL.
gurf
Phoo
Phoo
...
SHURP
...

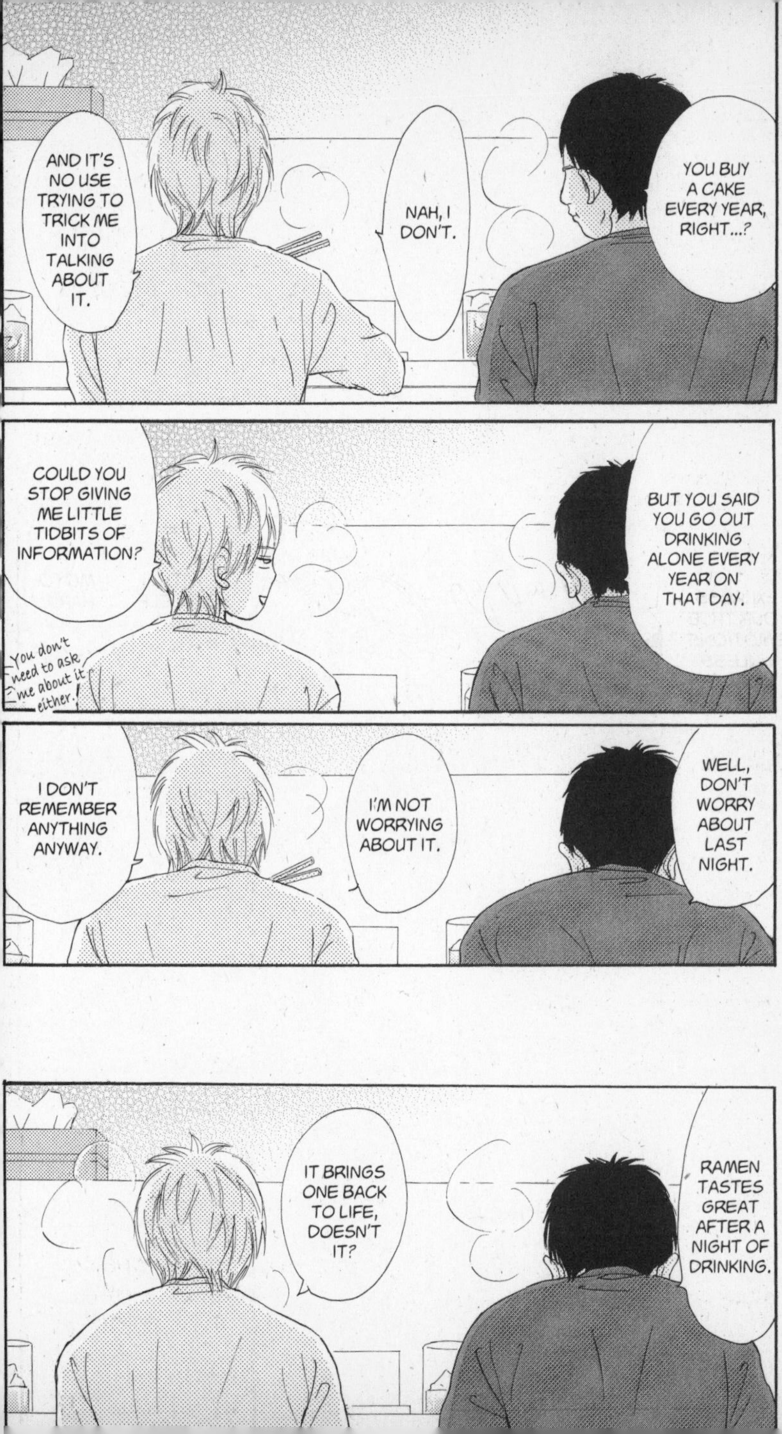
YOU BUY A CAKE EVERY YEAR, RIGHT...?
NAH, I DON'T.
AND IT'S NO USE TRYING TO TRICK ME INTO TALKING ABOUT IT.
BUT YOU SAID YOU GO OUT DRINKING ALONE EVERY YEAR ON THAT DAY.
COULD YOU STOP GIVING ME LITTLE TIDBITS OF INFORMATION?
You don't need to ask me about it either.
WELL, DON'T WORRY ABOUT LAST NIGHT.
I'M NOT WORRYING ABOUT IT.
I DON'T REMEMBER ANYTHING ANYWAY.
RAMEN TASTES GREAT AFTER A NIGHT OF DRINKING.
IT BRINGS ONE BACK TO LIFE, DOESN'T IT?

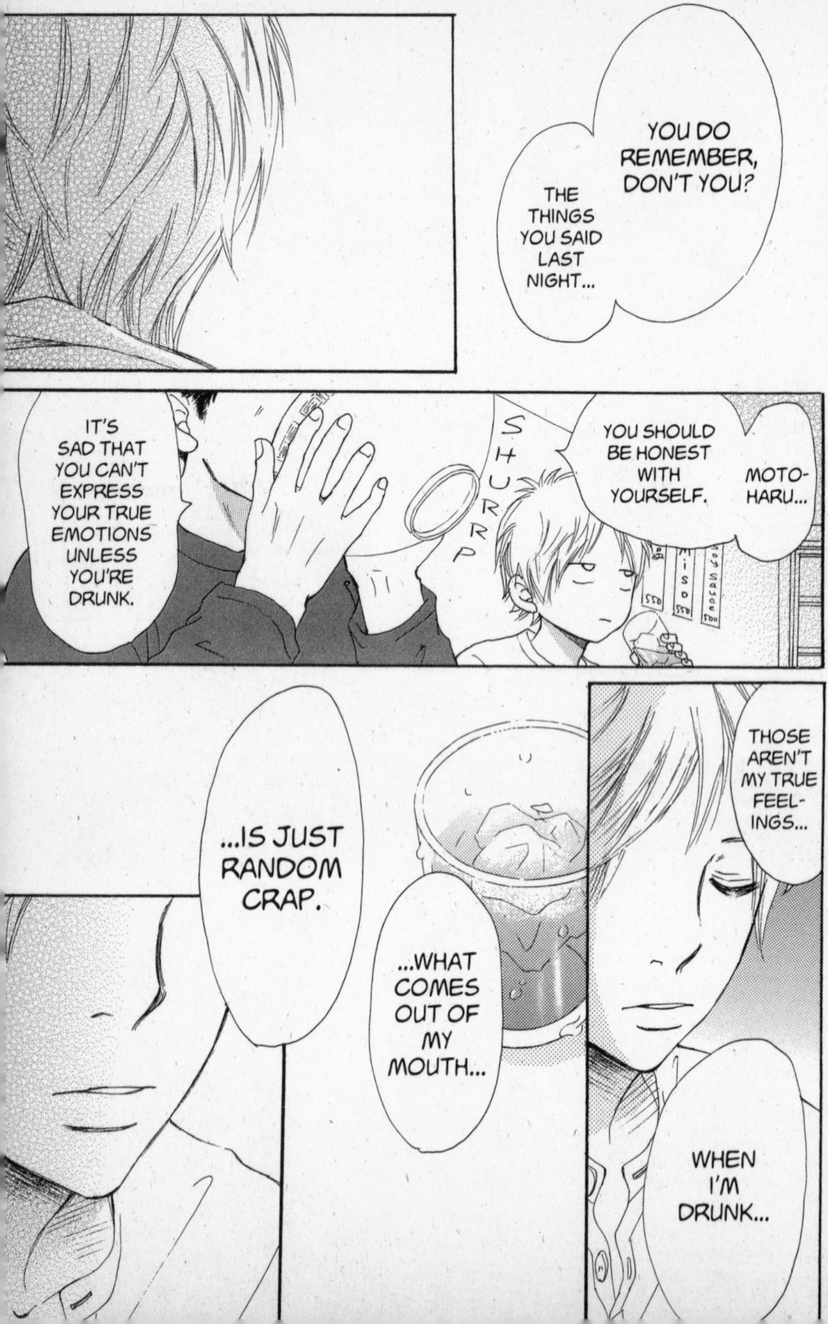
YOU DO REMEMBER, DON'T YOU?
THE THINGS YOU SAID LAST NIGHT...
MOTO-HARU...
YOU SHOULD BE HONEST WITH YOURSELF.
SHURRP
IT'S SAD THAT YOU CAN'T EXPRESS YOUR TRUE EMOTIONS UNLESS YOU'RE DRUNK.
THOSE AREN'T MY TRUE FEEL-INGS...
WHEN I'M DRUNK...
...WHAT COMES OUT OF MY MOUTH...
...IS JUST RANDOM CRAP.

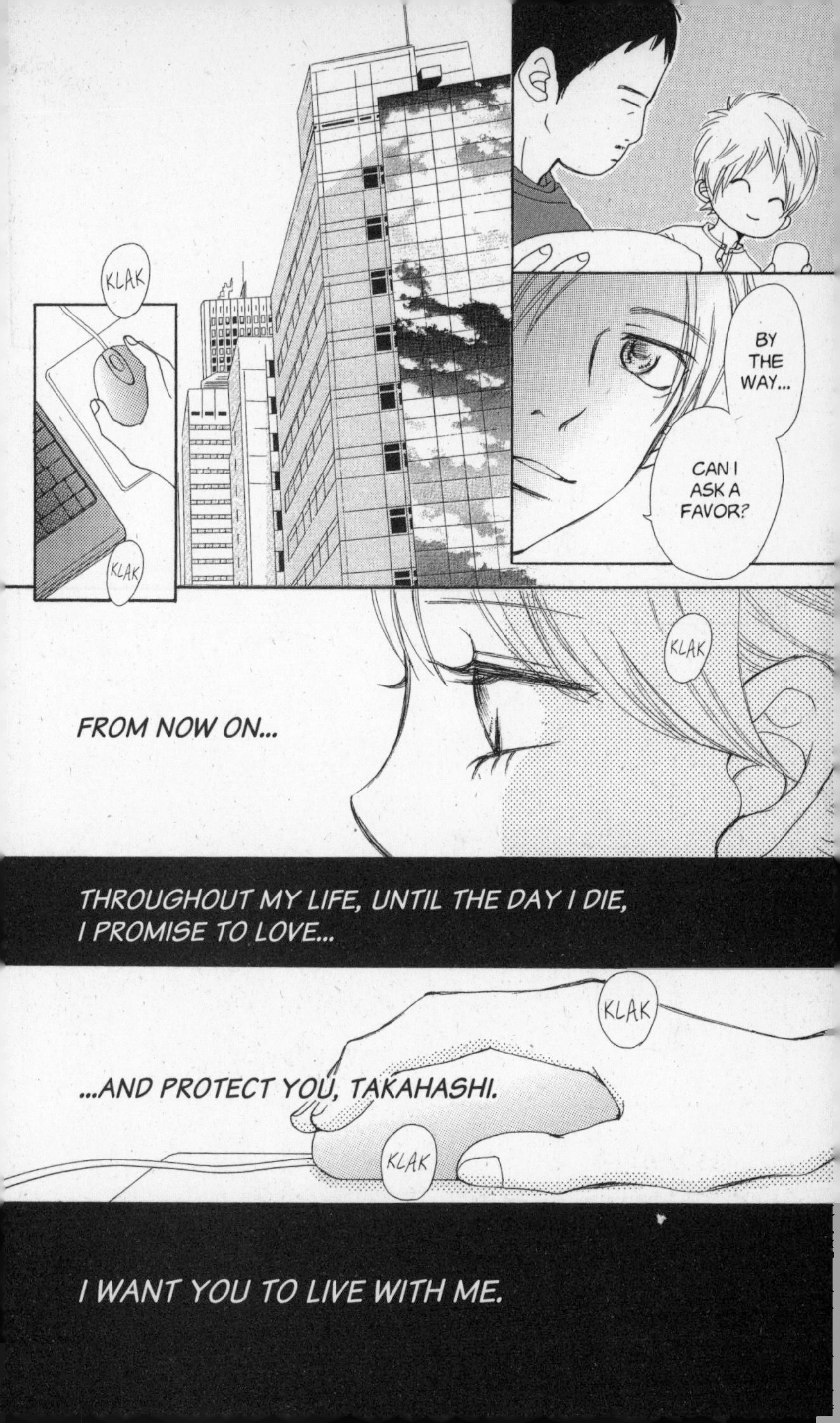
BY THE WAY...
CAN I ASK A FAVOR?
KLAK
KLAK
KLAK
FROM NOW ON...
THROUGHOUT MY LIFE, UNTIL THE DAY I DIE, I PROMISE TO LOVE...
KLAK
...AND PROTECT YOU, TAKAHASHI.
KLAK
I WANT YOU TO LIVE WITH ME.

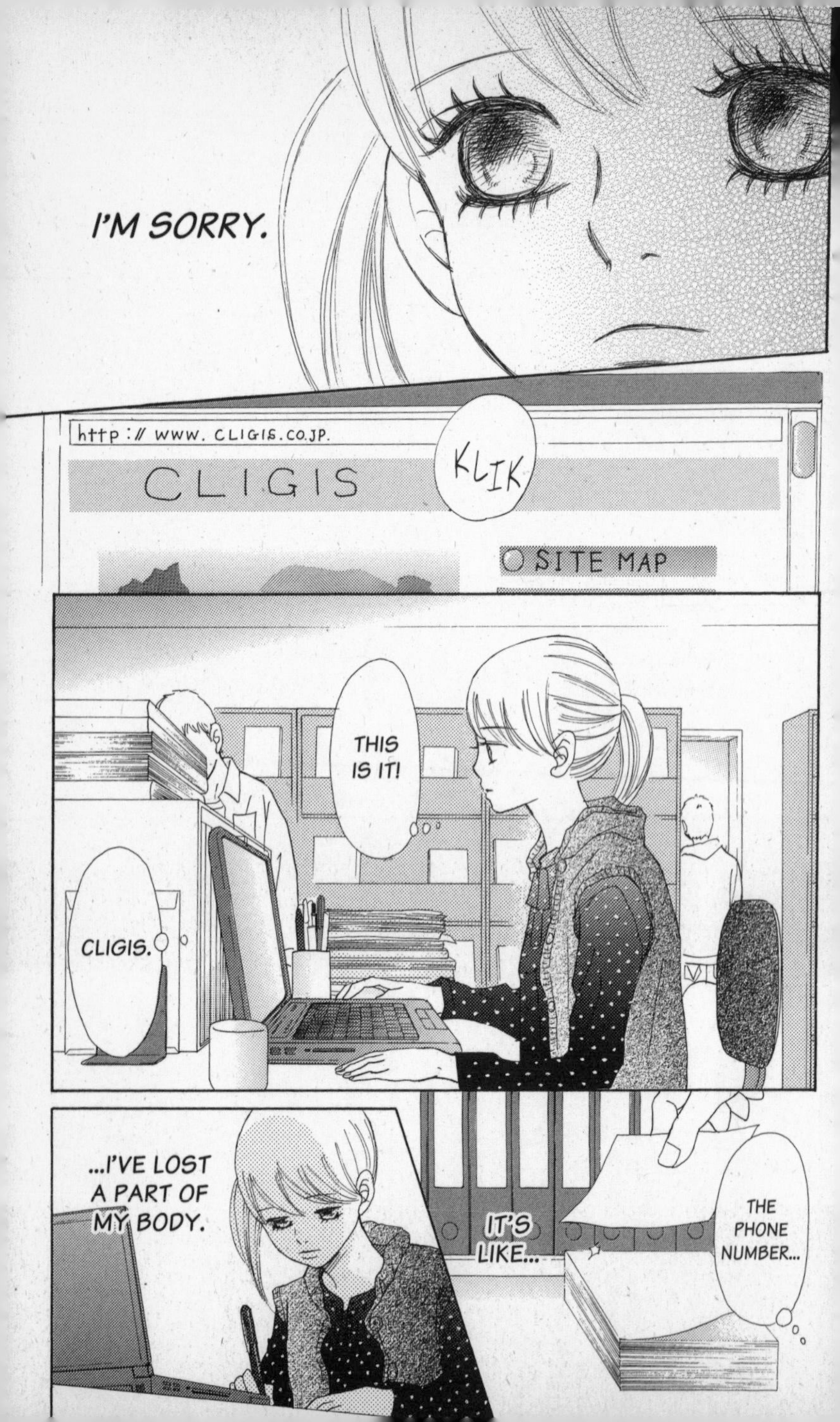
I'M SORRY.
KLIK
http://www.CLIGIS.co.jp.
CLIGIS
SITE MAP
THIS IS IT!
CLIGIS.
THE PHONE NUMBER...
IT'S LIKE...
...I'VE LOST A PART OF MY BODY.

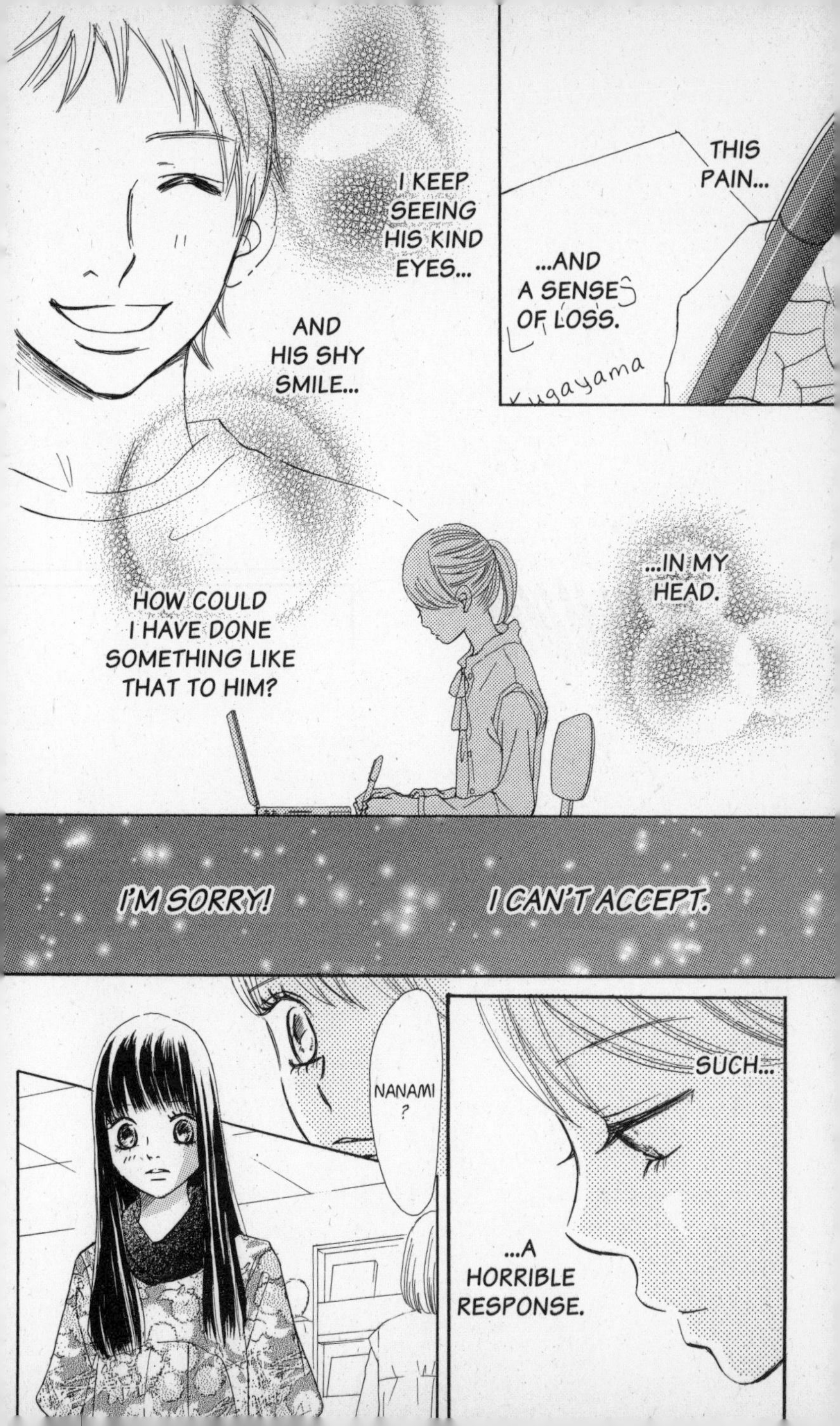
THIS PAIN...
...AND A SENSE OF LOSS.
Kugayama
I KEEP SEEING HIS KIND EYES...
AND HIS SHY SMILE...
...IN MY HEAD.
HOW COULD I HAVE DONE SOMETHING LIKE THAT TO HIM?
I'M SORRY!
I CAN'T ACCEPT.
SUCH...
...A HORRIBLE RESPONSE.
NANAMI ?

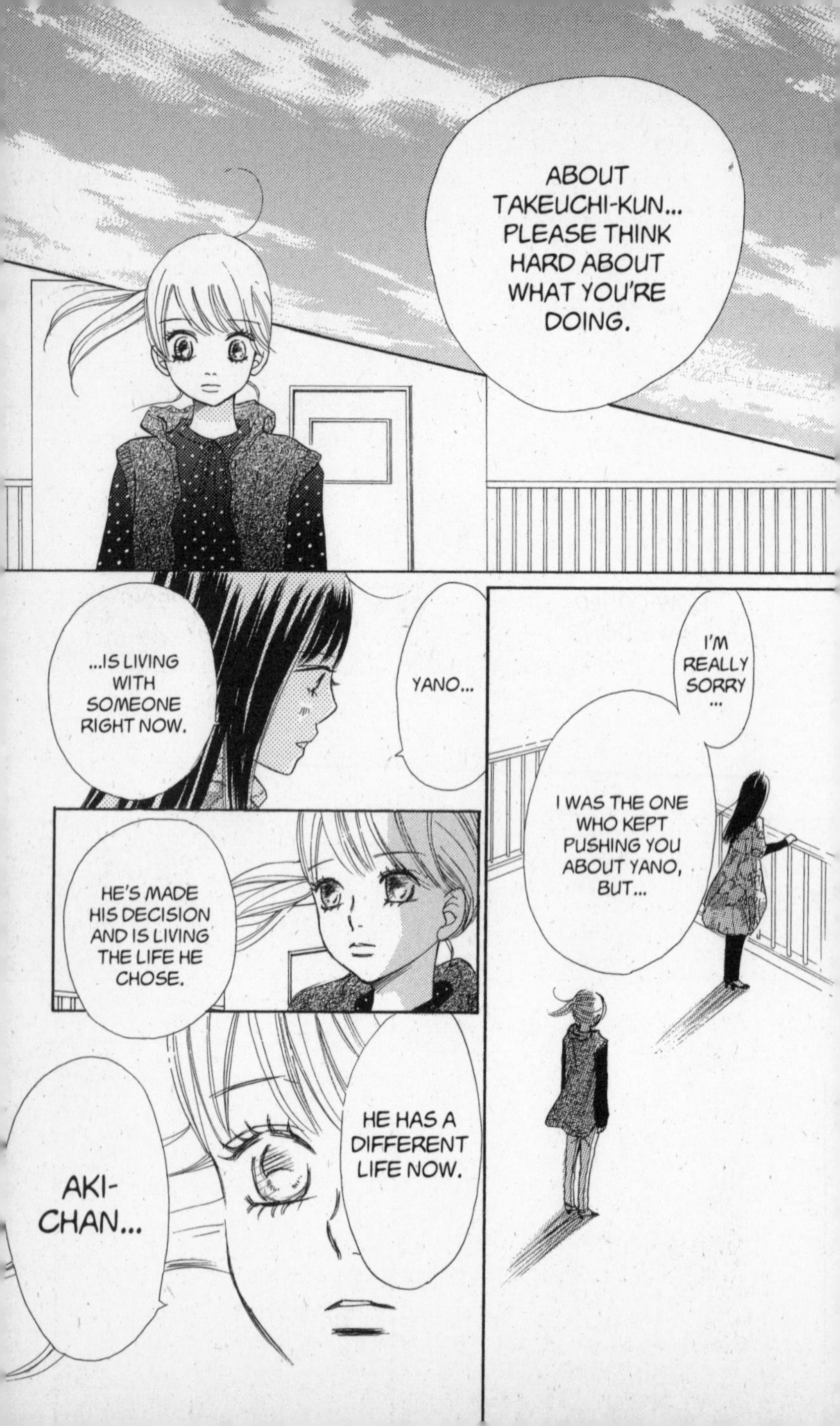
ABOUT TAKEUCHI-KUN... PLEASE THINK HARD ABOUT WHAT YOU'RE DOING.
I'M REALLY SORRY...
I WAS THE ONE WHO KEPT PUSHING YOU ABOUT YANO, BUT...
YANO...
...IS LIVING WITH SOMEONE RIGHT NOW.
HE'S MADE HIS DECISION AND IS LIVING THE LIFE HE CHOSE.
HE HAS A DIFFERENT LIFE NOW.
AKI-CHAN...

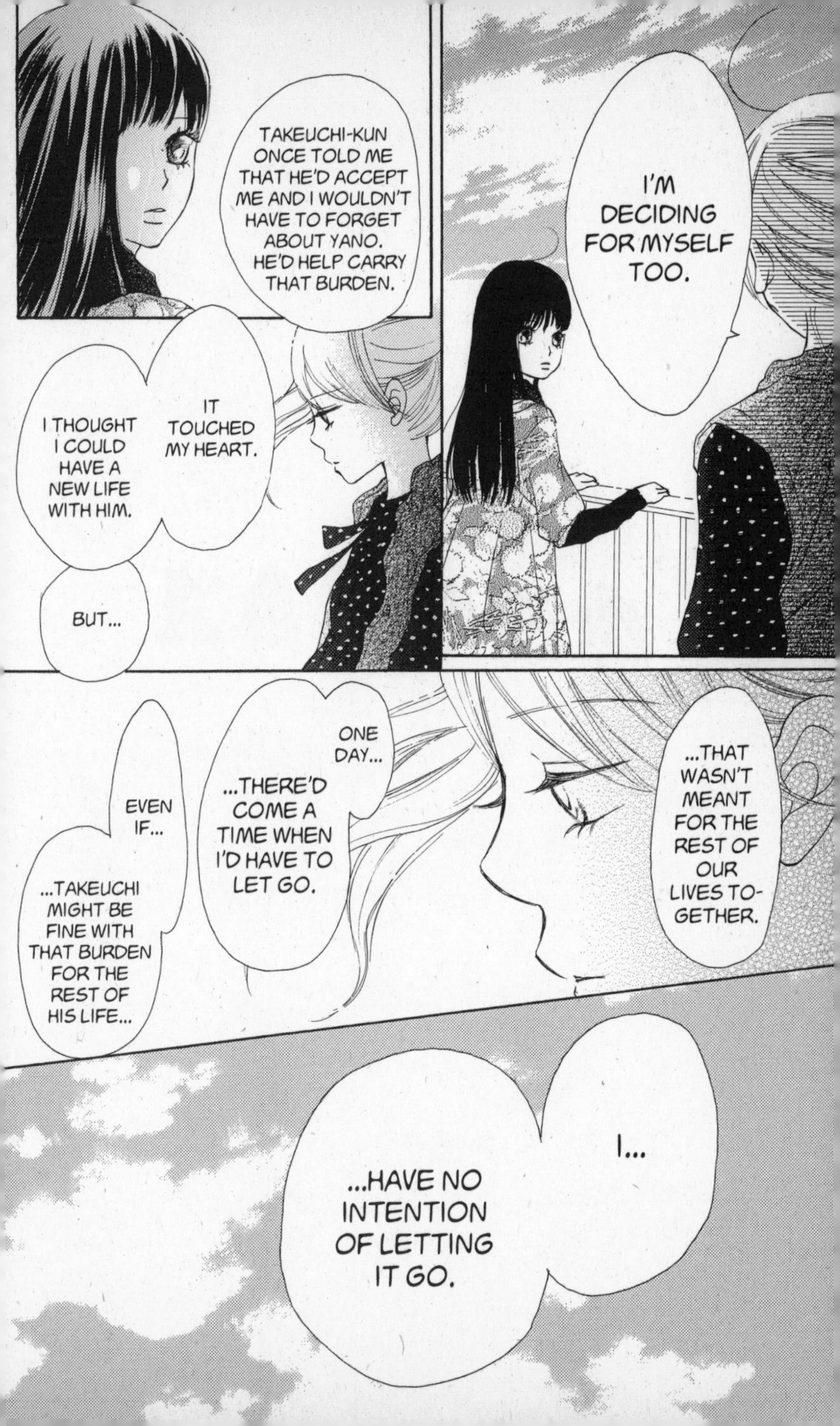
I'M DECIDING FOR MYSELF TOO.
TAKEUCHI-KUN ONCE TOLD ME THAT HE'D ACCEPT ME AND I WOULDN'T HAVE TO FORGET ABOUT YANO. HE'D HELP CARRY THAT BURDEN.
IT TOUCHED MY HEART.
I THOUGHT I COULD HAVE A NEW LIFE WITH HIM.
BUT...
...THAT WASN'T MEANT FOR THE REST OF OUR LIVES TO-GETHER.
ONE DAY...
...THERE'D COME A TIME WHEN I'D HAVE TO LET GO.
EVEN IF...
...TAKEUCHI MIGHT BE FINE WITH THAT BURDEN FOR THE REST OF HIS LIFE...
I...
...HAVE NO INTENTION OF LETTING IT GO.

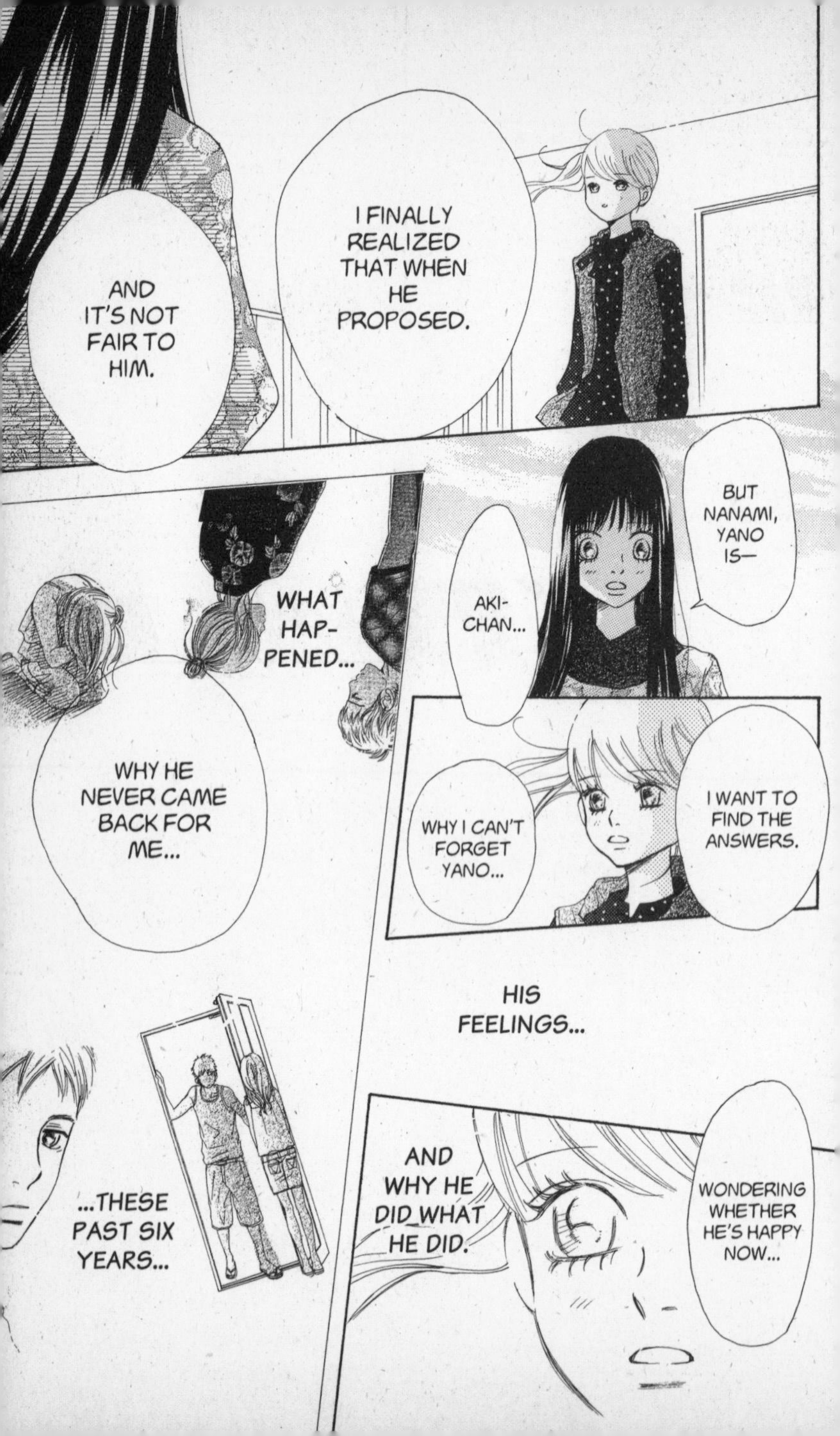
I FINALLY REALIZED THAT WHEN HE PROPOSED.
AND IT'S NOT FAIR TO HIM.
BUT NANAMI, YANO IS—
AKI-CHAN...
I WANT TO FIND THE ANSWERS.
WHY I CAN'T FORGET YANO...
HIS FEELINGS...
WONDERING WHETHER HE'S HAPPY NOW...
AND WHY HE DID WHAT HE DID.
WHAT HAPPENED...
WHY HE NEVER CAME BACK FOR ME...
...THESE PAST SIX YEARS...

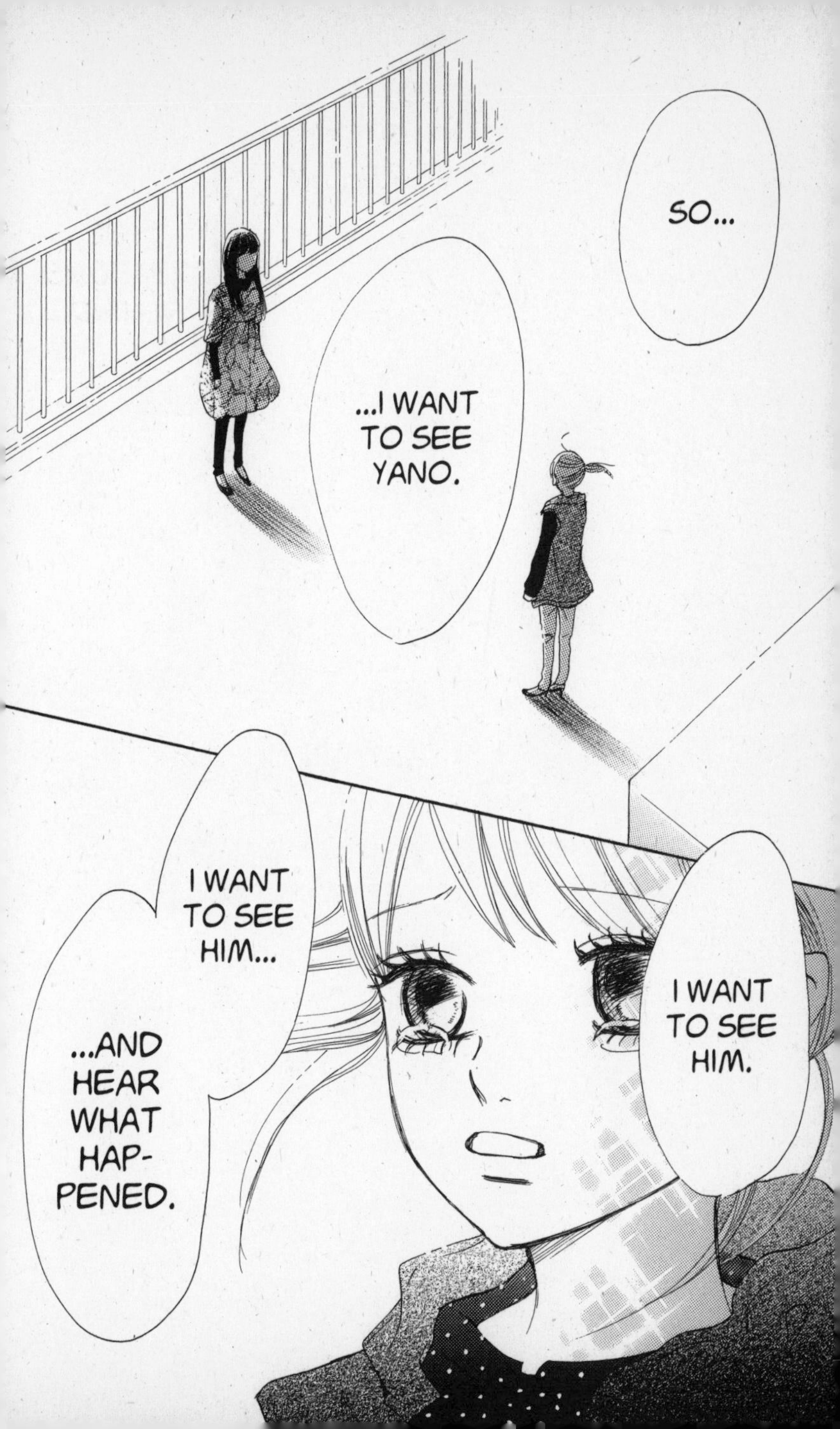
SO...
...I WANT TO SEE YANO.
I WANT TO SEE HIM.
I WANT TO SEE HIM...
...AND HEAR WHAT HAP-PENED.

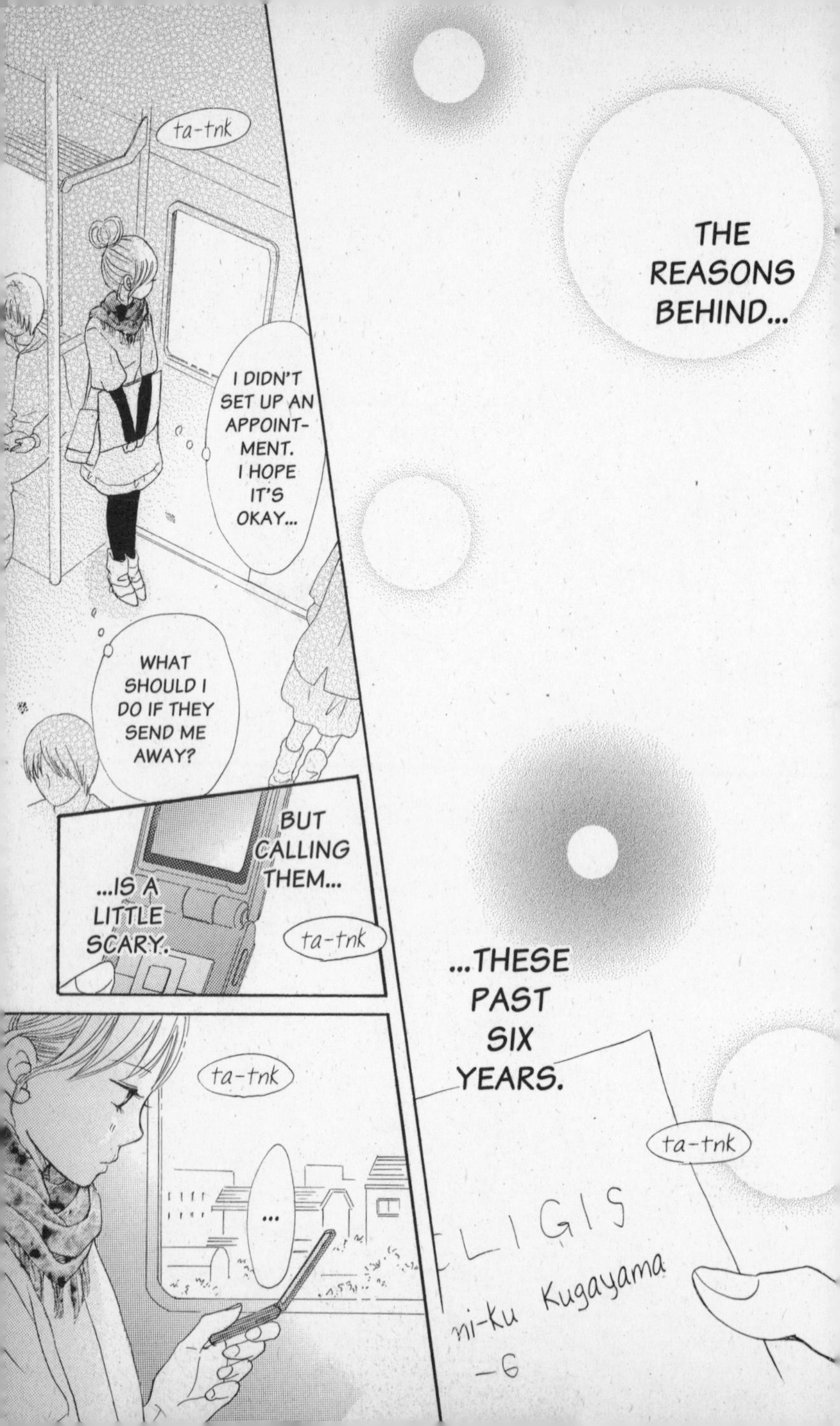
THE REASONS BEHIND...
...THESE PAST SIX YEARS.
ta-tnk
ta-tnk
I DIDN'T SET UP AN APPOINT-MENT. I HOPE IT'S OKAY...
WHAT SHOULD I DO IF THEY SEND ME AWAY?
BUT CALLING THEM...
...IS A LITTLE SCARY.
ta-tnk
ta-tnk
...

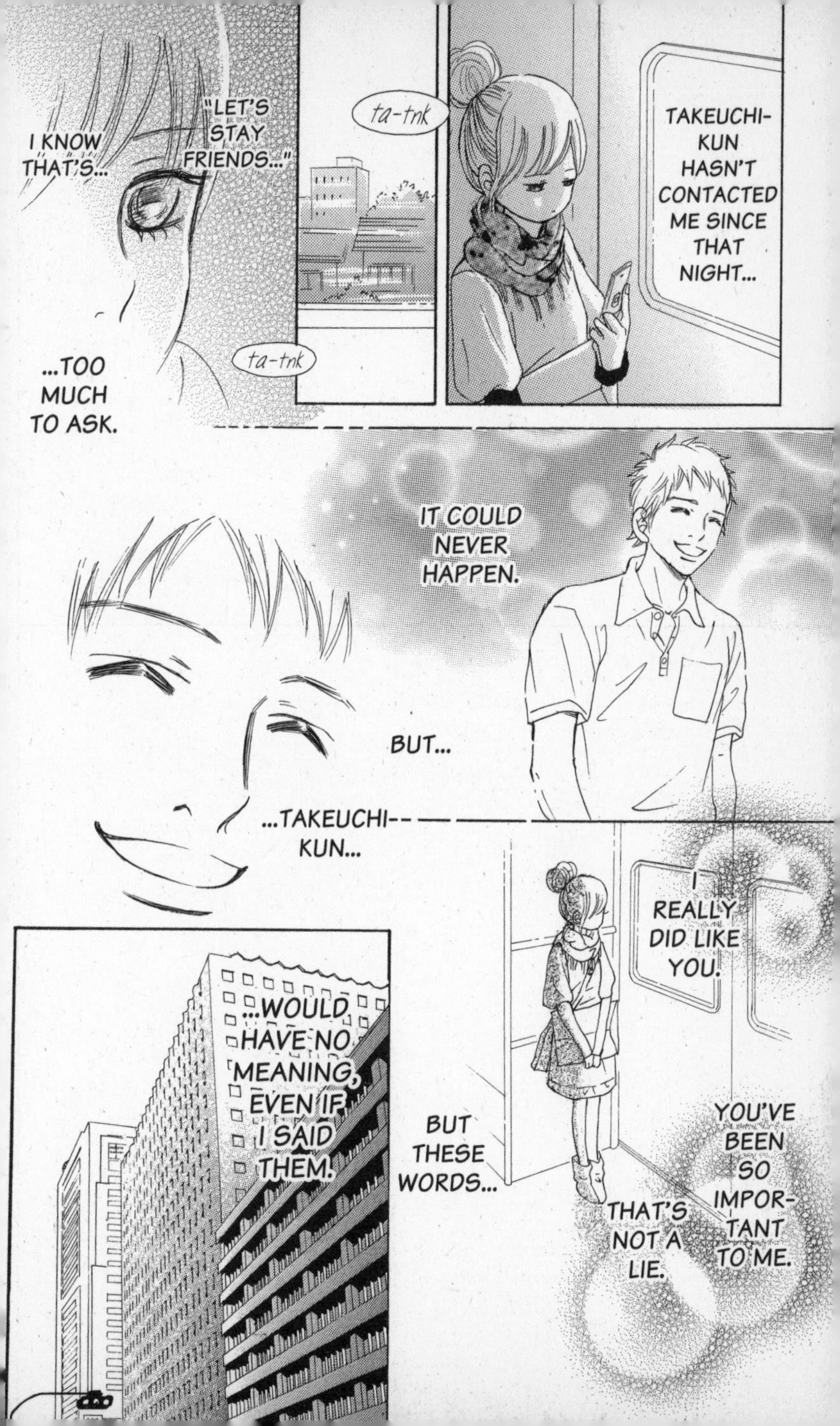
TAKEUCHI-KUN HASN'T CONTACTED ME SINCE THAT NIGHT...
ta-tnk
ta-tnk
"LET'S STAY FRIENDS..."
I KNOW THAT'S...
...TOO MUCH TO ASK.
IT COULD NEVER HAPPEN.
BUT...
...TAKEUCHI-KUN...
I REALLY DID LIKE YOU.
YOU'VE BEEN SO IMPORTANT TO ME.
THAT'S NOT A LIE.
BUT THESE WORDS...
...WOULD HAVE NO MEANING, EVEN IF I SAID THEM.

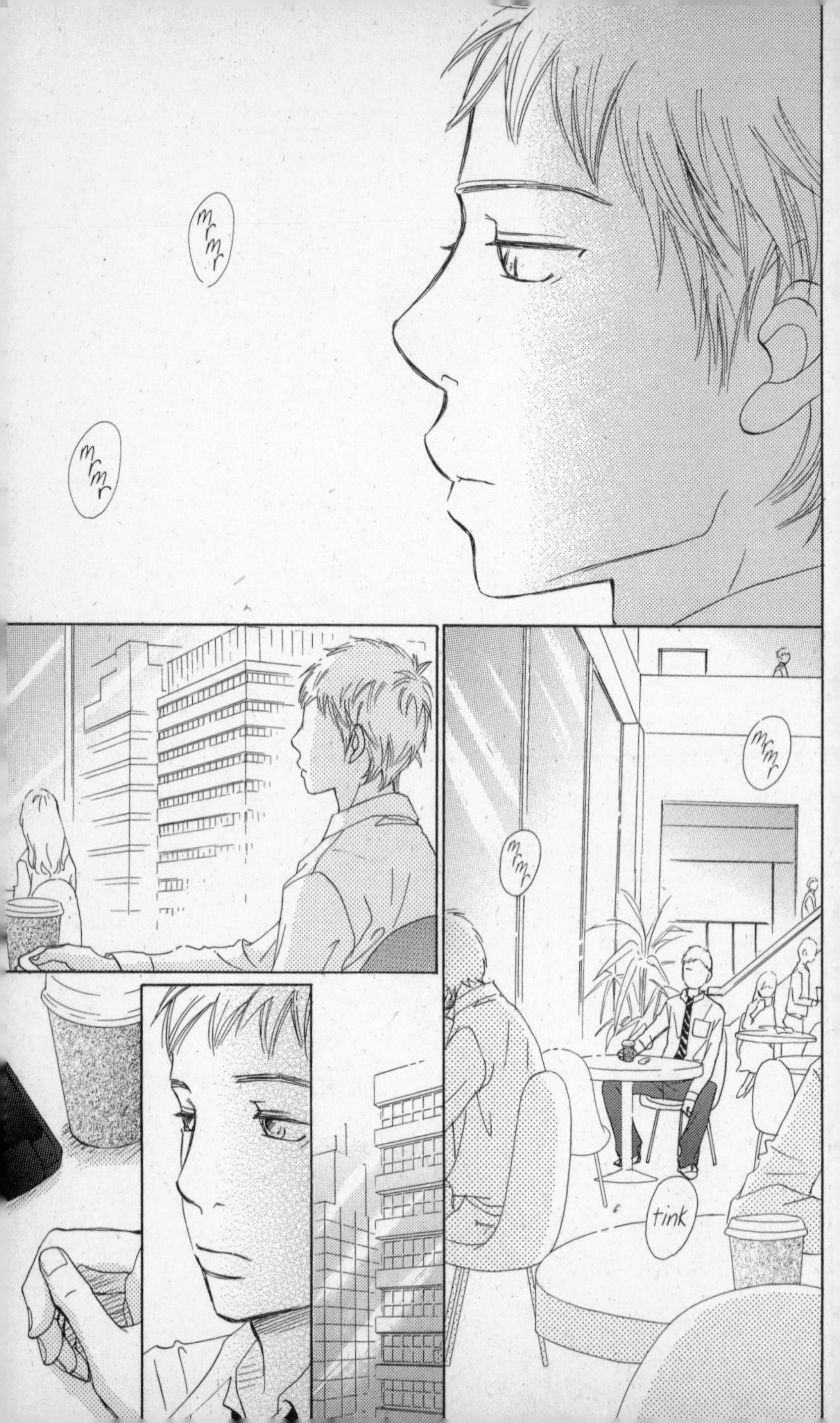
mrmr
mrmr
mrmr
mrmr
tink

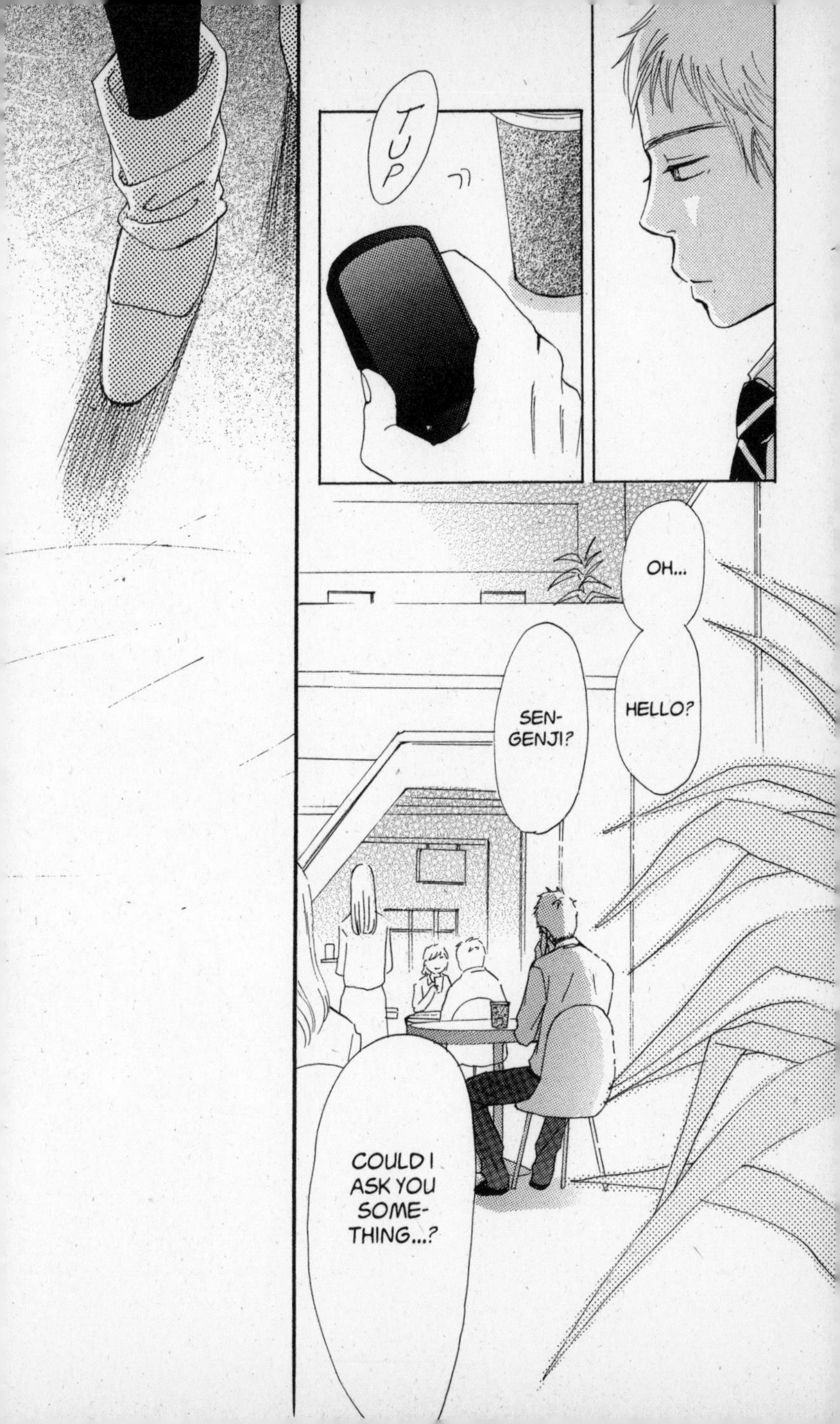
TUP
OH... HELLO?
SEN-GENJI?
COULD I ASK YOU SOME-THING...?

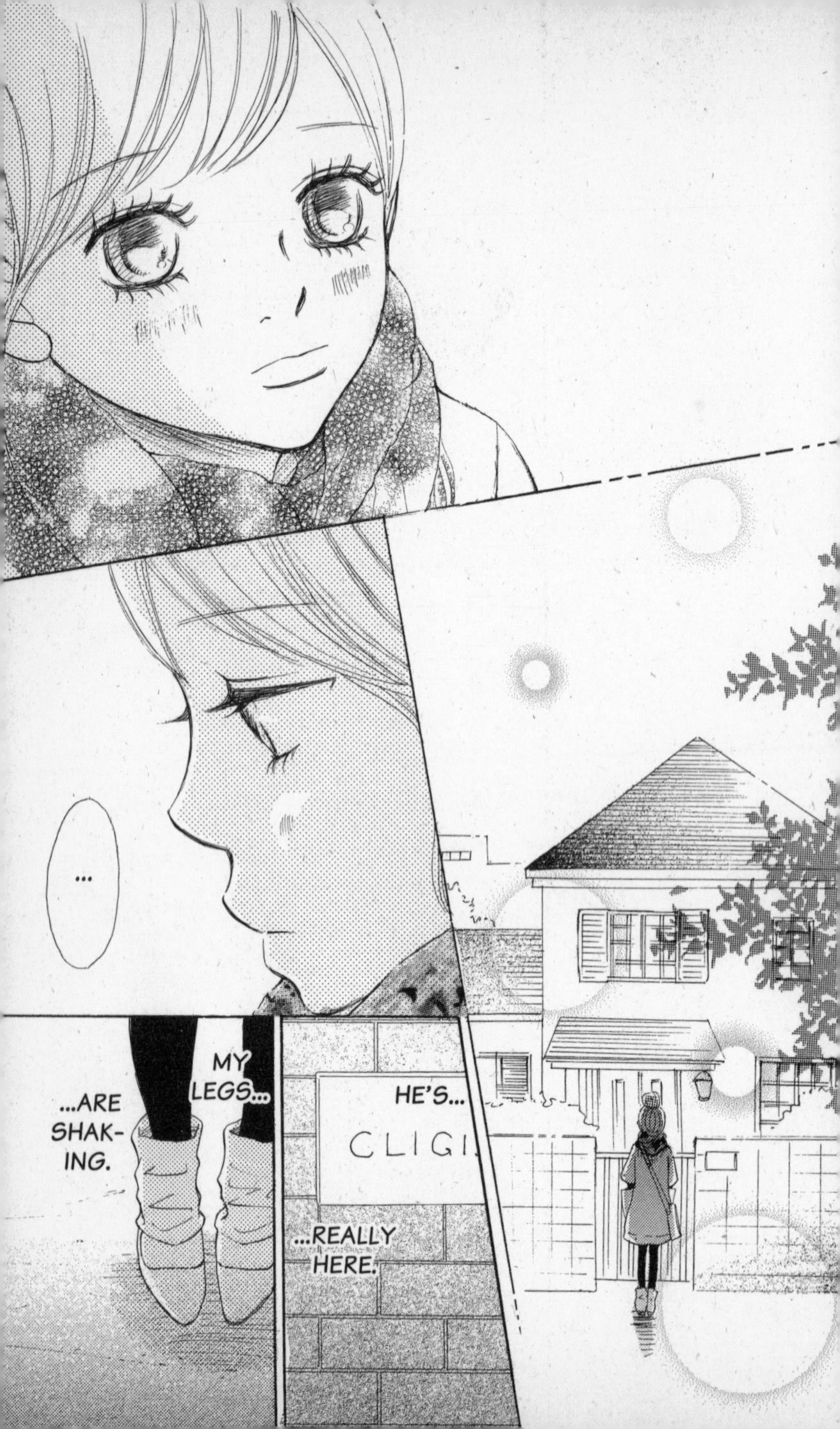
...
HE'S...
...REALLY HERE.
MY LEGS...
...ARE SHAK-ING.

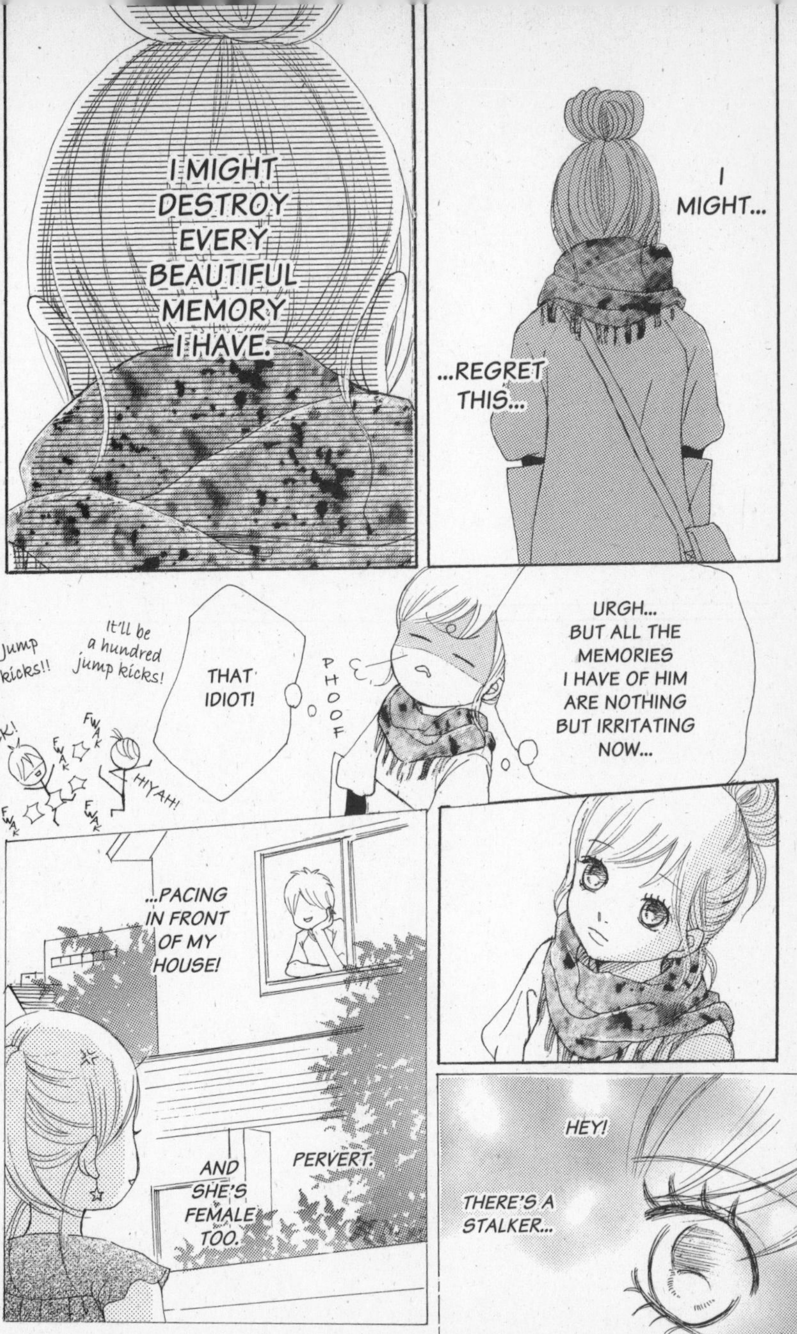
I MIGHT...
...REGRET THIS...
I MIGHT DESTROY EVERY BEAUTIFUL MEMORY I HAVE.
URGH... BUT ALL THE MEMORIES I HAVE OF HIM ARE NOTHING BUT IRRITATING NOW...
PHOOOF
THAT IDIOT!
It'll be a hundred jump kicks!
Jump kicks!!
FWAK
HIYAH!
FWAK
FWAK
FWAK
CK!
HEY!
THERE'S A STALKER...
...PACING IN FRONT OF MY HOUSE!
PERVERT.
AND SHE'S FEMALE TOO.

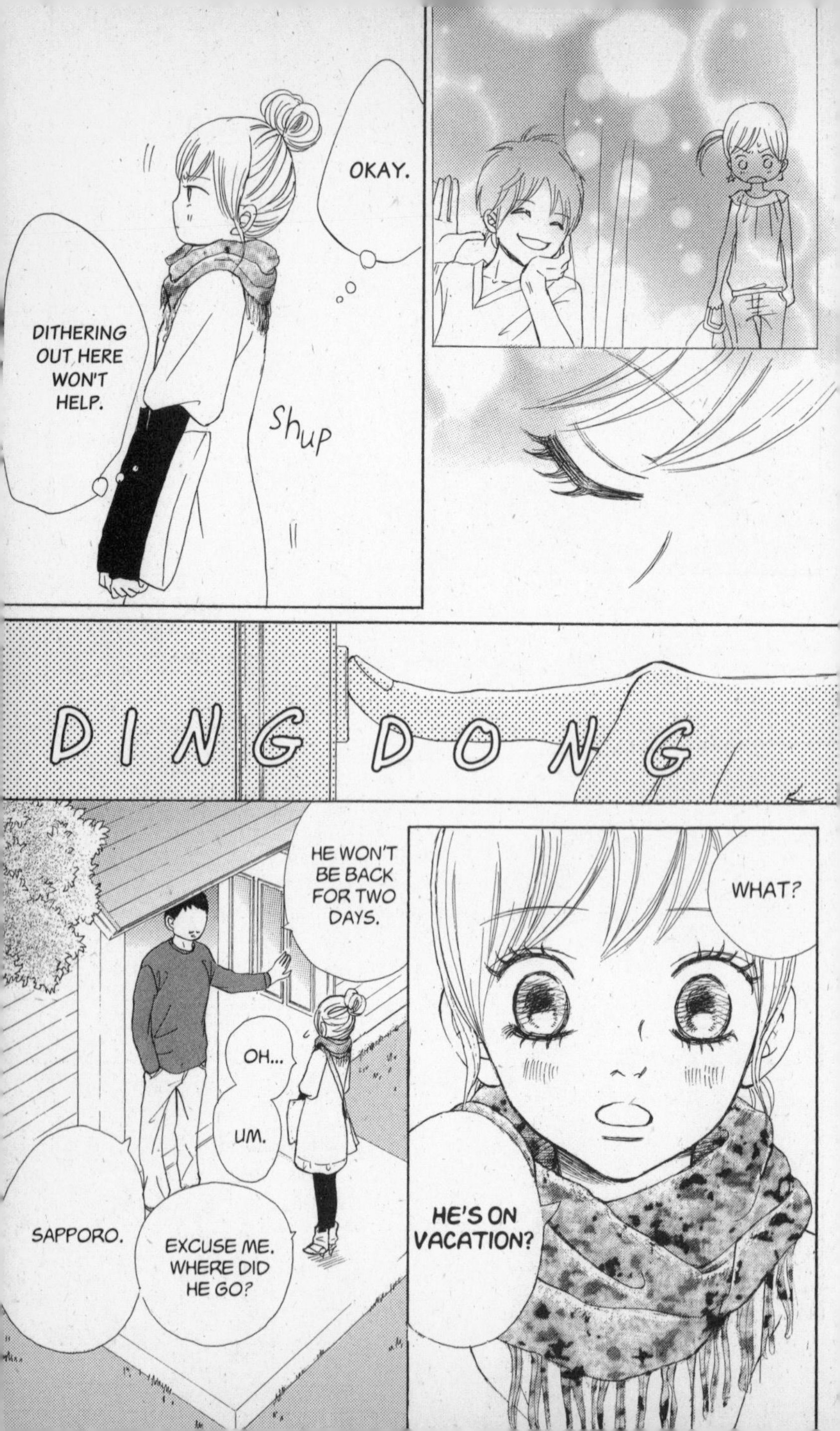
OKAY.
DITHERING OUT HERE WON'T HELP.
Shup
DING DONG
WHAT?
HE'S ON VACATION?
HE WON'T BE BACK FOR TWO DAYS.
OH...
UM.
EXCUSE ME. WHERE DID HE GO?
SAPPORO.

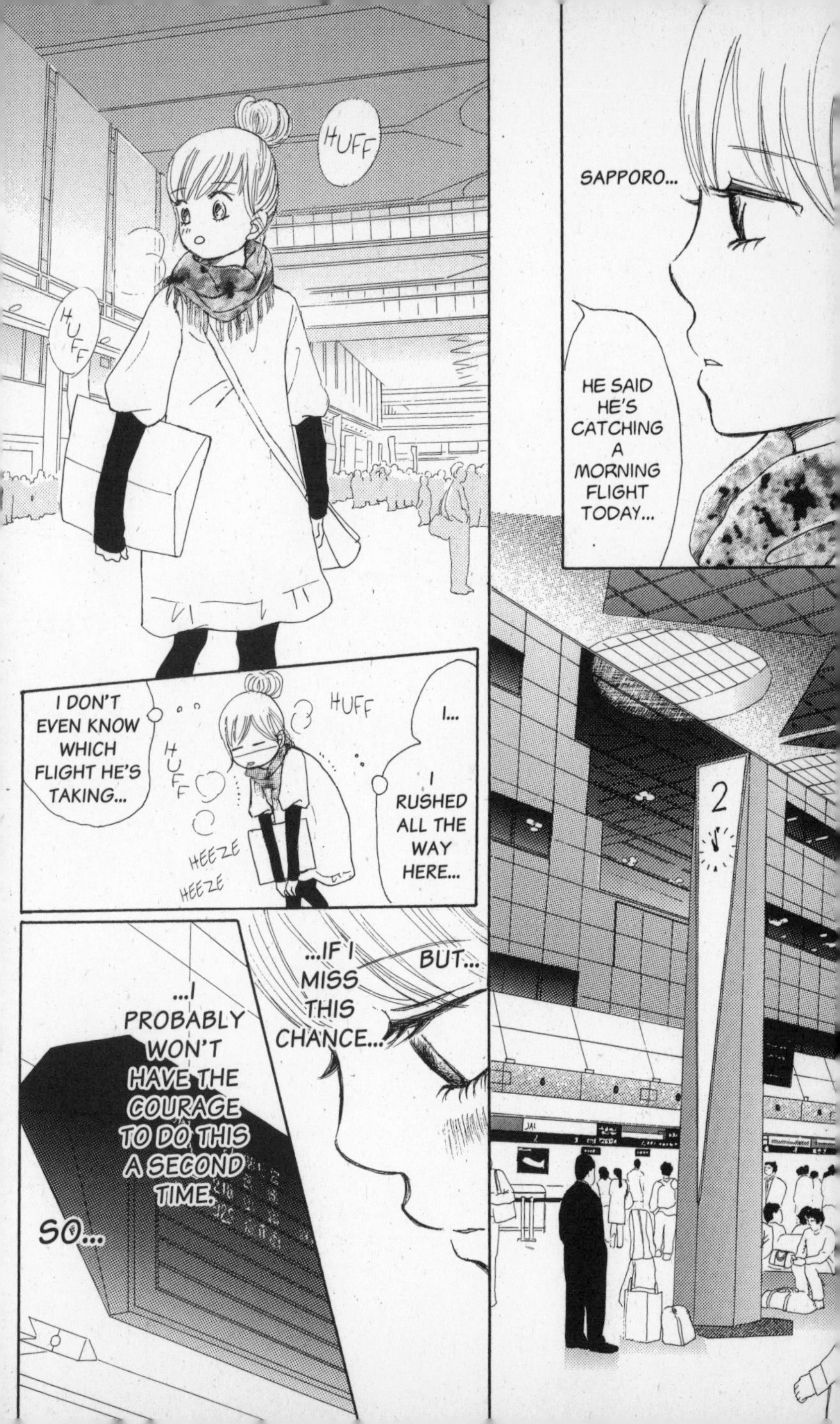
SAPPORO...
HE SAID HE'S CATCHING A MORNING FLIGHT TODAY...
HUFF
HUFF
I...
I RUSHED ALL THE WAY HERE...
HUFF
HUFF
HEEZE
HEEZE
I DON'T EVEN KNOW WHICH FLIGHT HE'S TAKING...
BUT...
...IF I MISS THIS CHANCE...
...I PROBABLY WON'T HAVE THE COURAGE TO DO THIS A SECOND TIME.
SO...

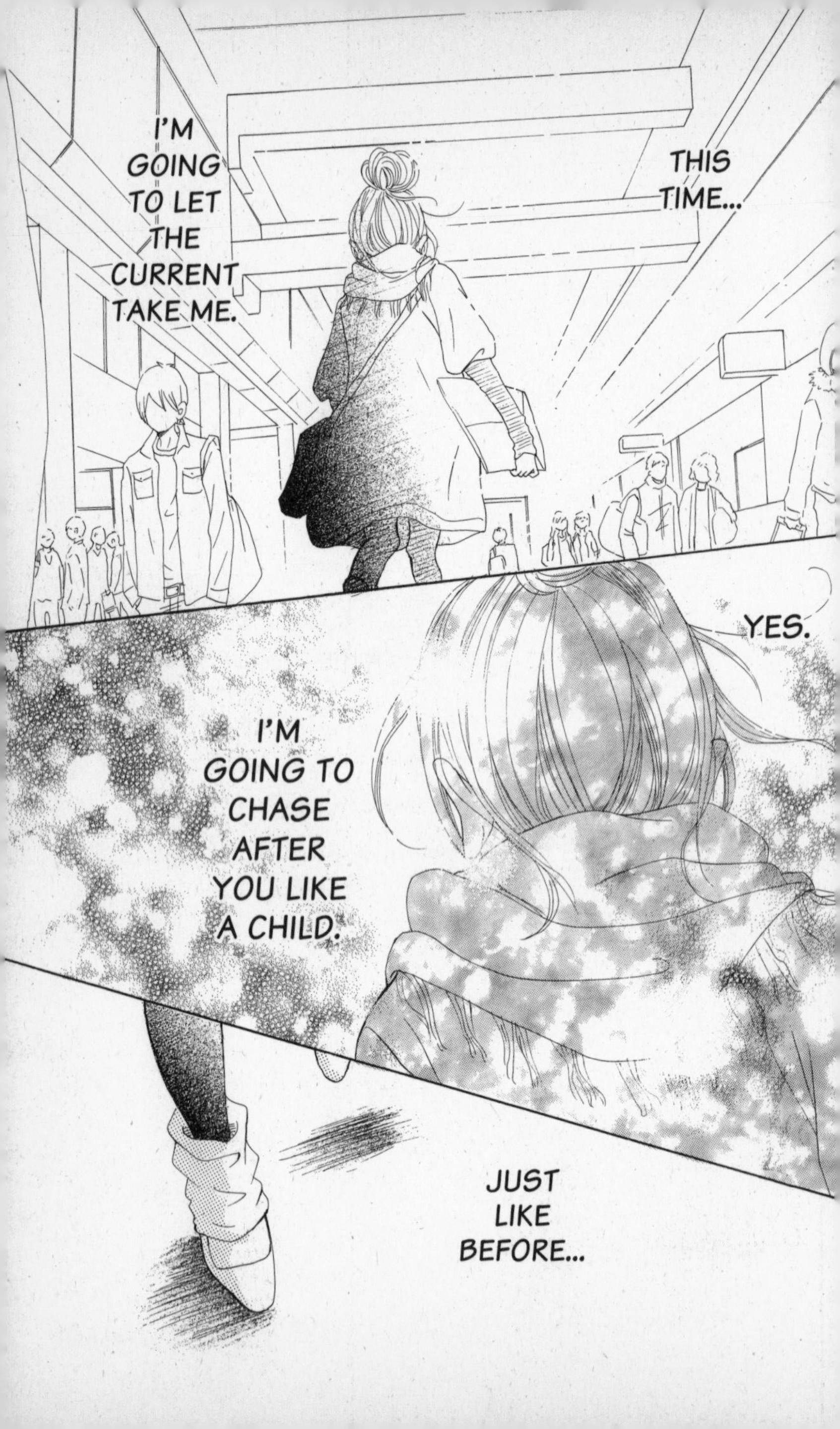
THIS TIME...
I'M GOING TO LET THE CURRENT TAKE ME.
YES.
I'M GOING TO CHASE AFTER YOU LIKE A CHILD.
JUST LIKE BEFORE...

JUST LIKE
I DID
BACK
THEN.

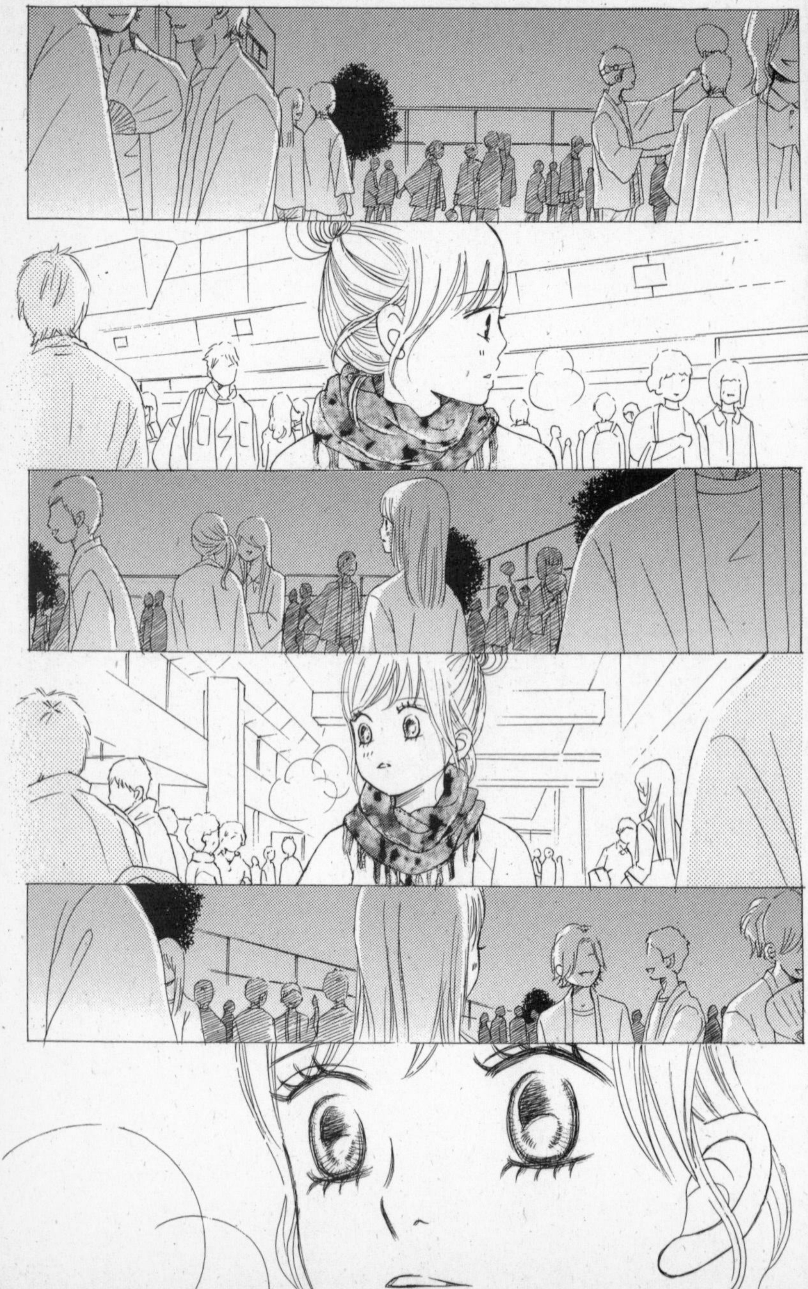

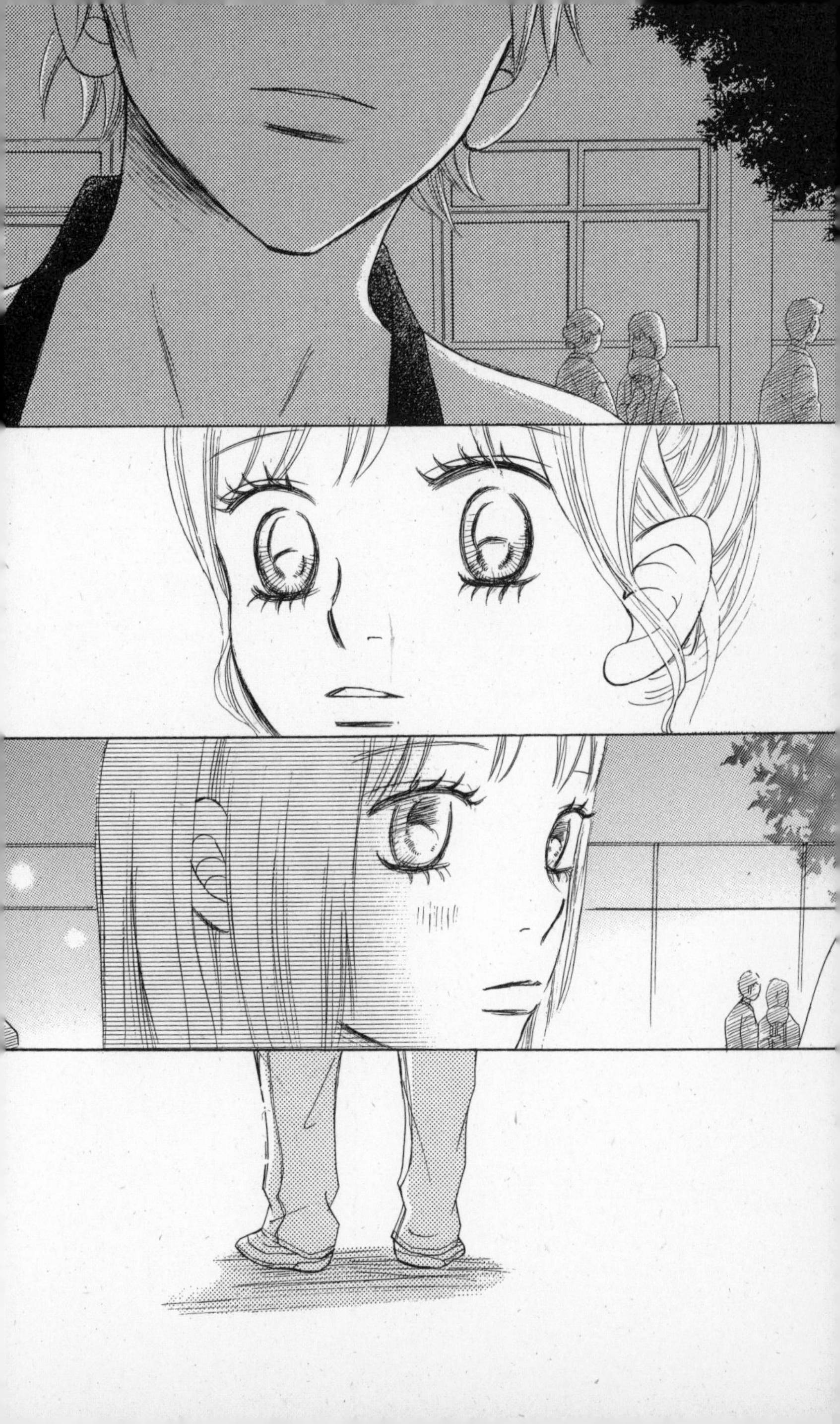

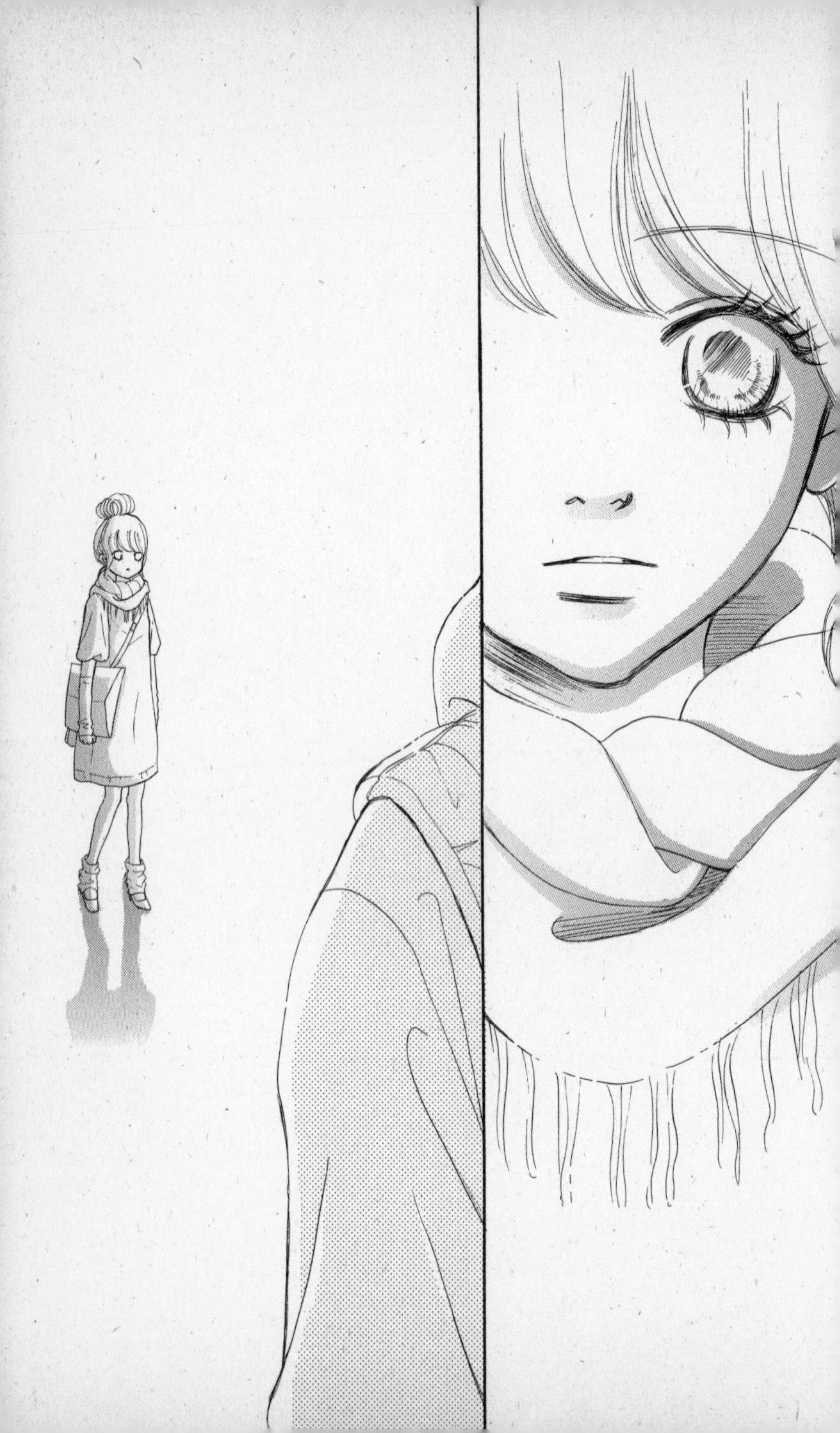

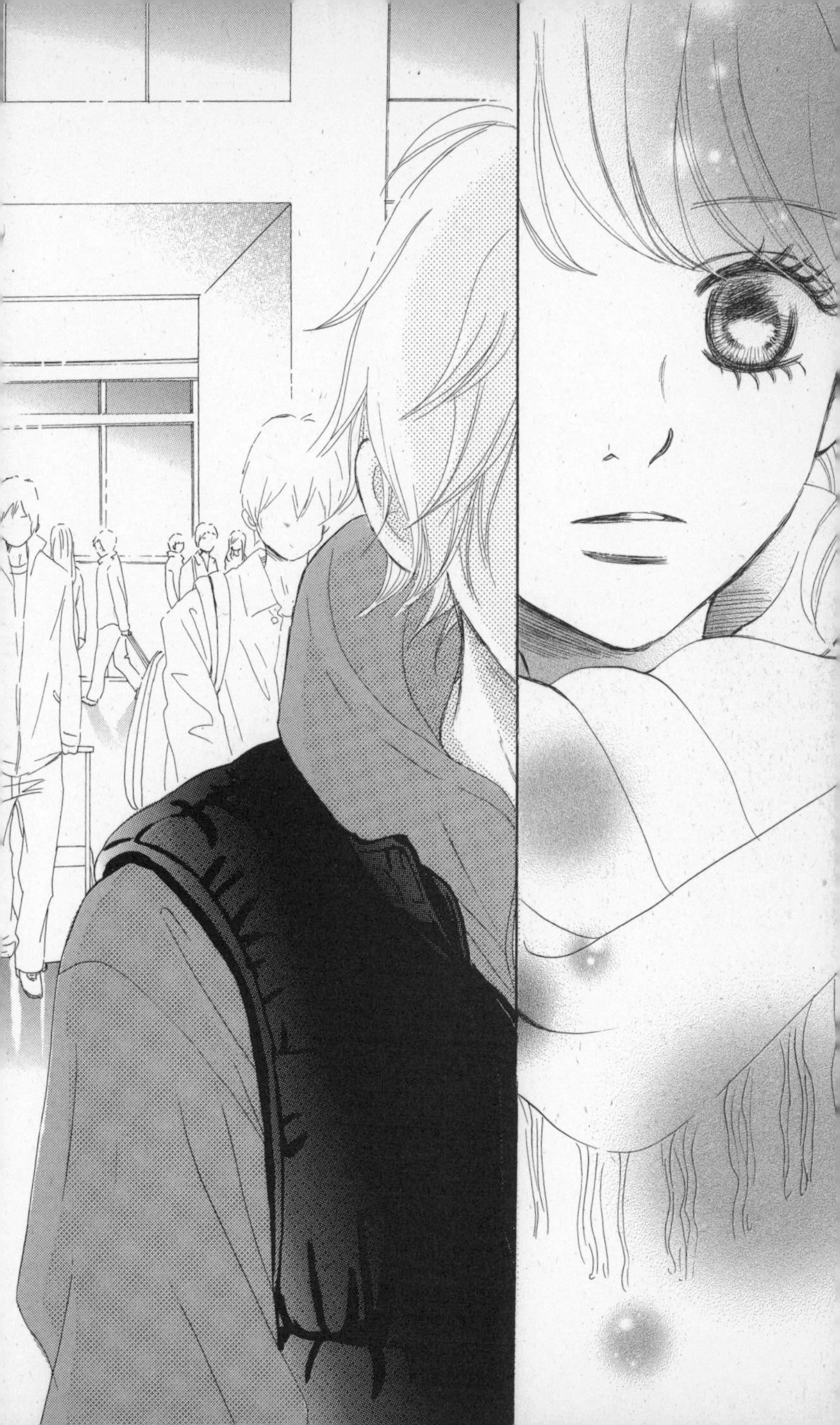

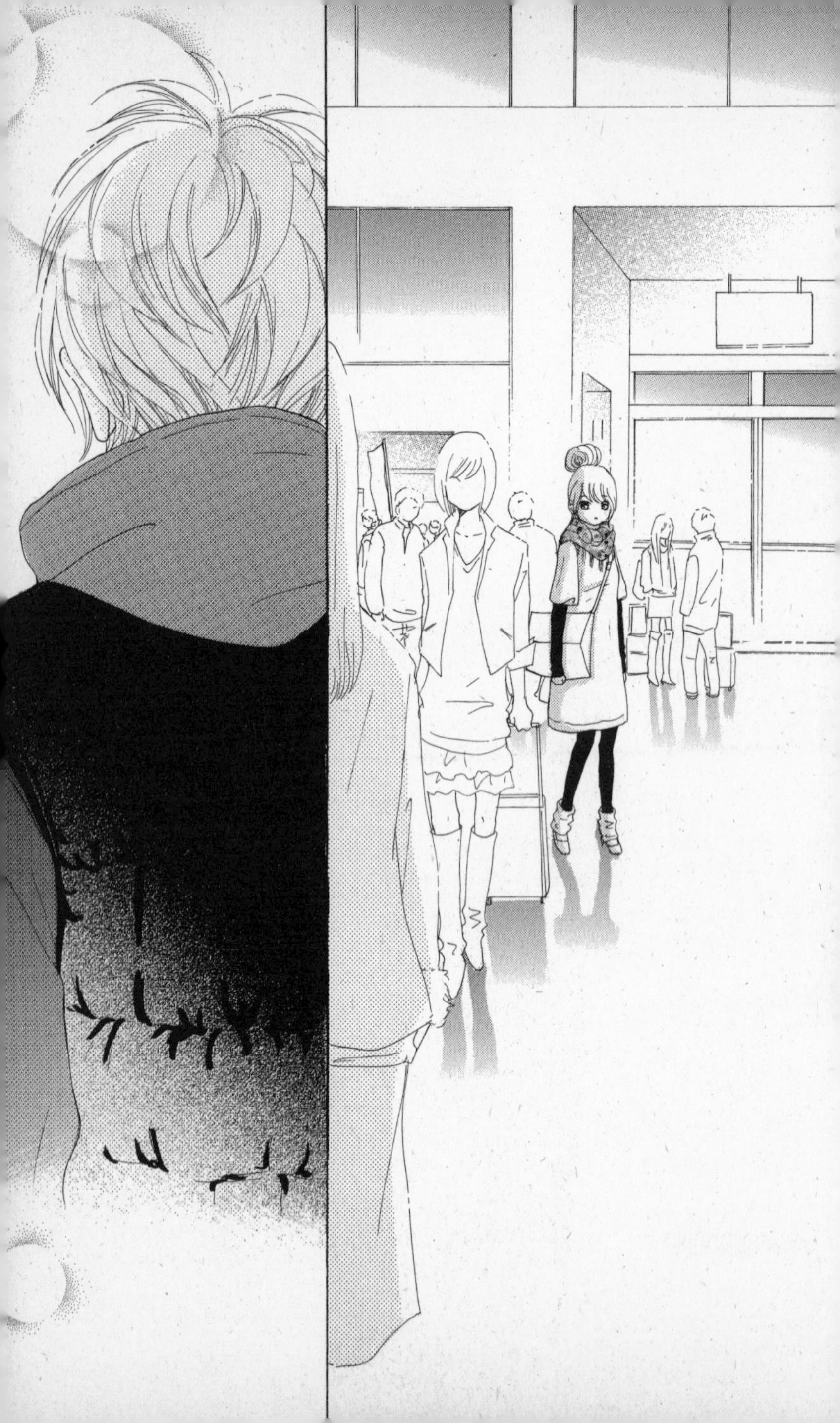

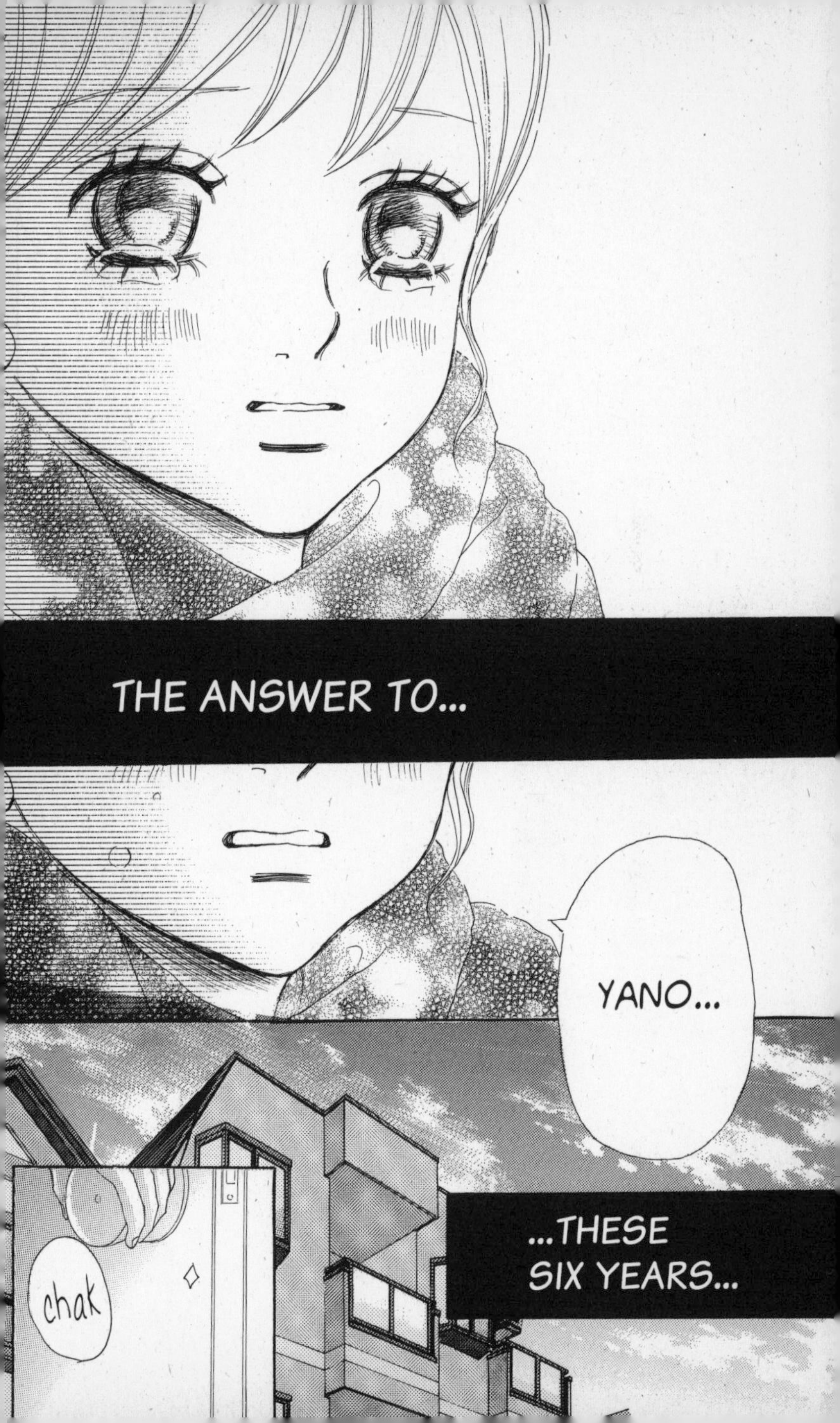
THE ANSWER TO...
YANO...
...THESE SIX YEARS...
chak

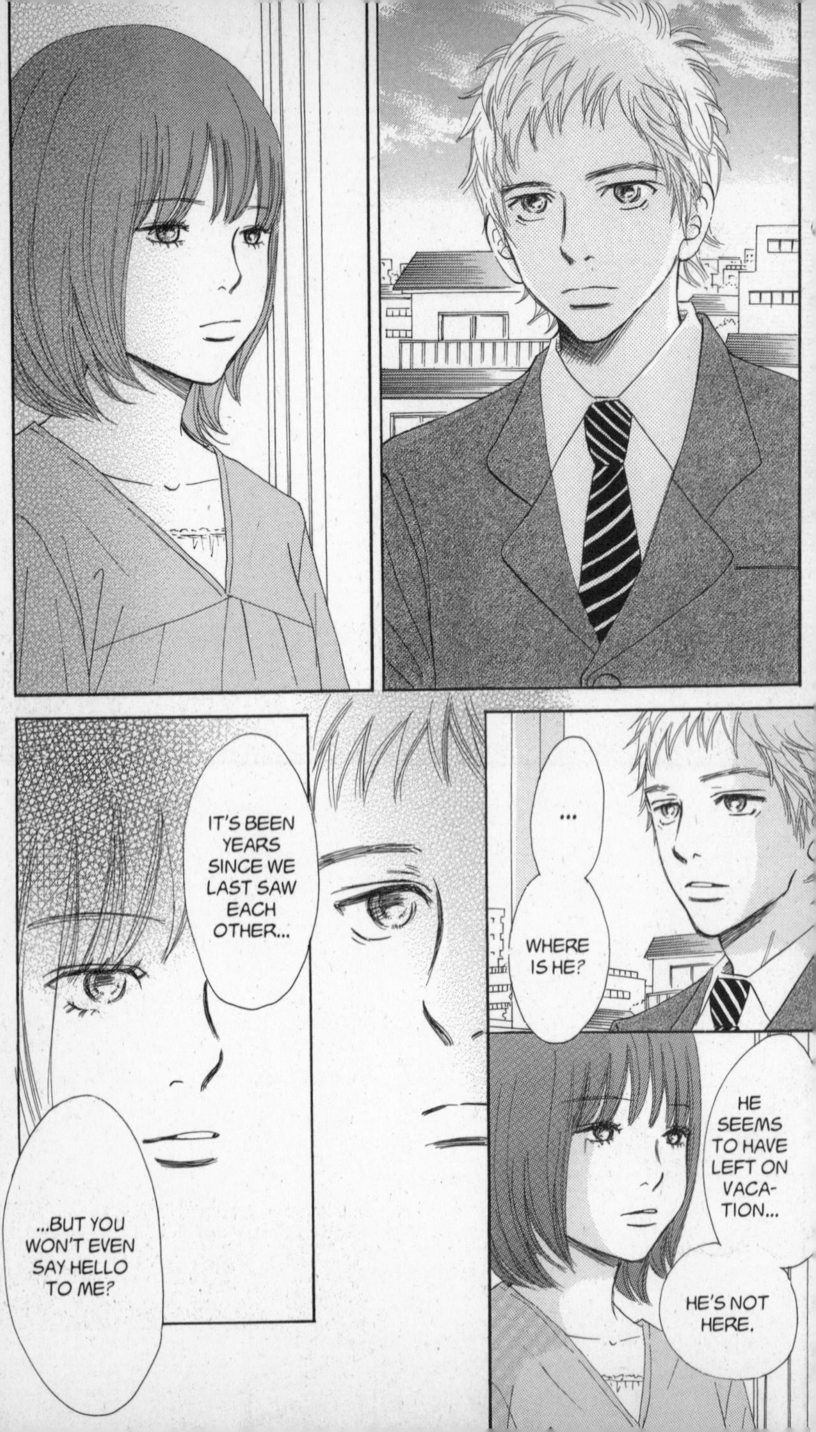
...
WHERE IS HE?
HE SEEMS TO HAVE LEFT ON VACATION...
HE'S NOT HERE.
IT'S BEEN YEARS SINCE WE LAST SAW EACH OTHER...
...BUT YOU WON'T EVEN SAY HELLO TO ME?

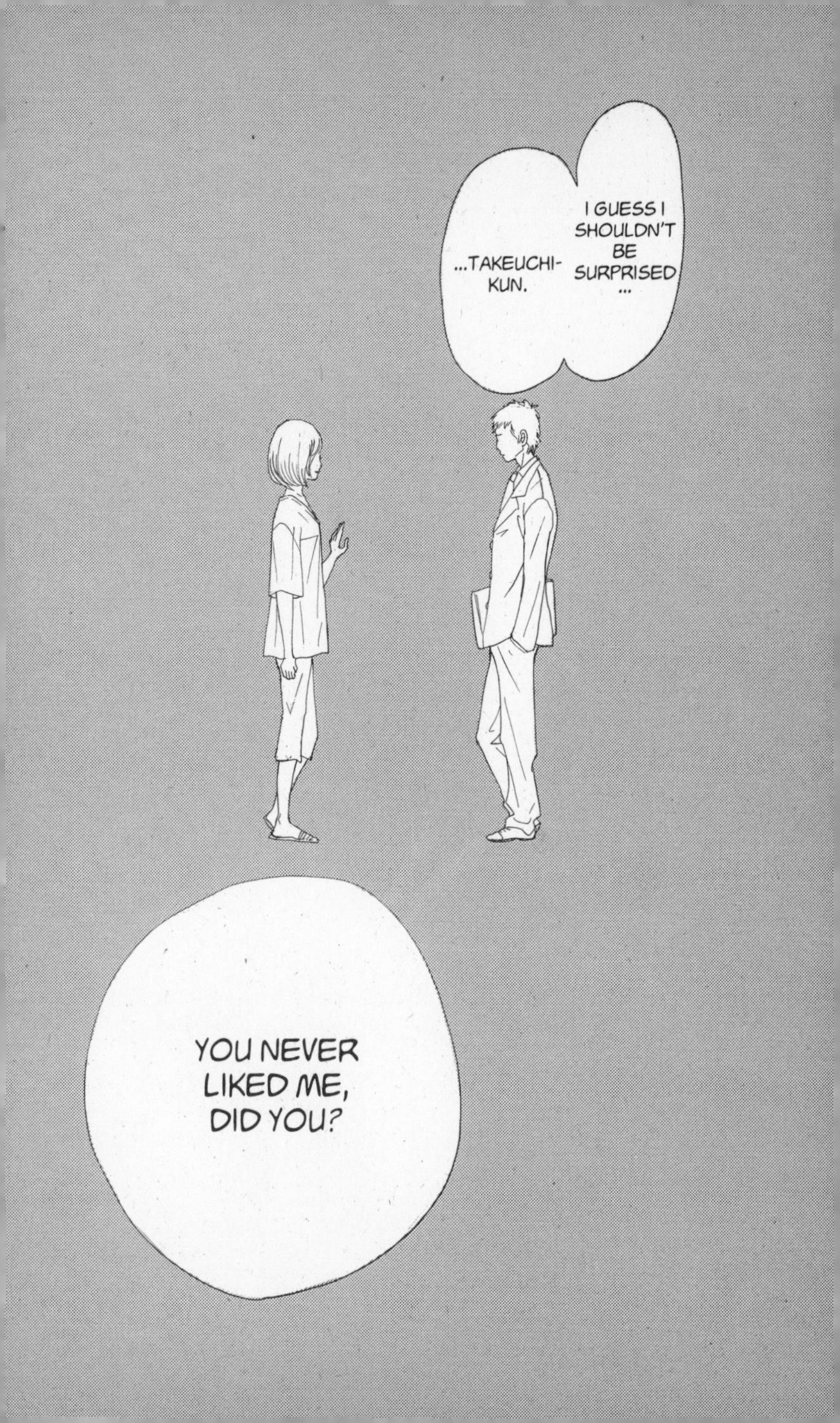
I GUESS I SHOULDN'T BE SURPRISED...
...TAKEUCHI-KUN.
YOU NEVER LIKED ME, DID YOU?

Chapter 52

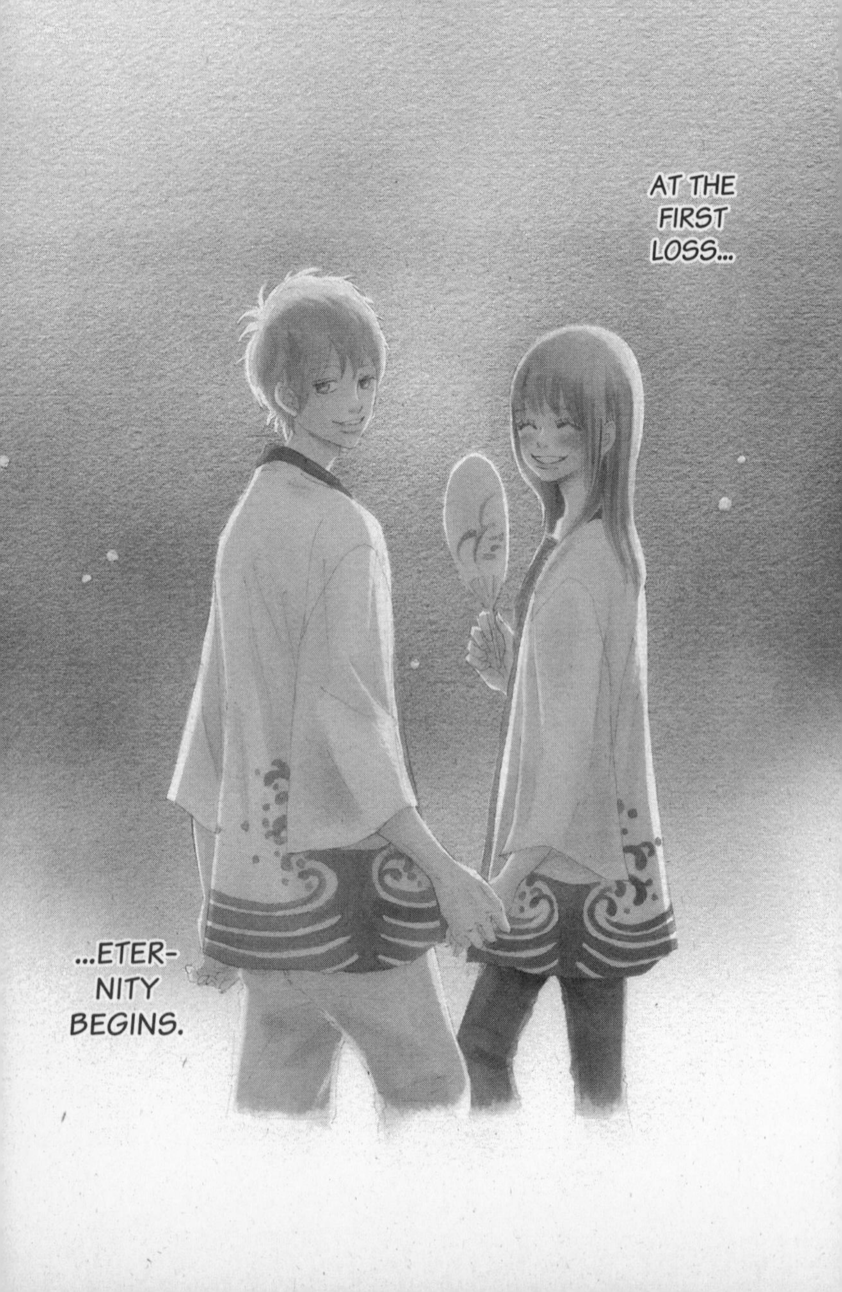
AT THE FIRST LOSS...
...ETERNITY BEGINS.

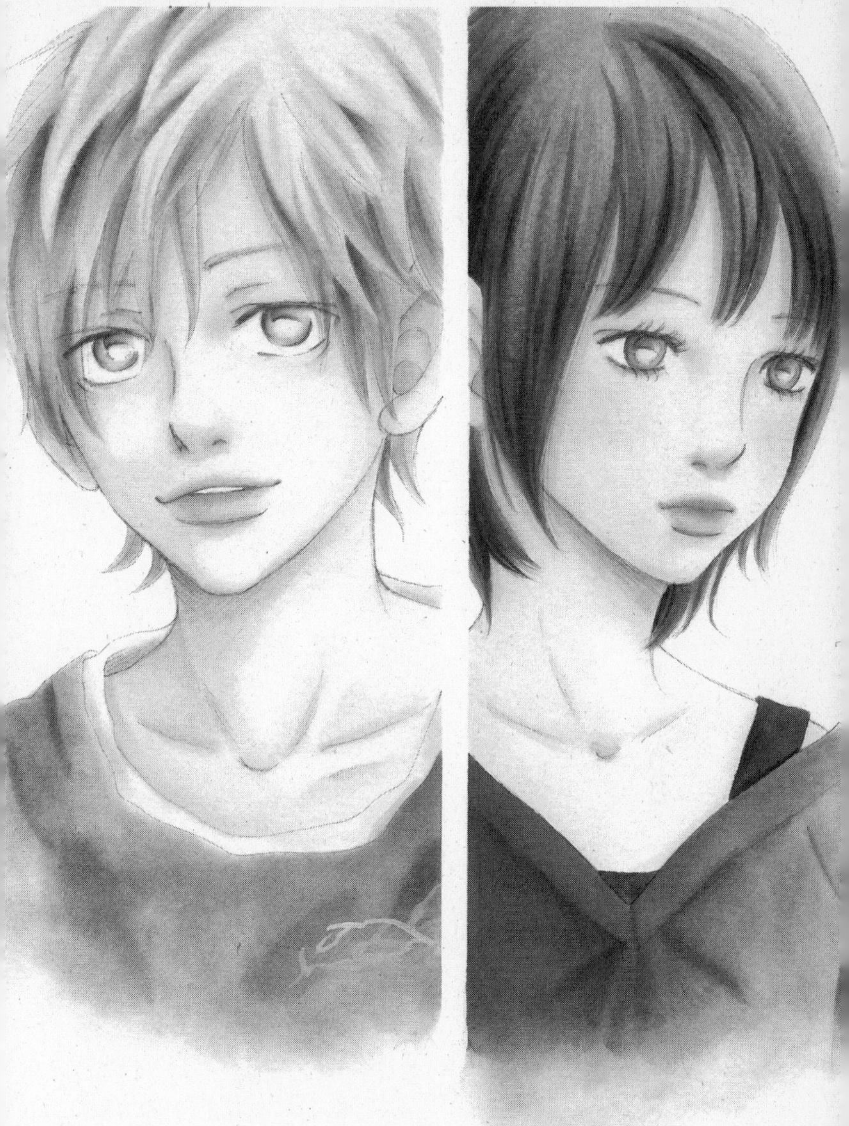

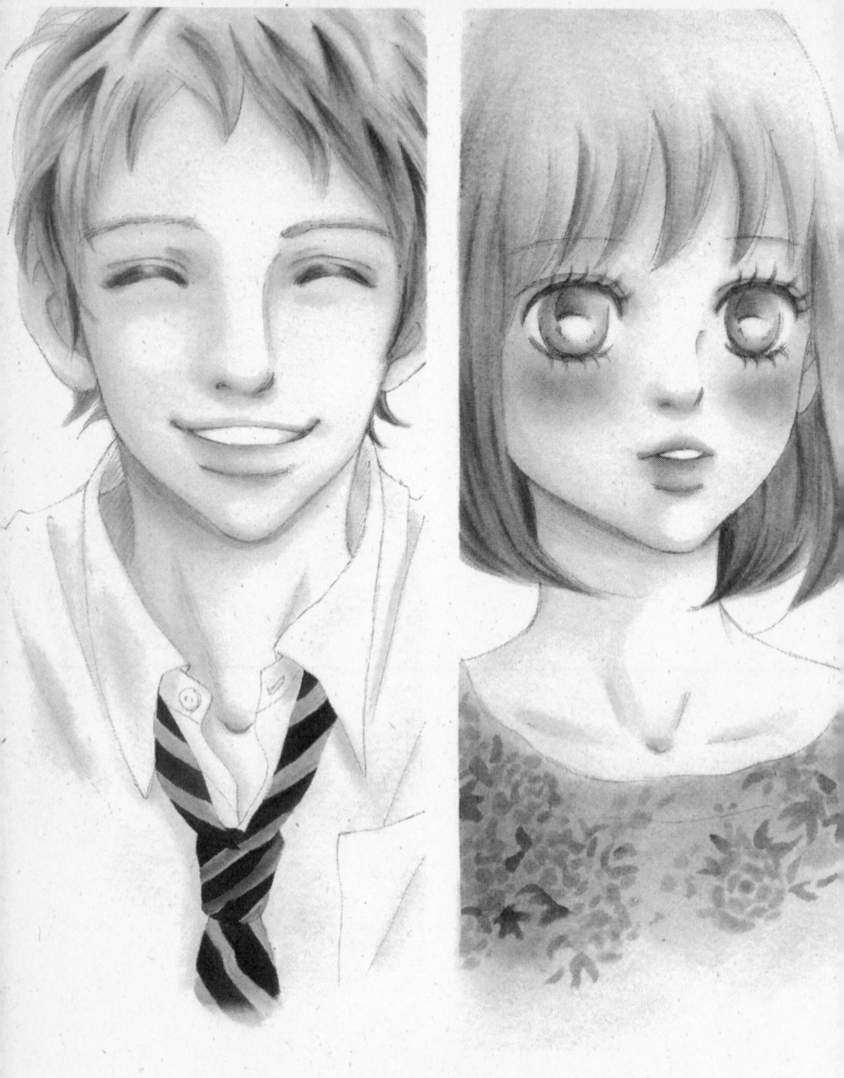

Chapter 52

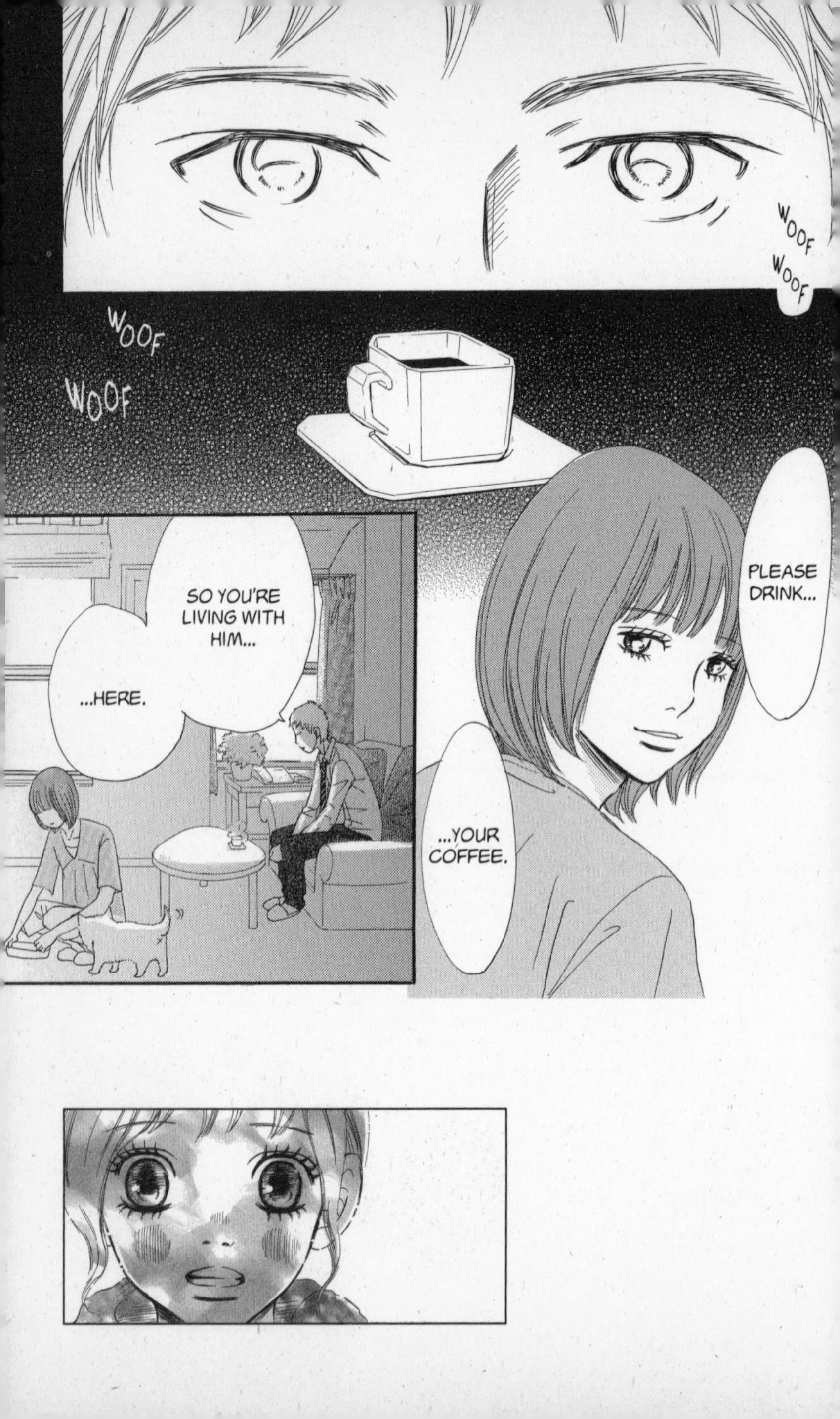
WOOF WOOF
WOOF
WOOF
PLEASE DRINK...
...YOUR COFFEE.
SO YOU'RE LIVING WITH HIM...
...HERE.

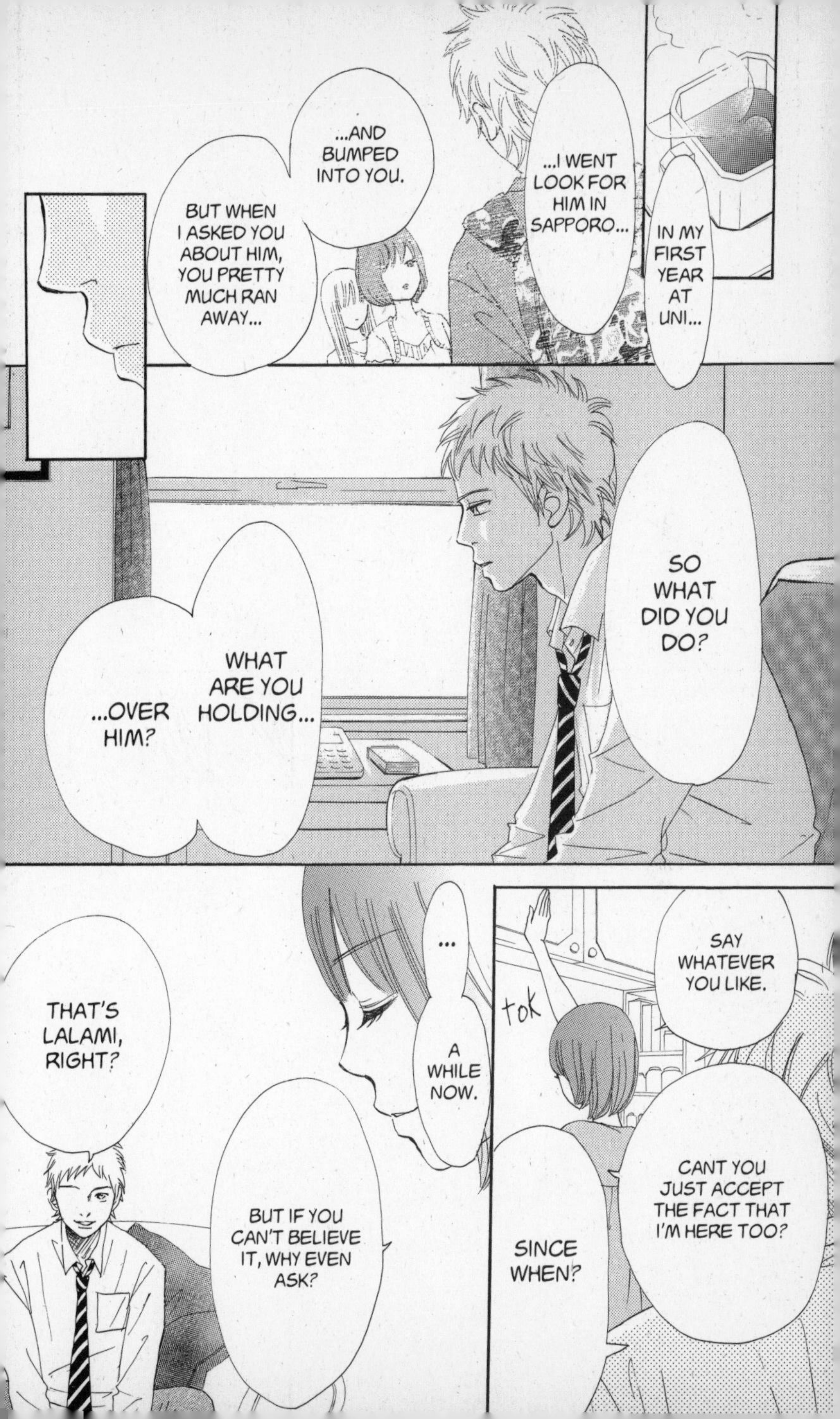
IN MY FIRST YEAR AT UNI...
...I WENT LOOK FOR HIM IN SAPPORO...
...AND BUMPED INTO YOU.
BUT WHEN I ASKED YOU ABOUT HIM, YOU PRETTY MUCH RAN AWAY...
SO WHAT DID YOU DO?
WHAT ARE YOU HOLDING...
...OVER HIM?
SAY WHATEVER YOU LIKE.
CANT YOU JUST ACCEPT THE FACT THAT I'M HERE TOO?
tok
SINCE WHEN?
...
A WHILE NOW.
THAT'S LALAMI, RIGHT?
BUT IF YOU CAN'T BELIEVE IT, WHY EVEN ASK?

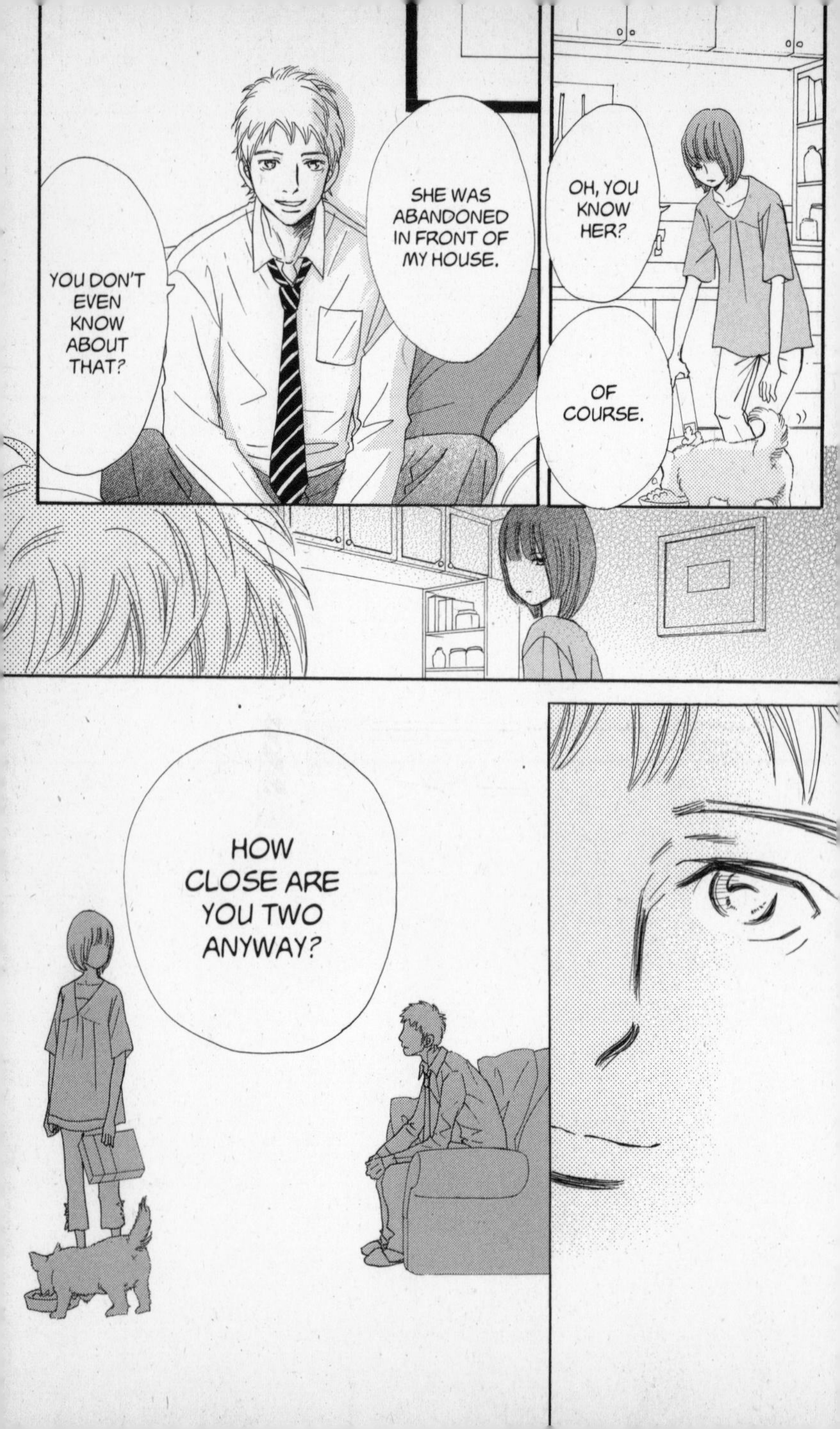
OH, YOU KNOW HER?
OF COURSE.
SHE WAS ABANDONED IN FRONT OF MY HOUSE.
YOU DON'T EVEN KNOW ABOUT THAT?
HOW CLOSE ARE YOU TWO ANYWAY?

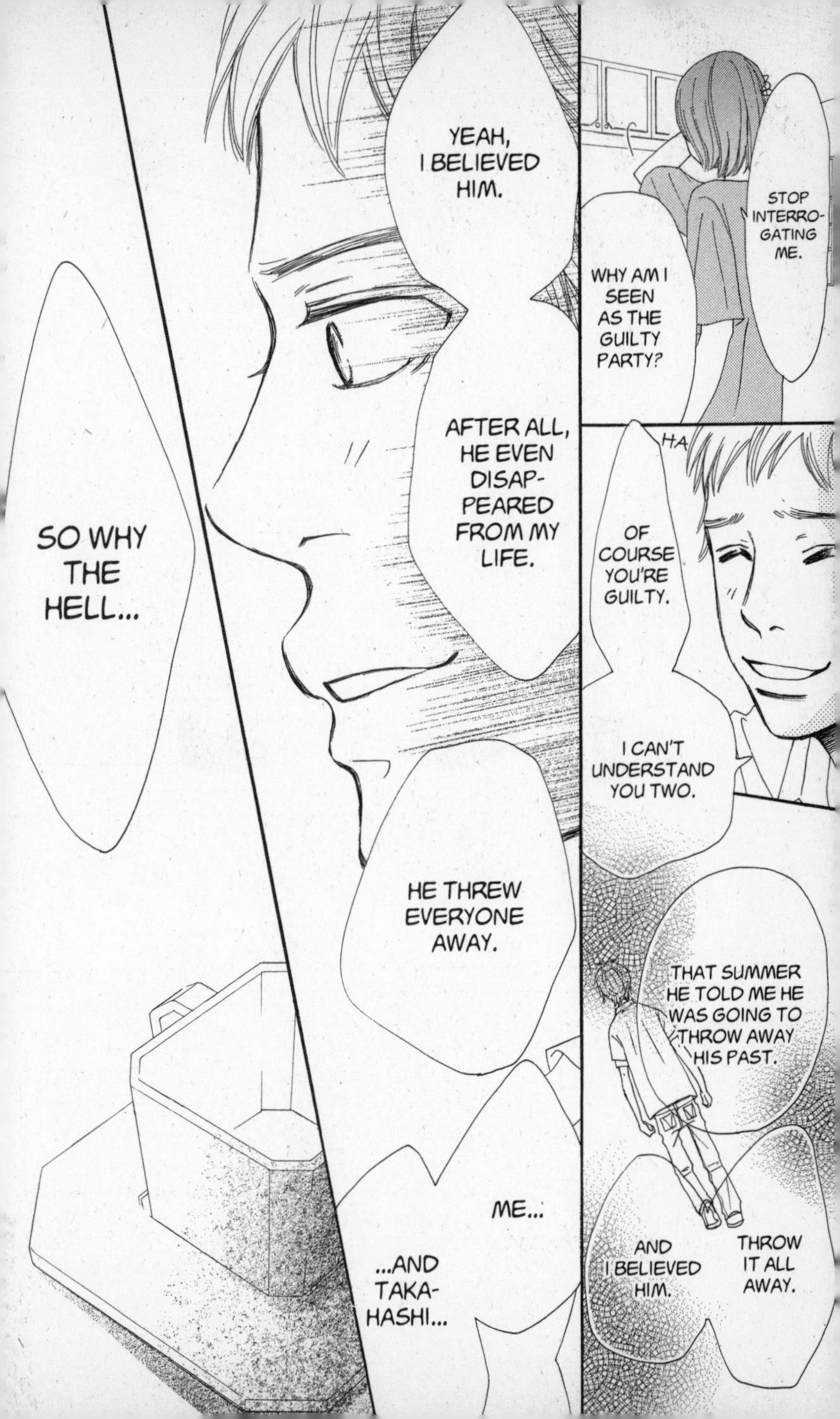
STOP INTERRO-GATING ME.
WHY AM I SEEN AS THE GUILTY PARTY?
HA
OF COURSE YOU'RE GUILTY.
I CAN'T UNDERSTAND YOU TWO.
THAT SUMMER HE TOLD ME HE WAS GOING TO THROW AWAY HIS PAST.
THROW IT ALL AWAY.
AND I BELIEVED HIM.
YEAH, I BELIEVED HIM.
AFTER ALL, HE EVEN DISAP-PEARED FROM MY LIFE.
HE THREW EVERYONE AWAY.
ME...
...AND TAKA-HASHI...
SO WHY THE HELL...

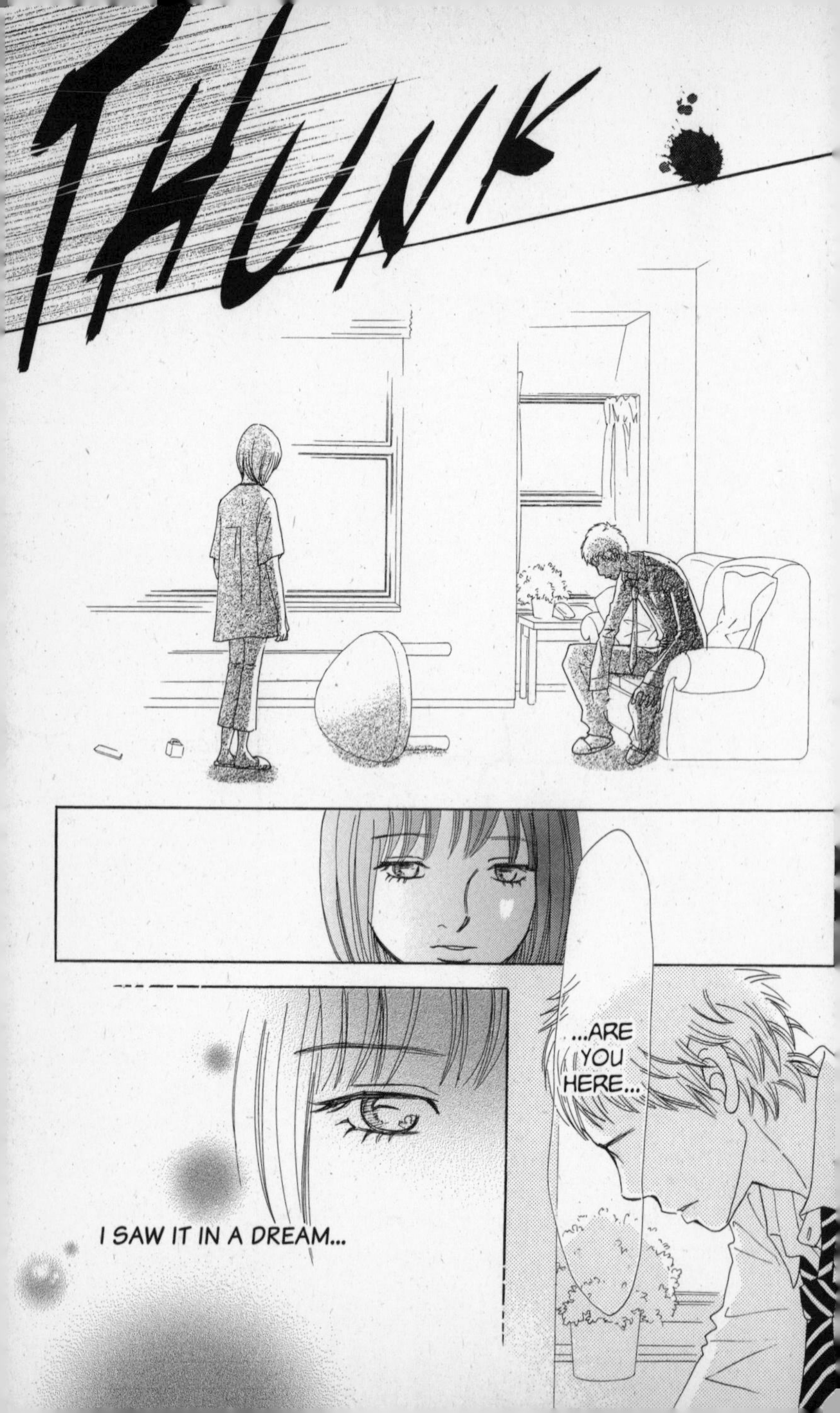
THUNK
...ARE YOU HERE...
I SAW IT IN A DREAM...

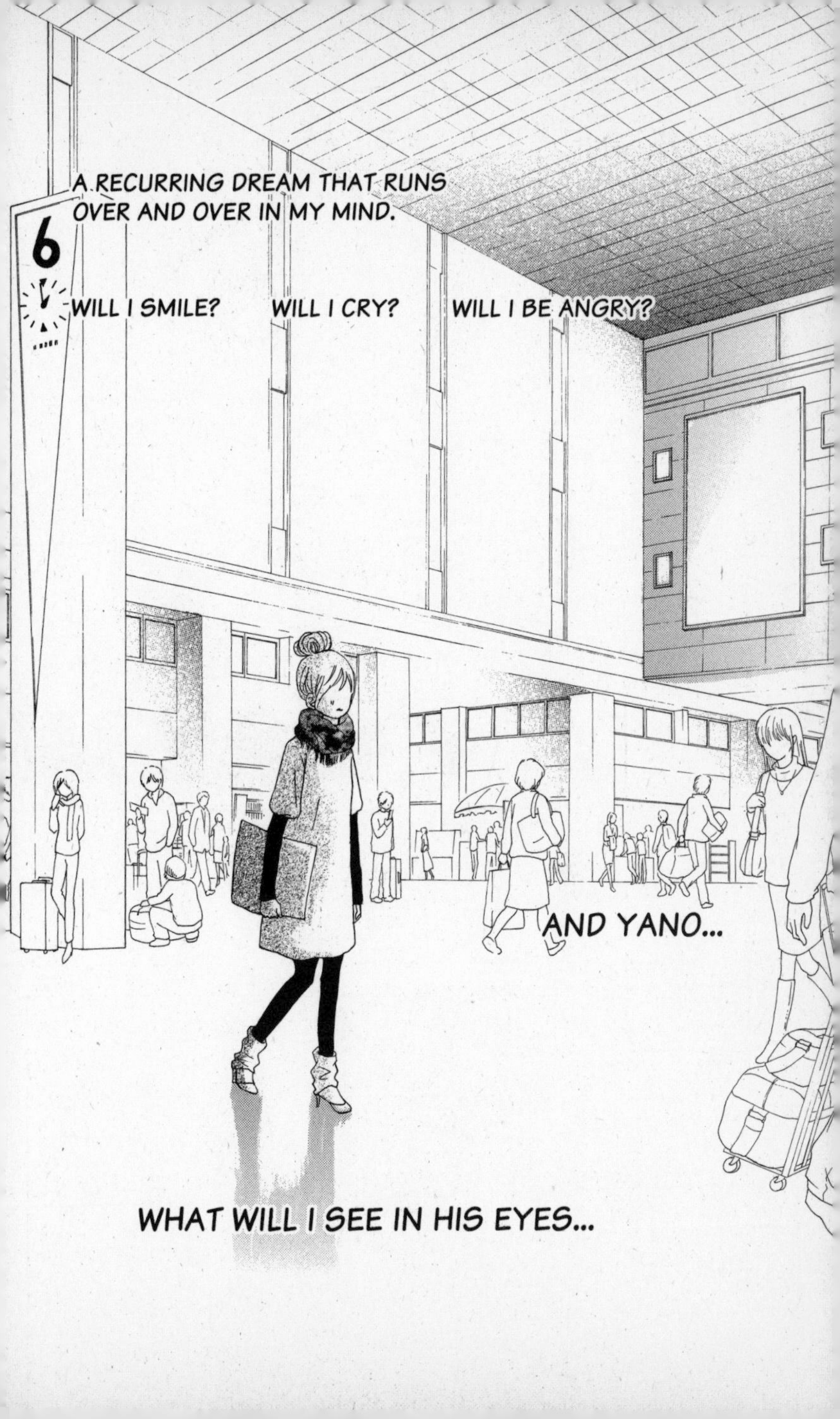
6
A RECURRING DREAM THAT RUNS OVER AND OVER IN MY MIND.
WILL I SMILE?
WILL I CRY?
WILL I BE ANGRY?
AND YANO...
WHAT WILL I SEE IN HIS EYES...

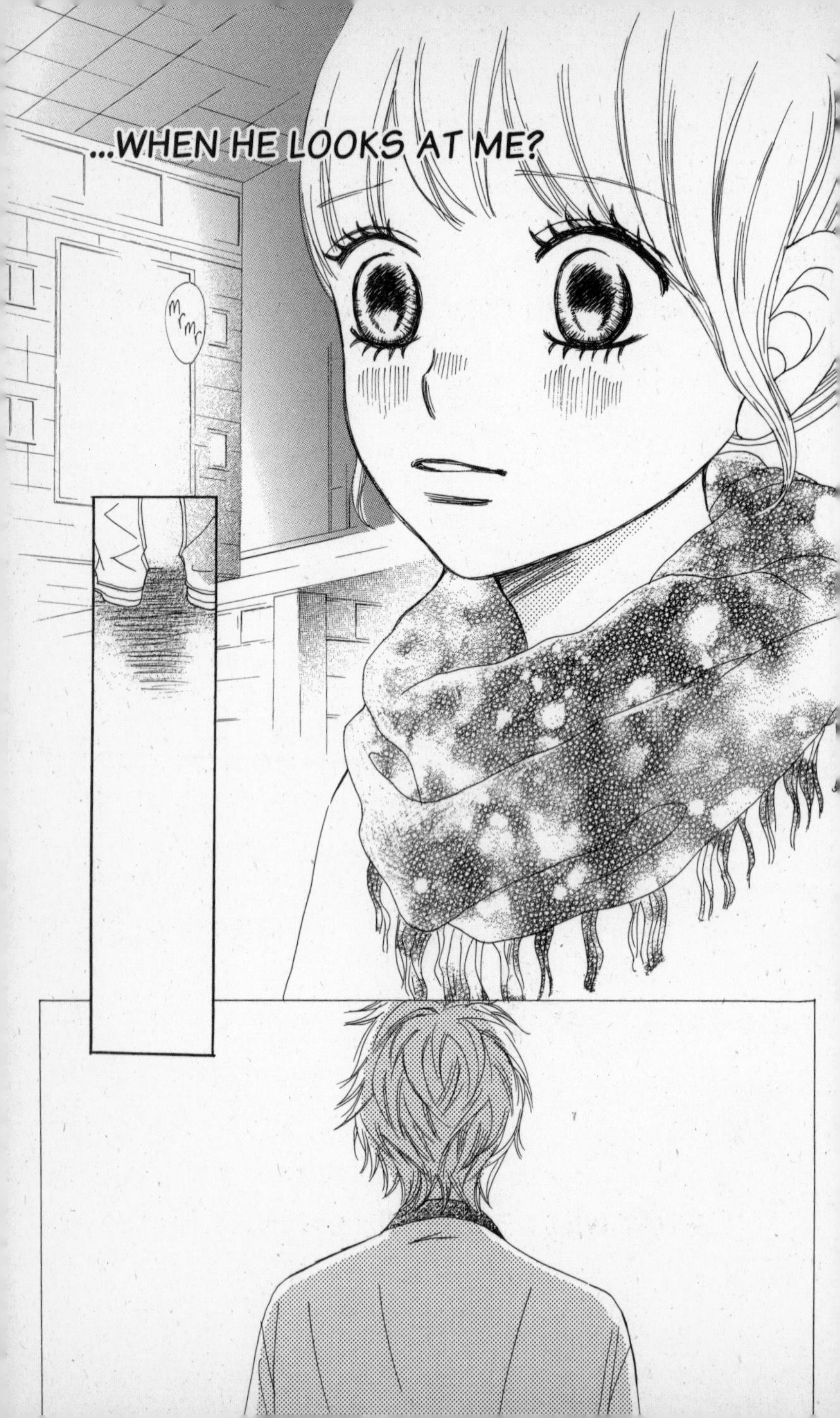
...WHEN HE LOOKS AT ME?
mrmr

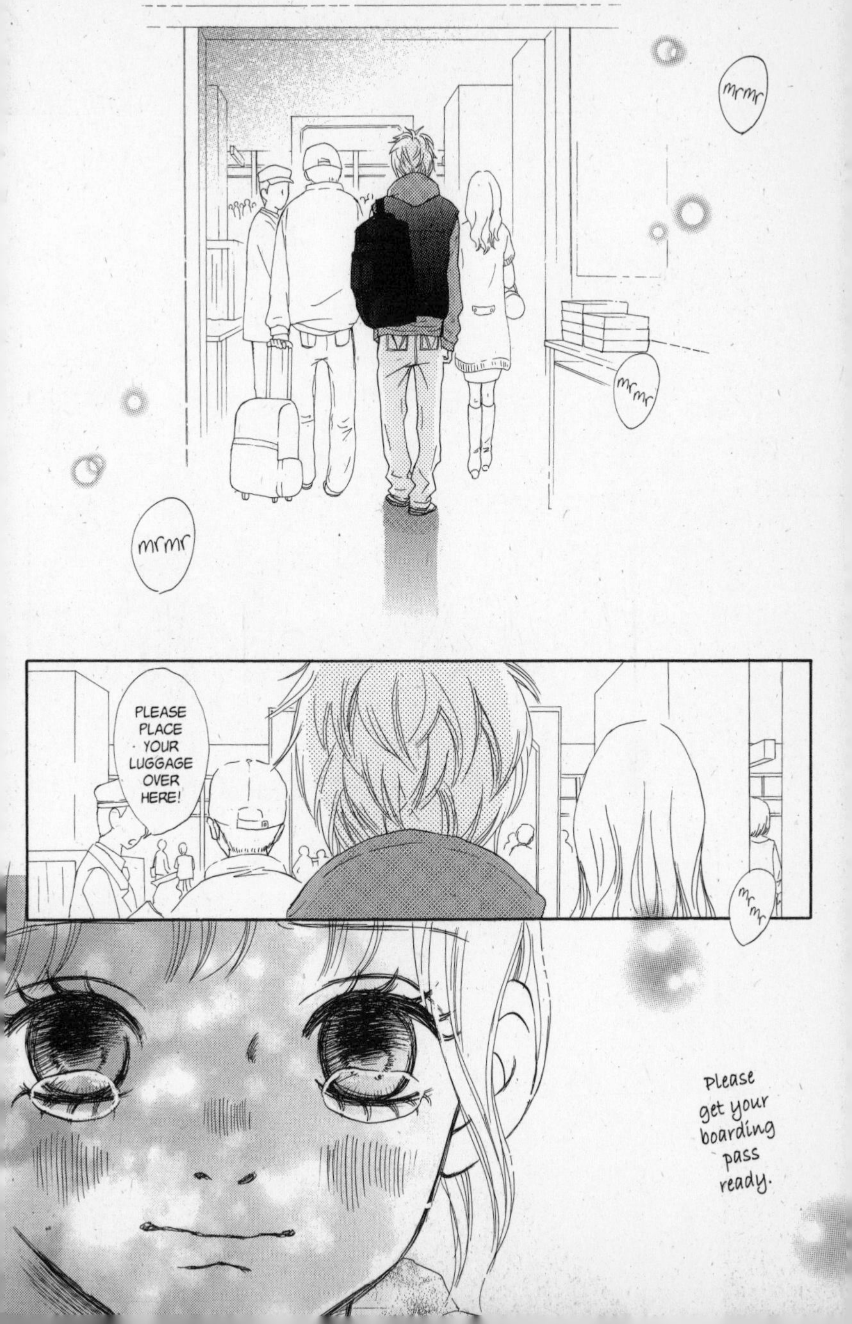

mrmr
mrmr
mrmr
mrmr
PLEASE PLACE YOUR LUGGAGE OVER HERE!
Please get your boarding pass ready.

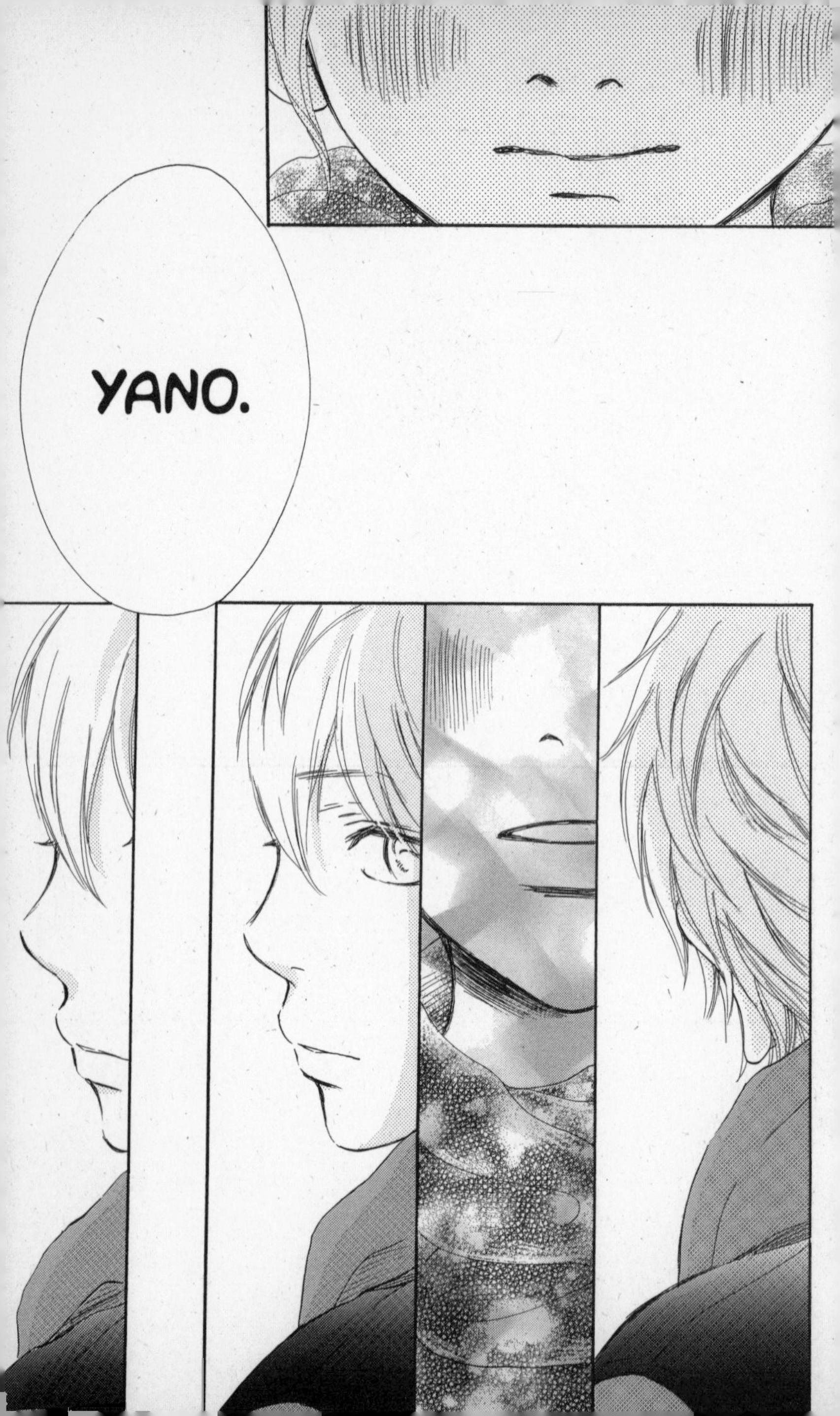
YANO.

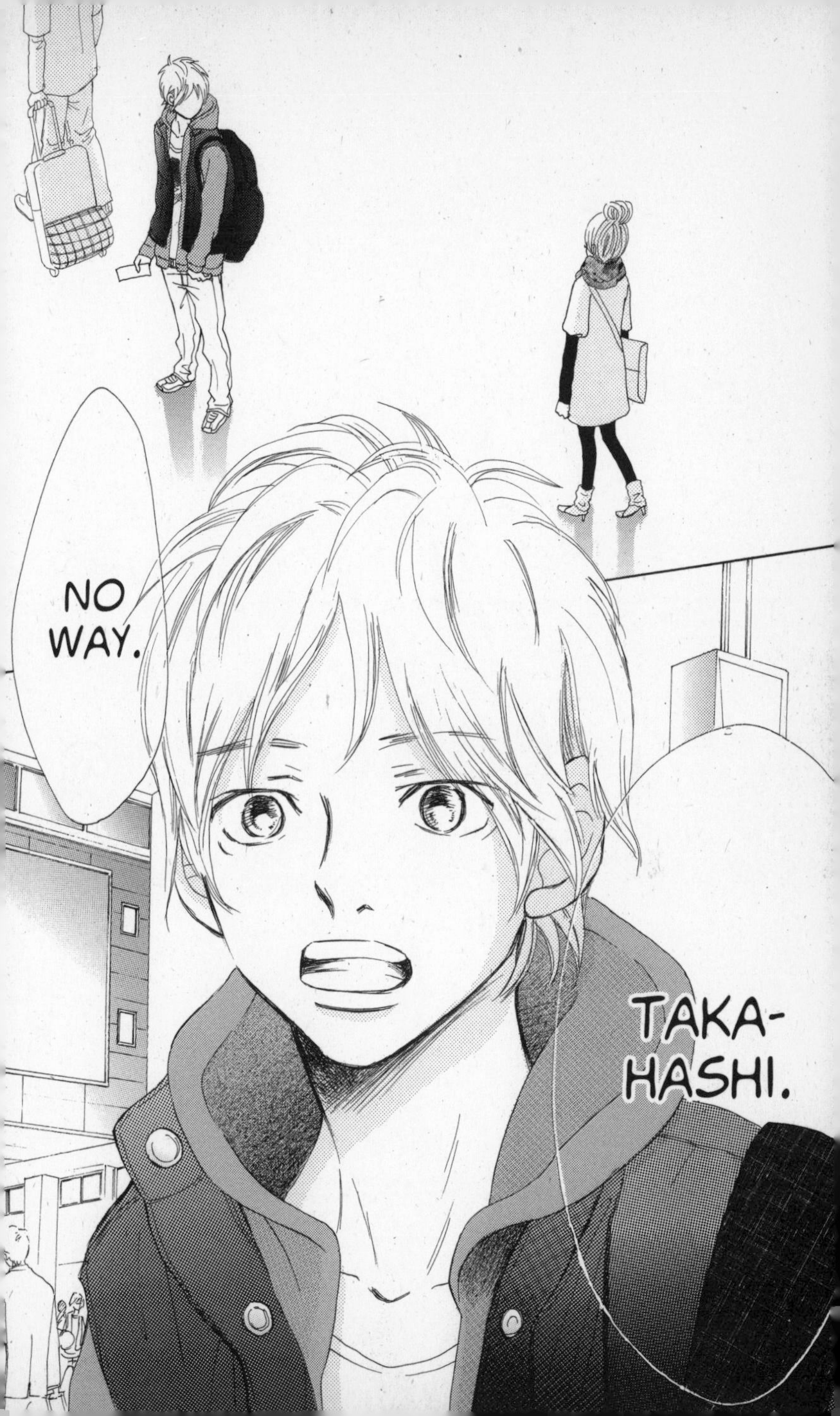
TAKA-HASHI.
NO WAY.

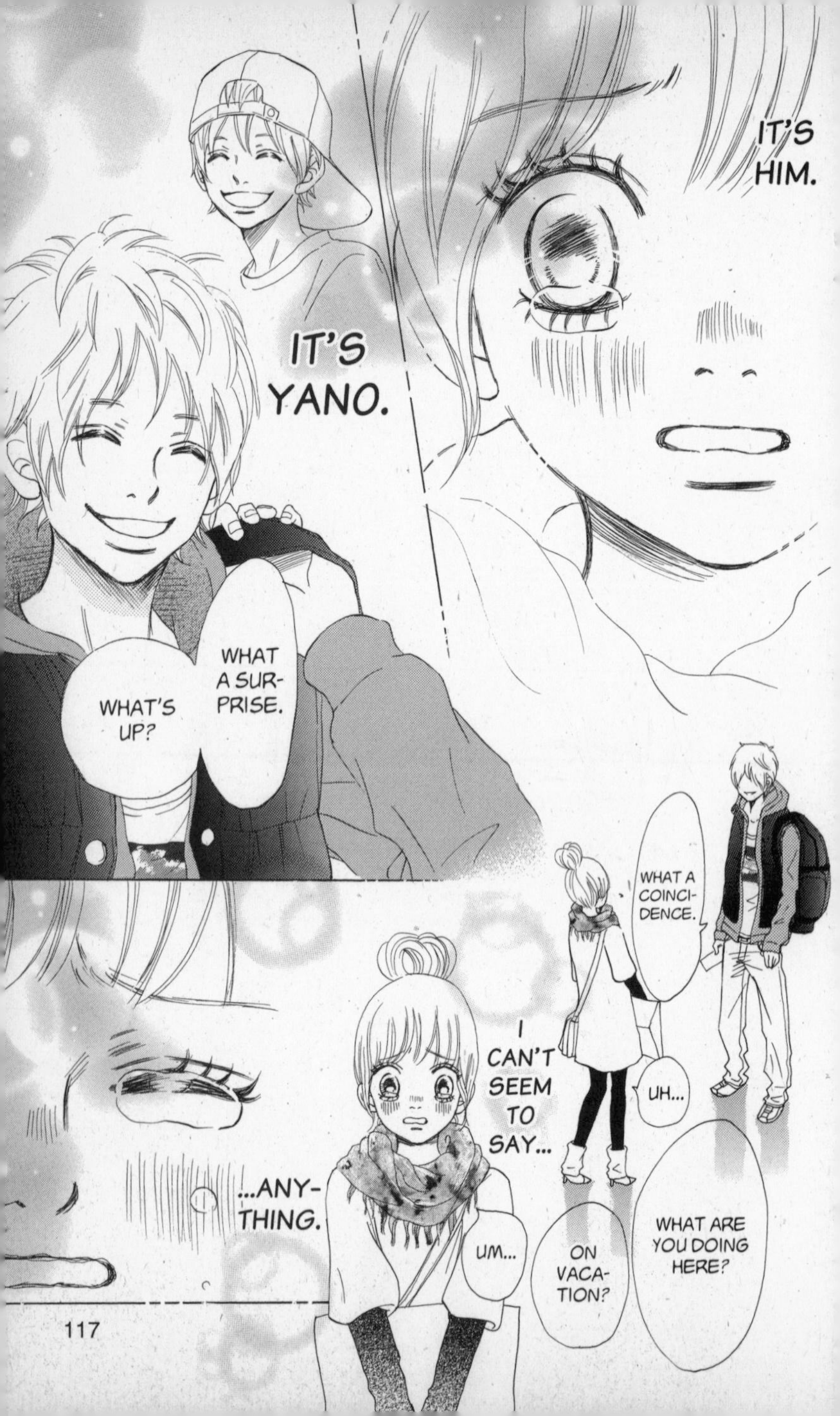
IT'S HIM.
IT'S YANO.
WHAT A SURPRISE.
WHAT'S UP?
WHAT A COINCIDENCE.
UH...
WHAT ARE YOU DOING HERE?
ON VACATION?
UM...
I CAN'T SEEM TO SAY...
...ANYTHING.

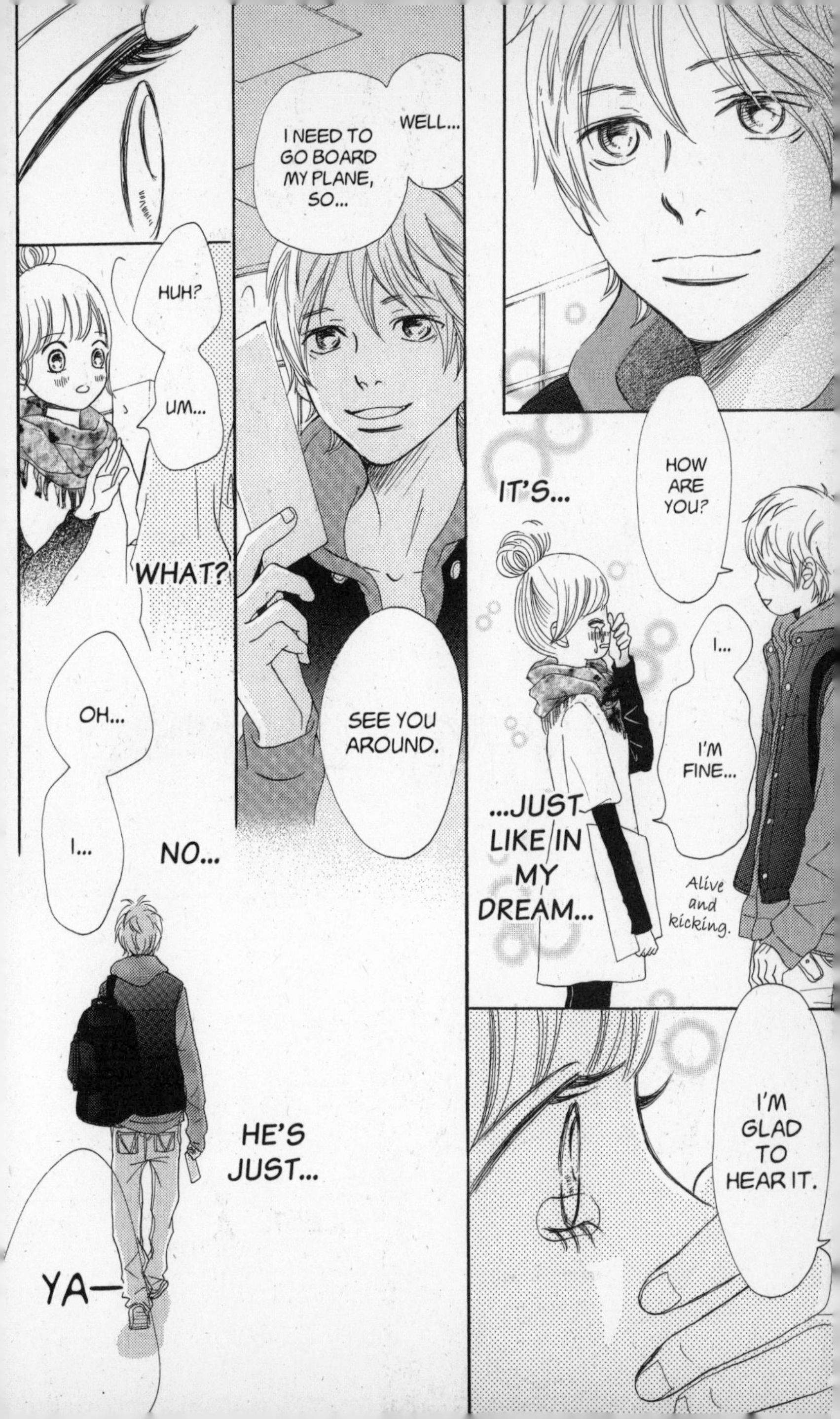
HOW ARE YOU?
IT'S...
I...
I'M FINE...
Alive and kicking.
...JUST LIKE IN MY DREAM...
I'M GLAD TO HEAR IT.
WELL...
I NEED TO GO BOARD MY PLANE, SO...
SEE YOU AROUND.
HUH?
UM...
WHAT?
OH...
I...
NO...
HE'S JUST...
YA—

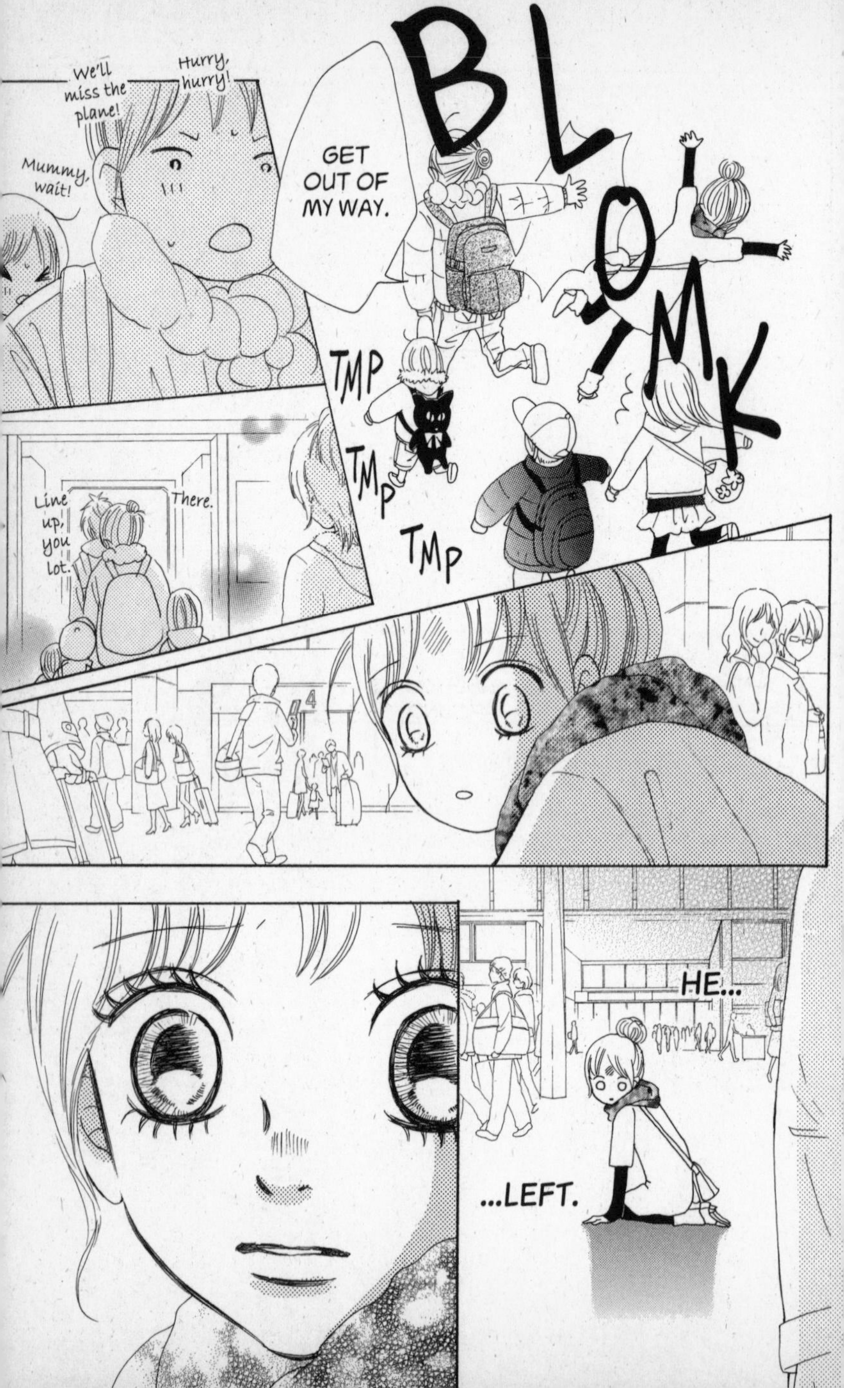
BLOMK
GET OUT OF MY WAY.
TMP
TMP
TMP
Hurry, hurry!
We'll miss the plane!
Mummy, wait!
There.
Line up, you lot.
HE...
...LEFT.

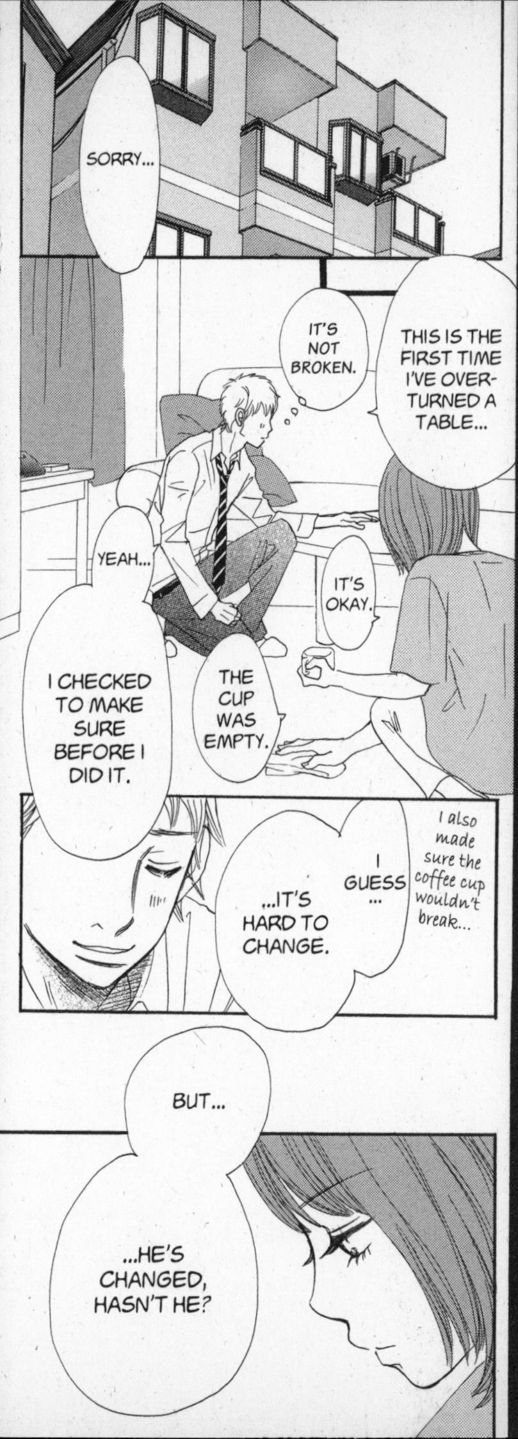
SORRY...
THIS IS THE FIRST TIME I'VE OVER-TURNED A TABLE...
IT'S NOT BROKEN.
IT'S OKAY.
THE CUP WAS EMPTY.
YEAH...
I CHECKED TO MAKE SURE BEFORE I DID IT.
I also made sure the coffee cup wouldn't break...
I GUESS...
...IT'S HARD TO CHANGE.
BUT...
...HE'S CHANGED, HASN'T HE?

WHAT THE HELL?!

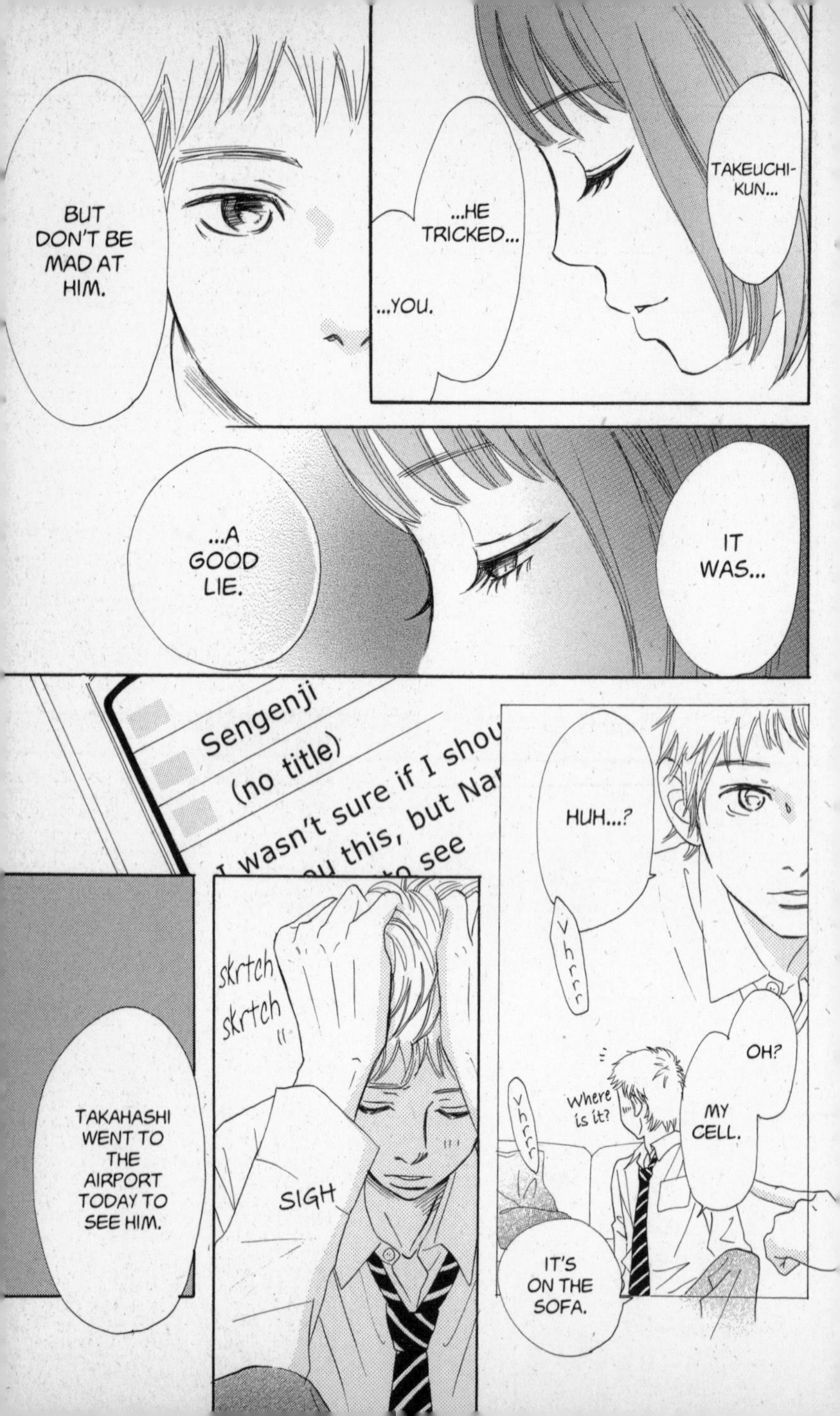
TAKEUCHI-KUN...
...HE TRICKED...
...YOU.
BUT DON'T BE MAD AT HIM.
IT WAS...
...A GOOD LIE.
HUH...?
Vhrrr
OH?
MY CELL.
Where is it?
Vhrrr
IT'S ON THE SOFA.
Sengenji
(no title)
I wasn't sure if I shou
ou this, but Na
to see
skrtch skrtch
SIGH
TAKAHASHI WENT TO THE AIRPORT TODAY TO SEE HIM.

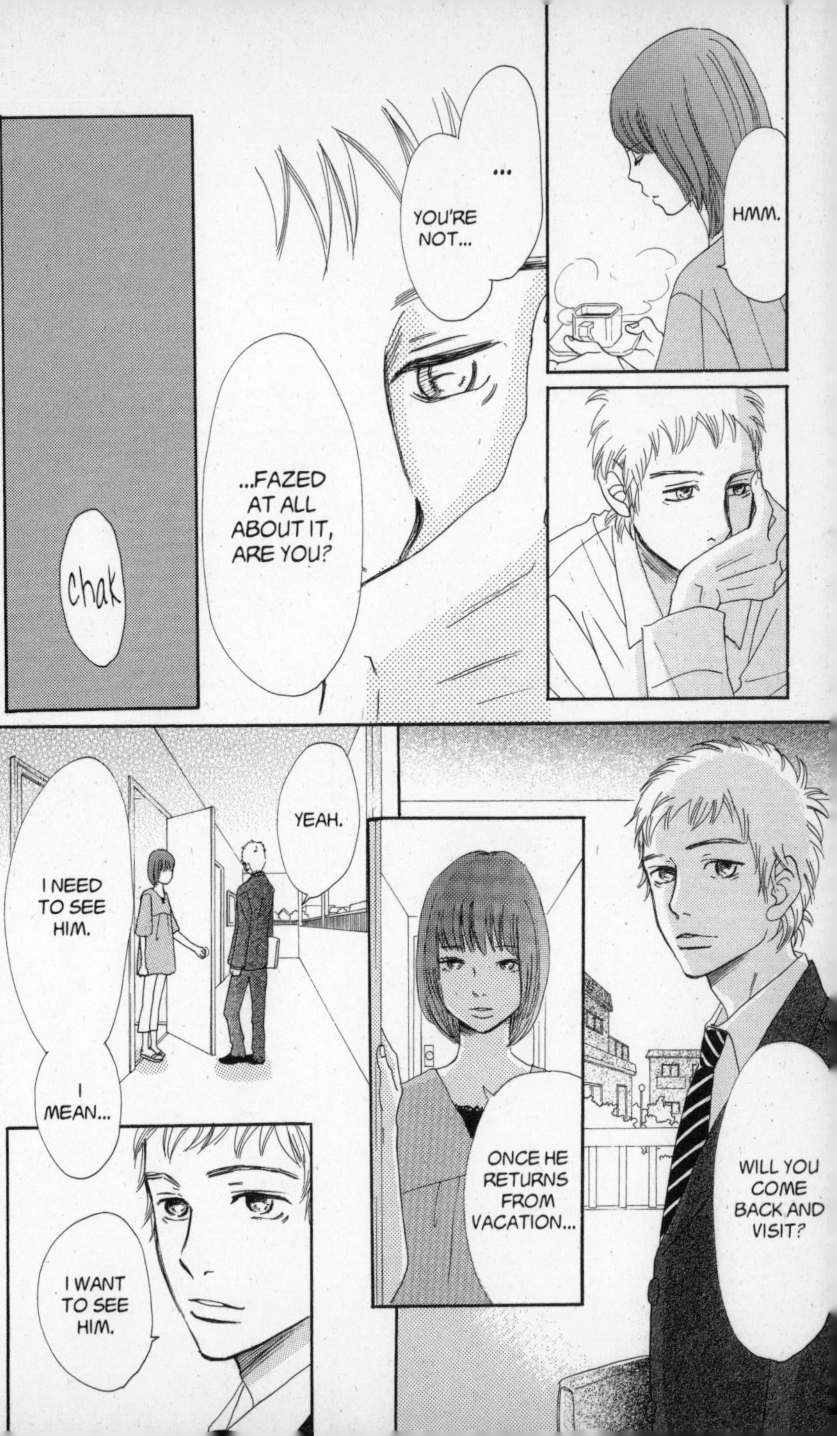
HMM.
...
YOU'RE NOT...
...FAZED AT ALL ABOUT IT, ARE YOU?
Chak
WILL YOU COME BACK AND VISIT?
ONCE HE RETURNS FROM VACATION...
YEAH.
I NEED TO SEE HIM.
I MEAN...
I WANT TO SEE HIM.

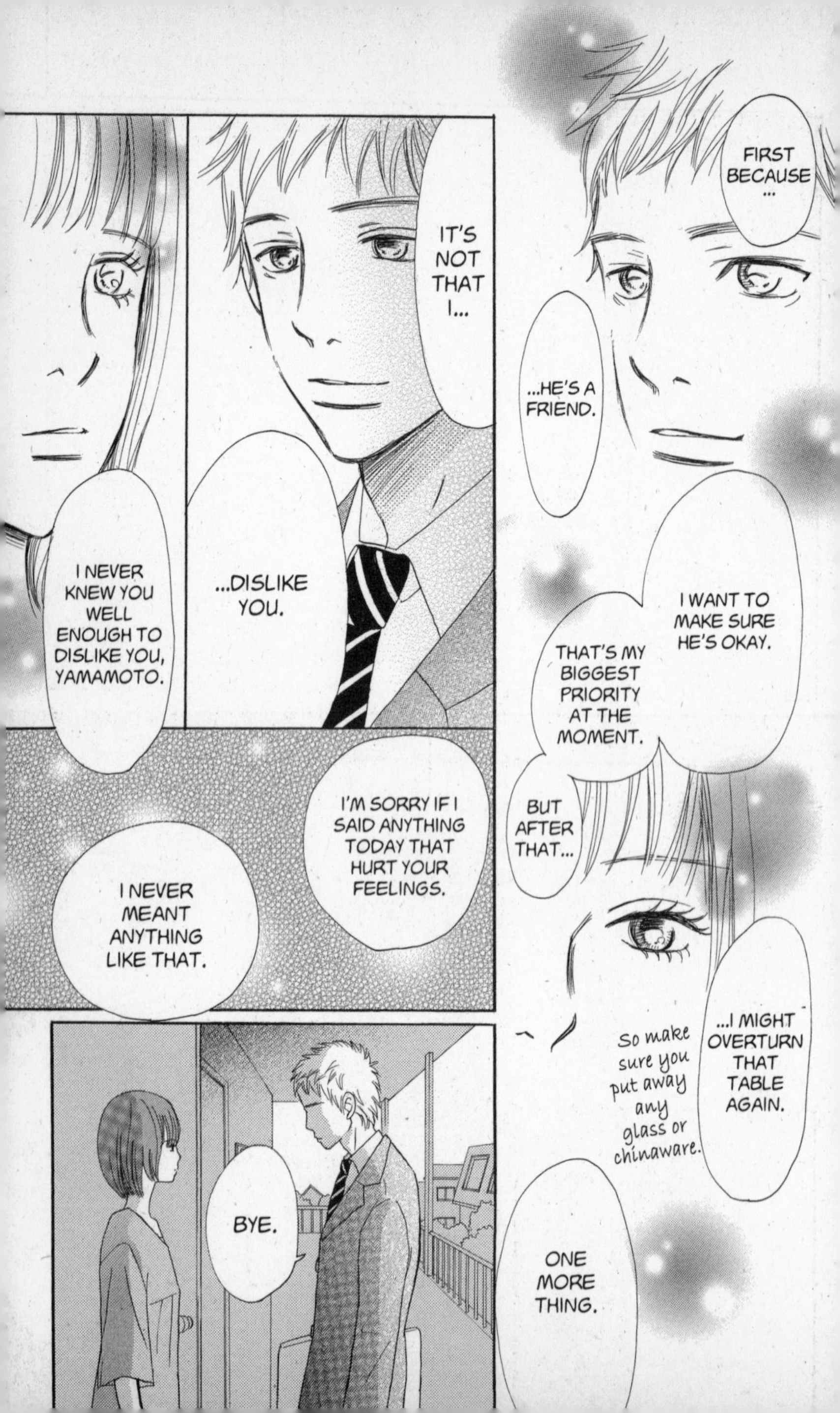
FIRST BECAUSE...
...HE'S A FRIEND.
I WANT TO MAKE SURE HE'S OKAY.
THAT'S MY BIGGEST PRIORITY AT THE MOMENT.
BUT AFTER THAT...
...I MIGHT OVERTURN THAT TABLE AGAIN.
So make sure you put away any glass or chinaware.
ONE MORE THING.
IT'S NOT THAT I...
...DISLIKE YOU.
I NEVER KNEW YOU WELL ENOUGH TO DISLIKE YOU, YAMAMOTO.
I'M SORRY IF I SAID ANYTHING TODAY THAT HURT YOUR FEELINGS.
I NEVER MEANT ANYTHING LIKE THAT.
BYE.

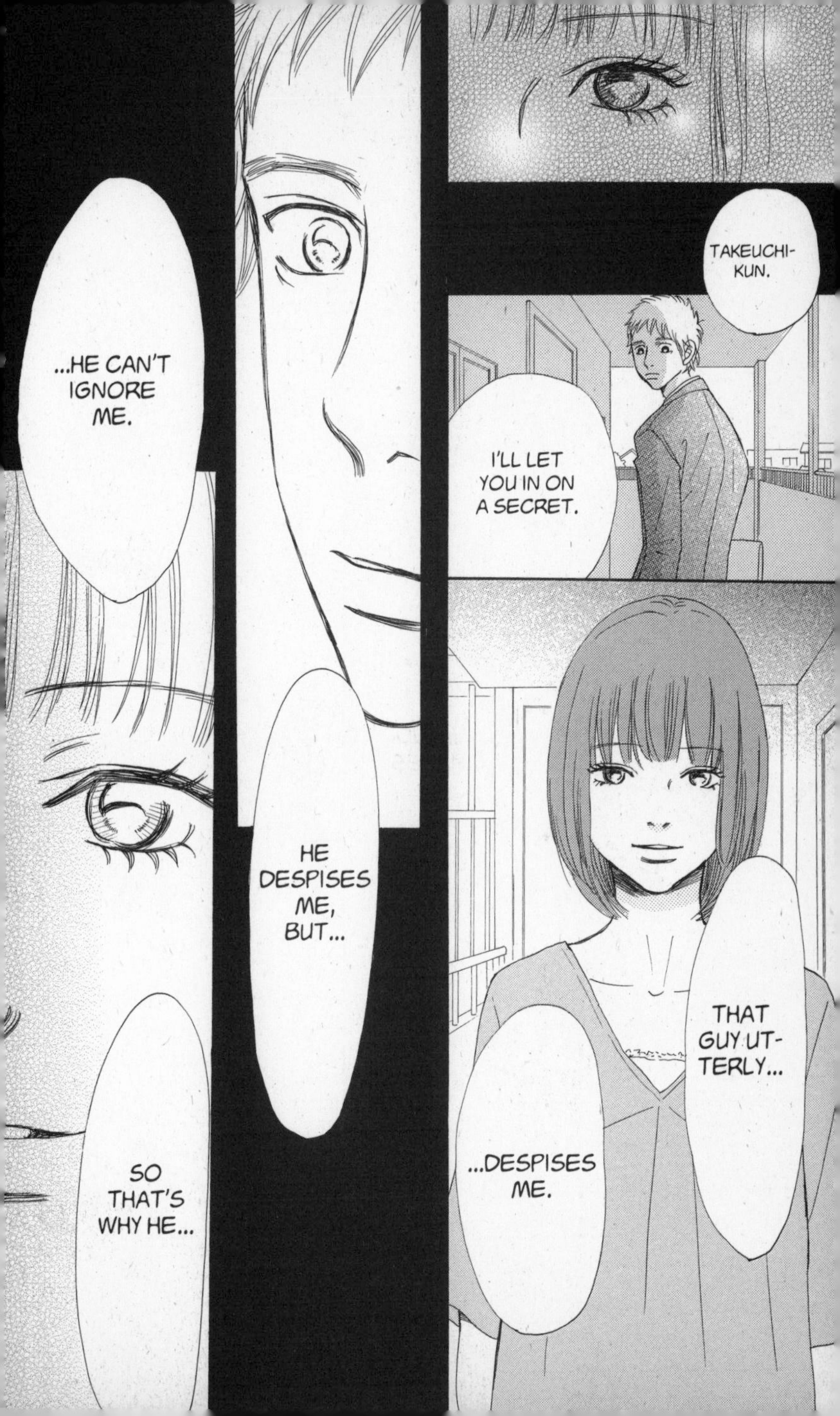
TAKEUCHI-KUN.
I'LL LET YOU IN ON A SECRET.
THAT GUY UTTERLY...
...DESPISES ME.
HE DESPISES ME, BUT...
...HE CAN'T IGNORE ME.
SO THAT'S WHY HE...

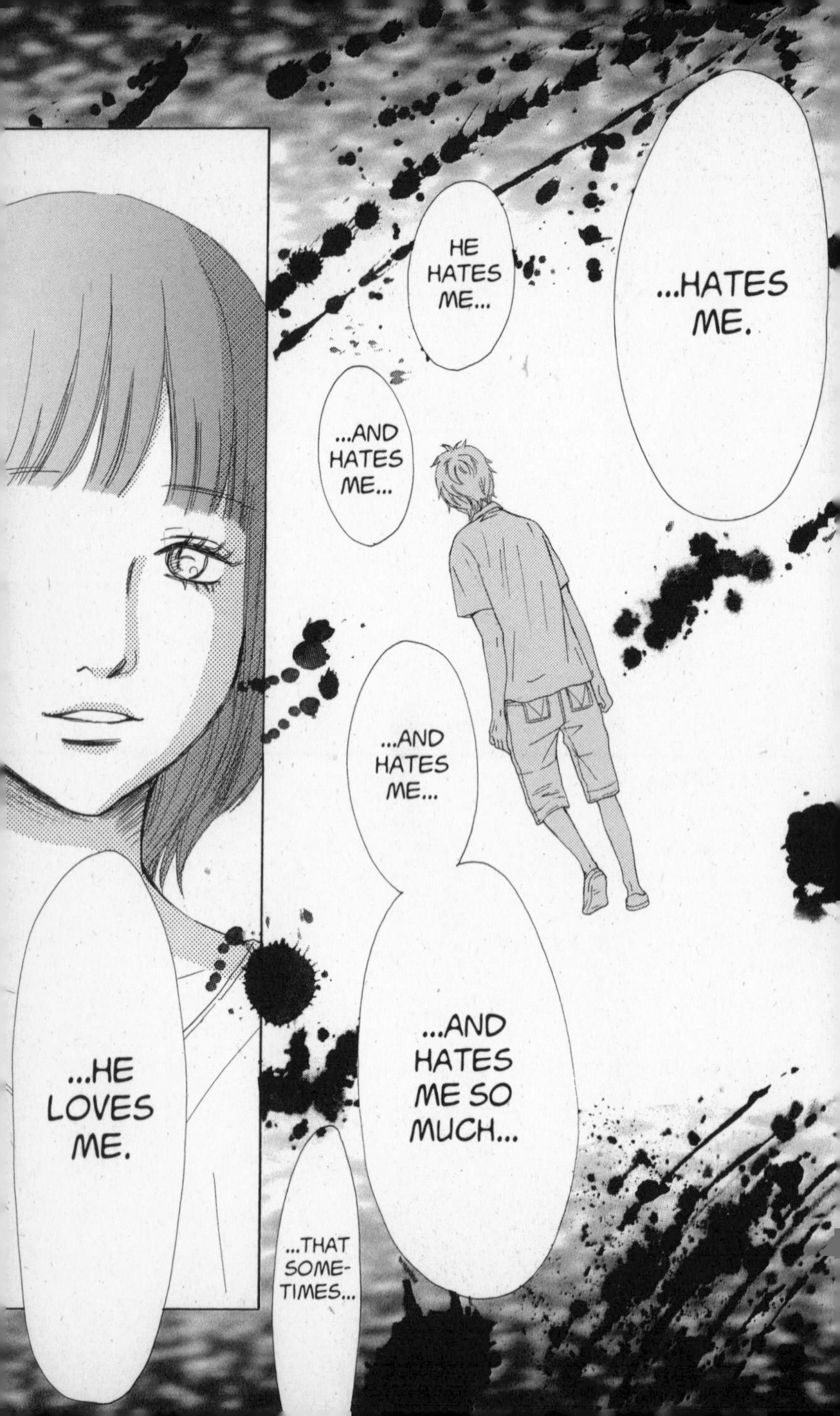
...HATES ME.
HE HATES ME...
...AND HATES ME...
...AND HATES ME...
...AND HATES ME SO MUCH...
...THAT SOME-TIMES...
...HE LOVES ME.

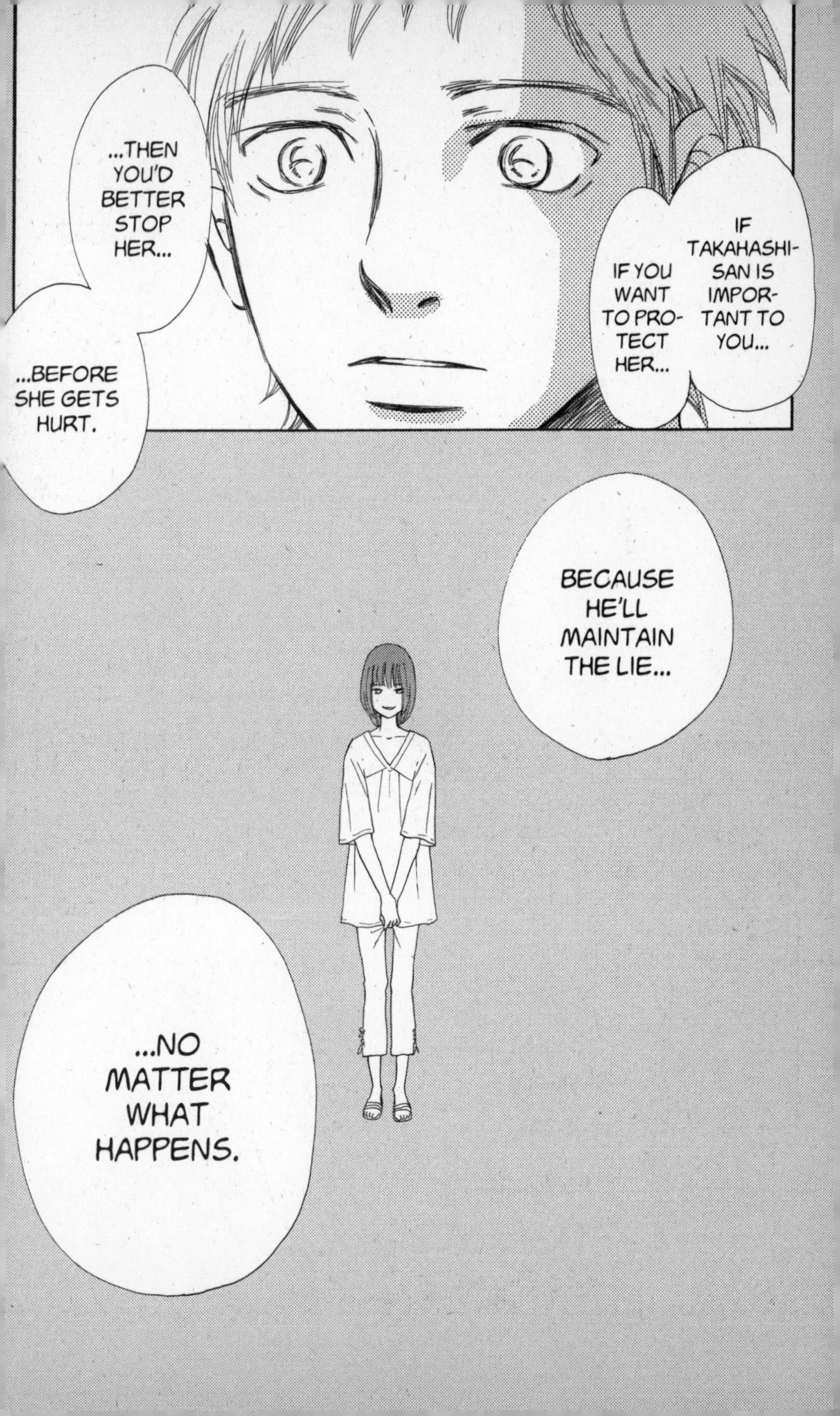
IF TAKAHASHI-SAN IS IMPORTANT TO YOU...
IF YOU WANT TO PROTECT HER...
...THEN YOU'D BETTER STOP HER...
...BEFORE SHE GETS HURT.
BECAUSE HE'LL MAINTAIN THE LIE...
...NO MATTER WHAT HAPPENS.

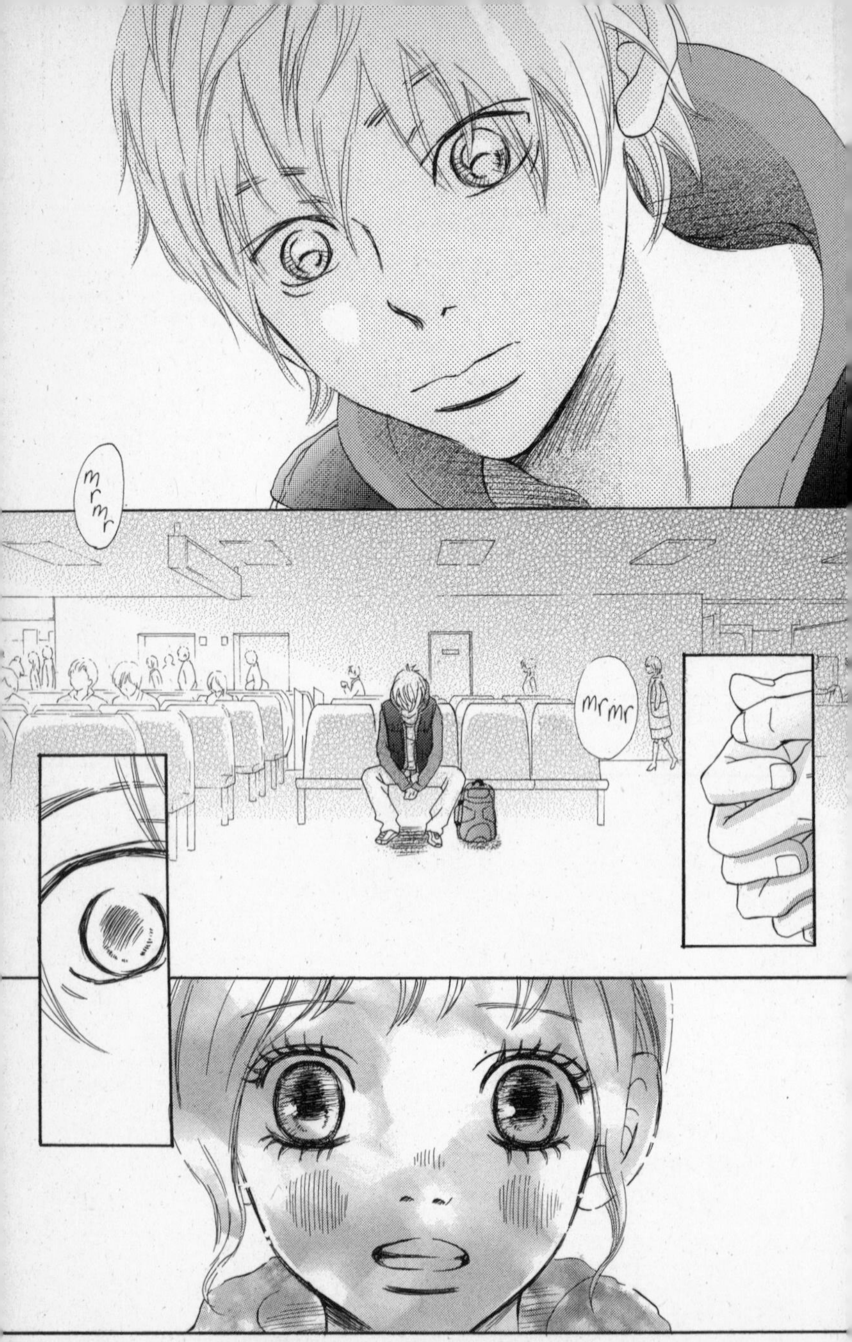
mrmr
mrmr

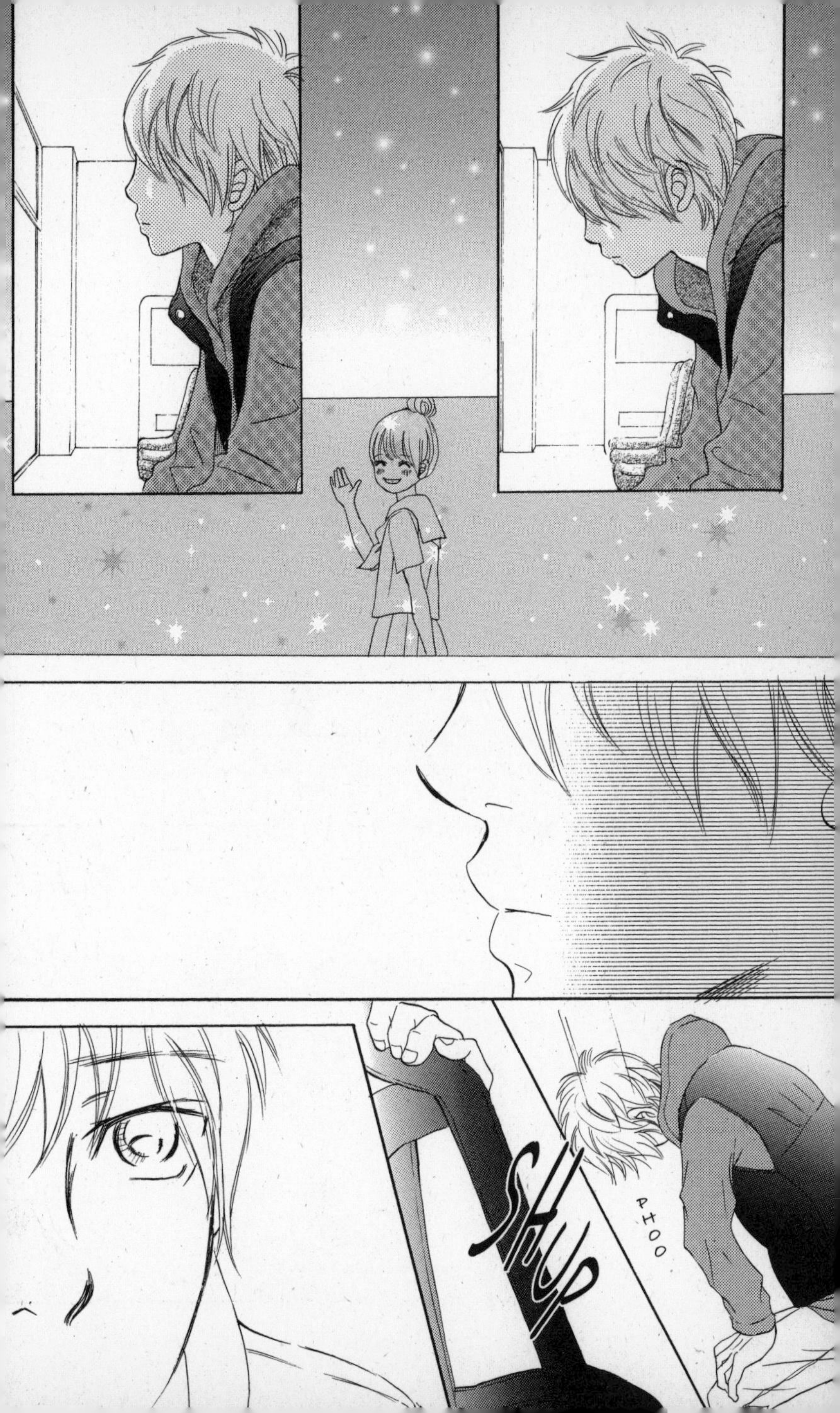
PHOO
SHUP

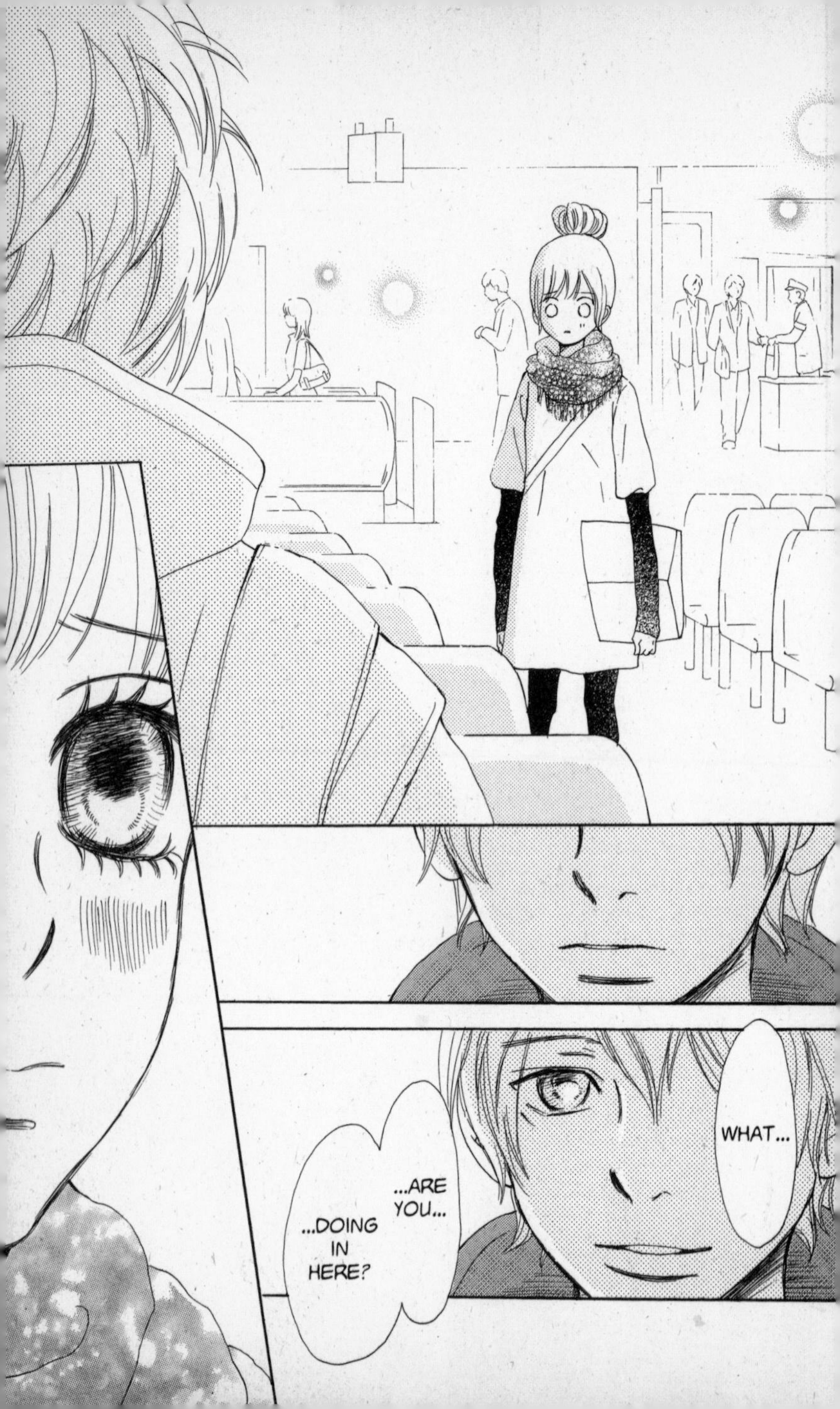
WHAT...
...ARE YOU...
...DOING IN HERE?

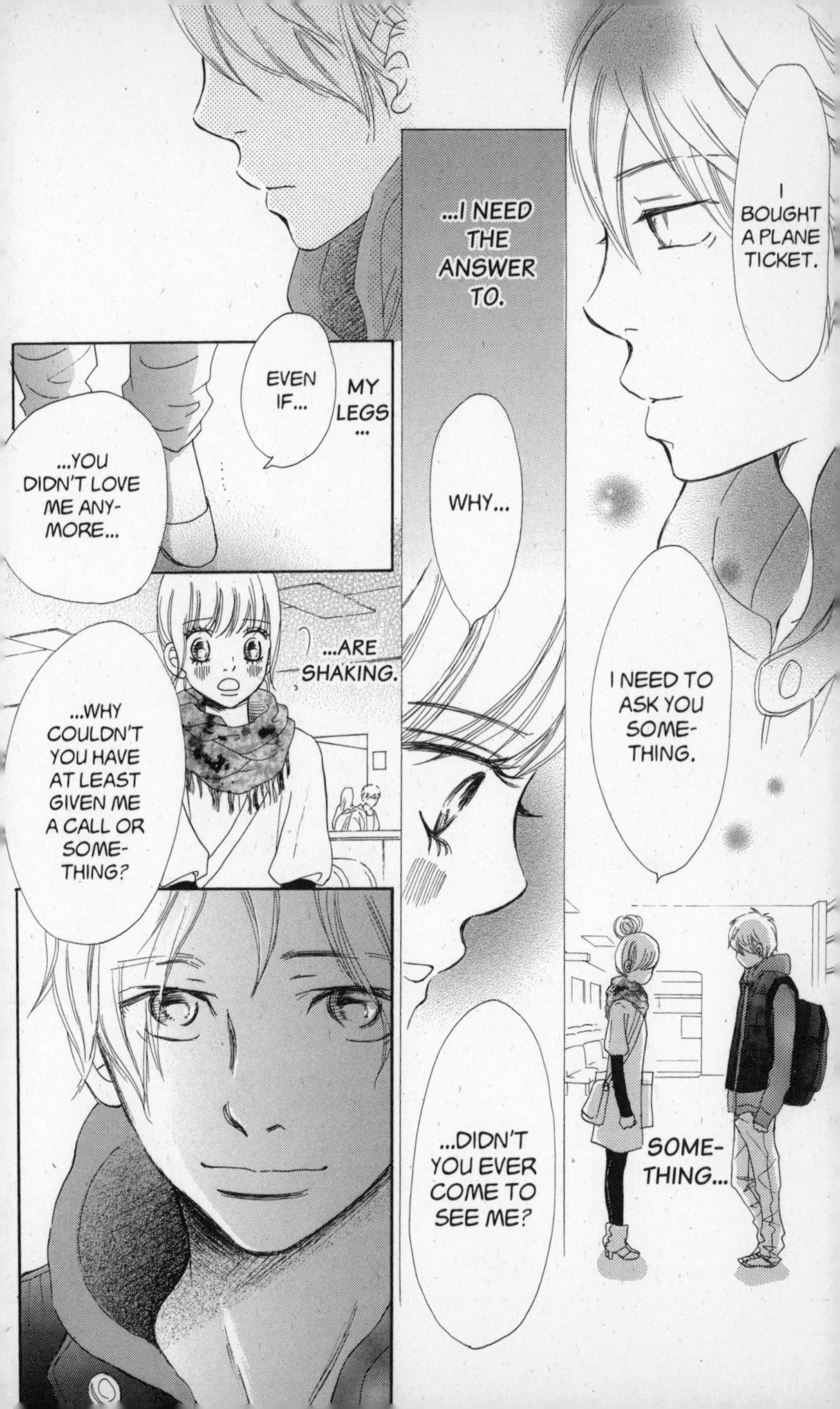
I BOUGHT A PLANE TICKET.
I NEED TO ASK YOU SOMETHING.
SOMETHING...
...I NEED THE ANSWER TO.
WHY...
...DIDN'T YOU EVER COME TO SEE ME?
EVEN IF...
MY LEGS...
...YOU DIDN'T LOVE ME ANYMORE...
...ARE SHAKING.
...WHY COULDN'T YOU HAVE AT LEAST GIVEN ME A CALL OR SOMETHING?

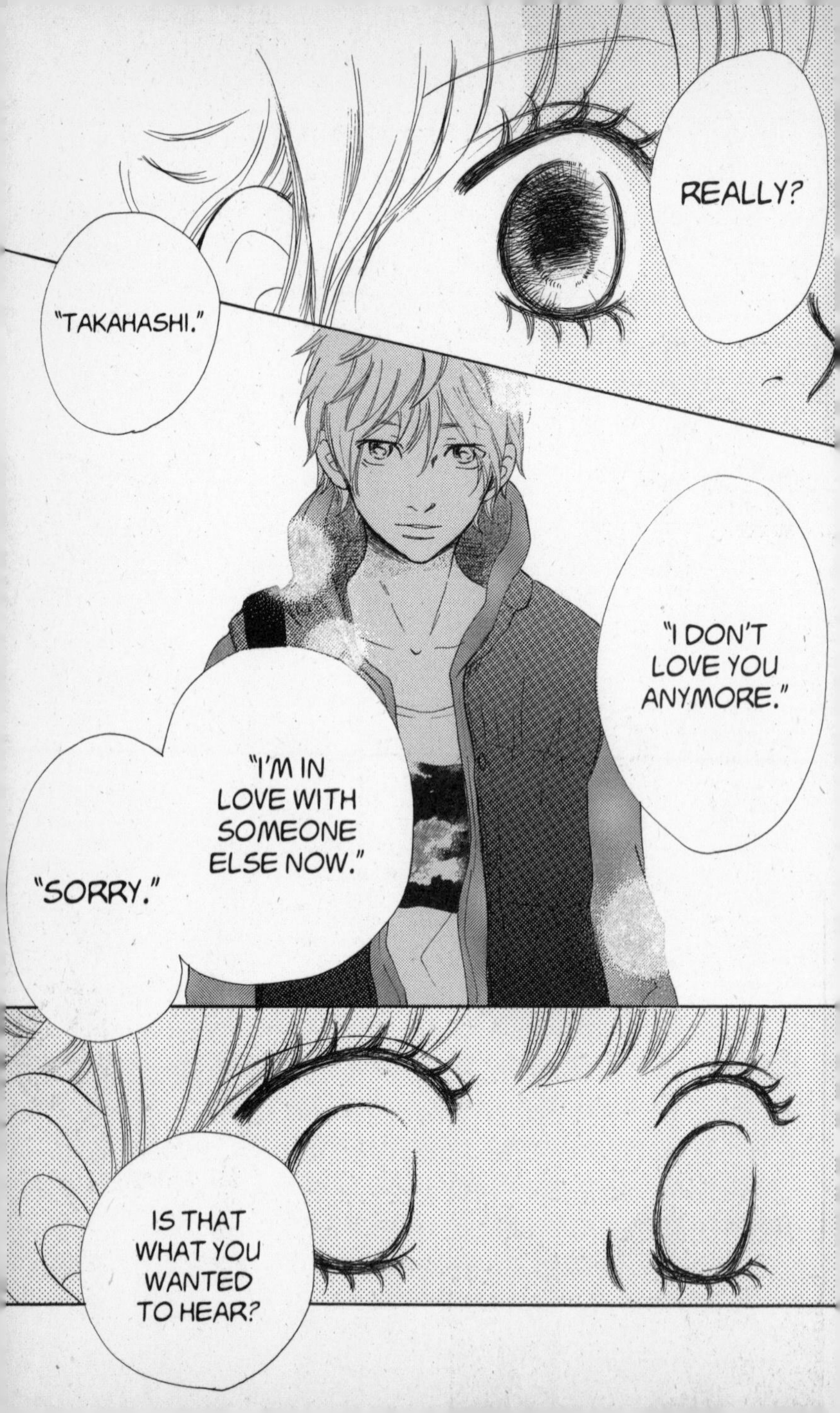
REALLY?
"TAKAHASHI."
"I DON'T LOVE YOU ANYMORE."
"I'M IN LOVE WITH SOMEONE ELSE NOW."
"SORRY."
IS THAT WHAT YOU WANTED TO HEAR?

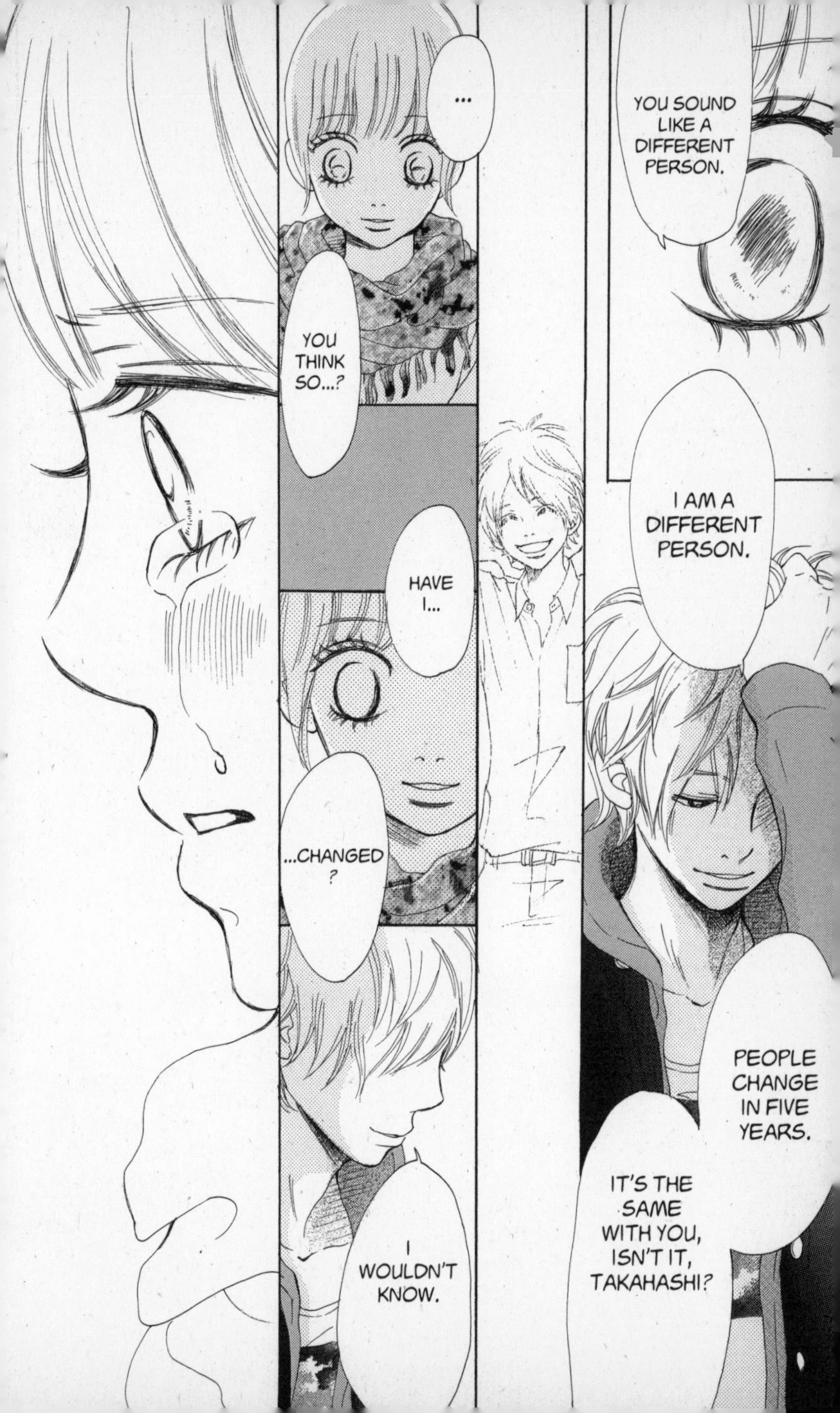

YOU SOUND LIKE A DIFFERENT PERSON.
I AM A DIFFERENT PERSON.
PEOPLE CHANGE IN FIVE YEARS.
IT'S THE SAME WITH YOU, ISN'T IT, TAKAHASHI?
...
YOU THINK SO...?
HAVE I...
...CHANGED?
I WOULDN'T KNOW.

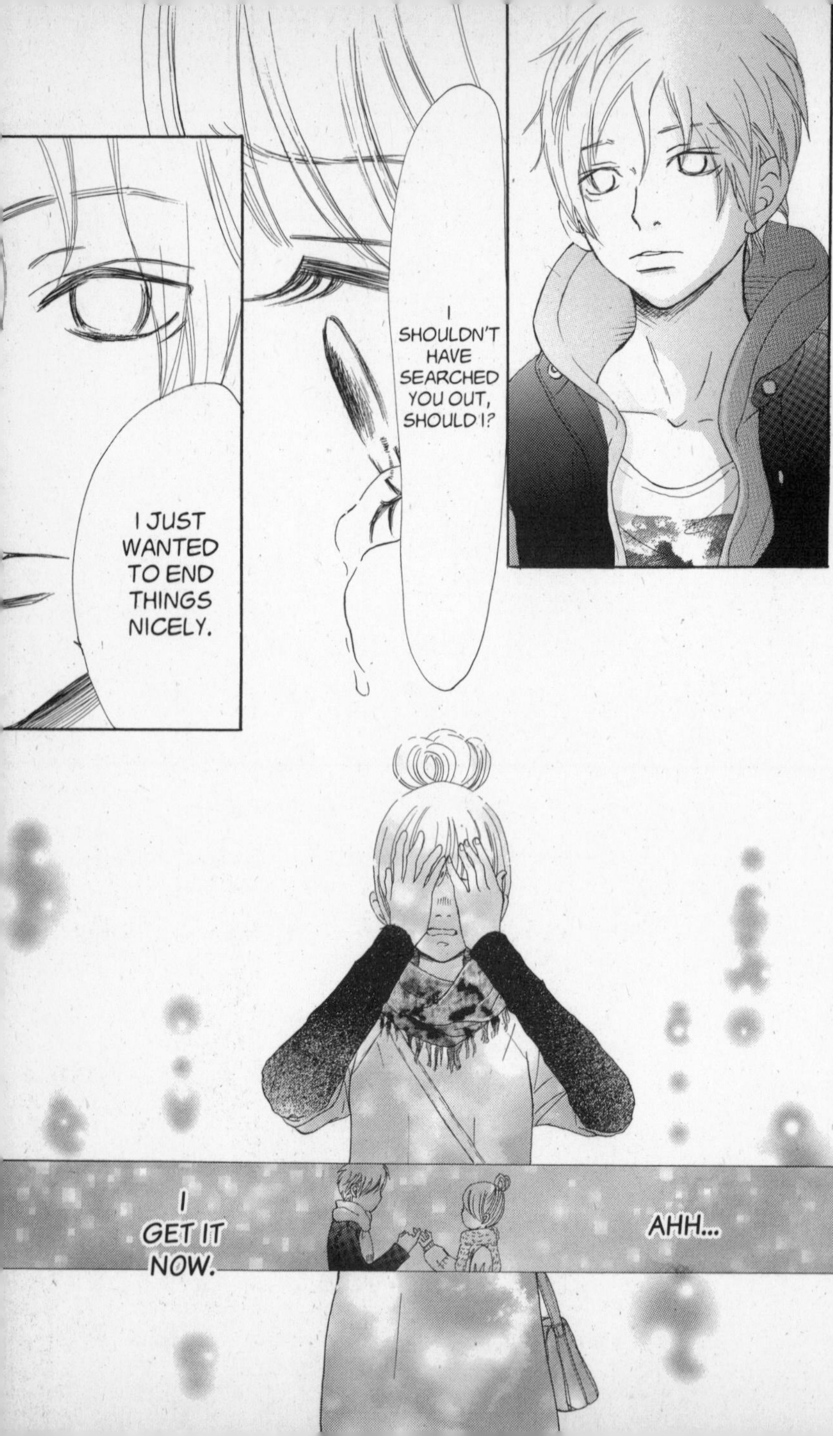
I SHOULDN'T HAVE SEARCHED YOU OUT, SHOULD I?
I JUST WANTED TO END THINGS NICELY.
AHH...
I GET IT NOW.

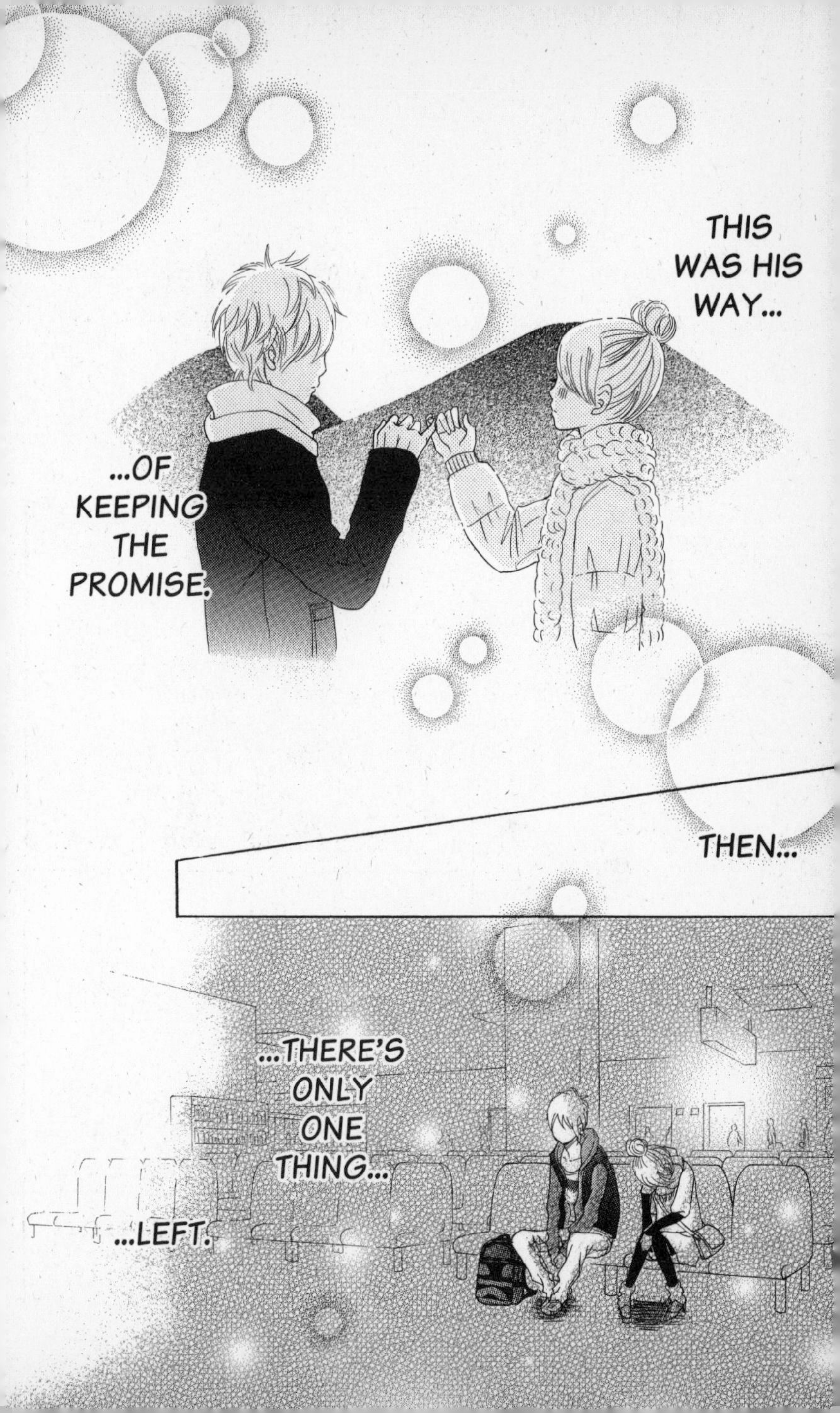
THIS WAS HIS WAY...
...OF KEEPING THE PROMISE.
THEN...
...THERE'S ONLY ONE THING...
...LEFT.

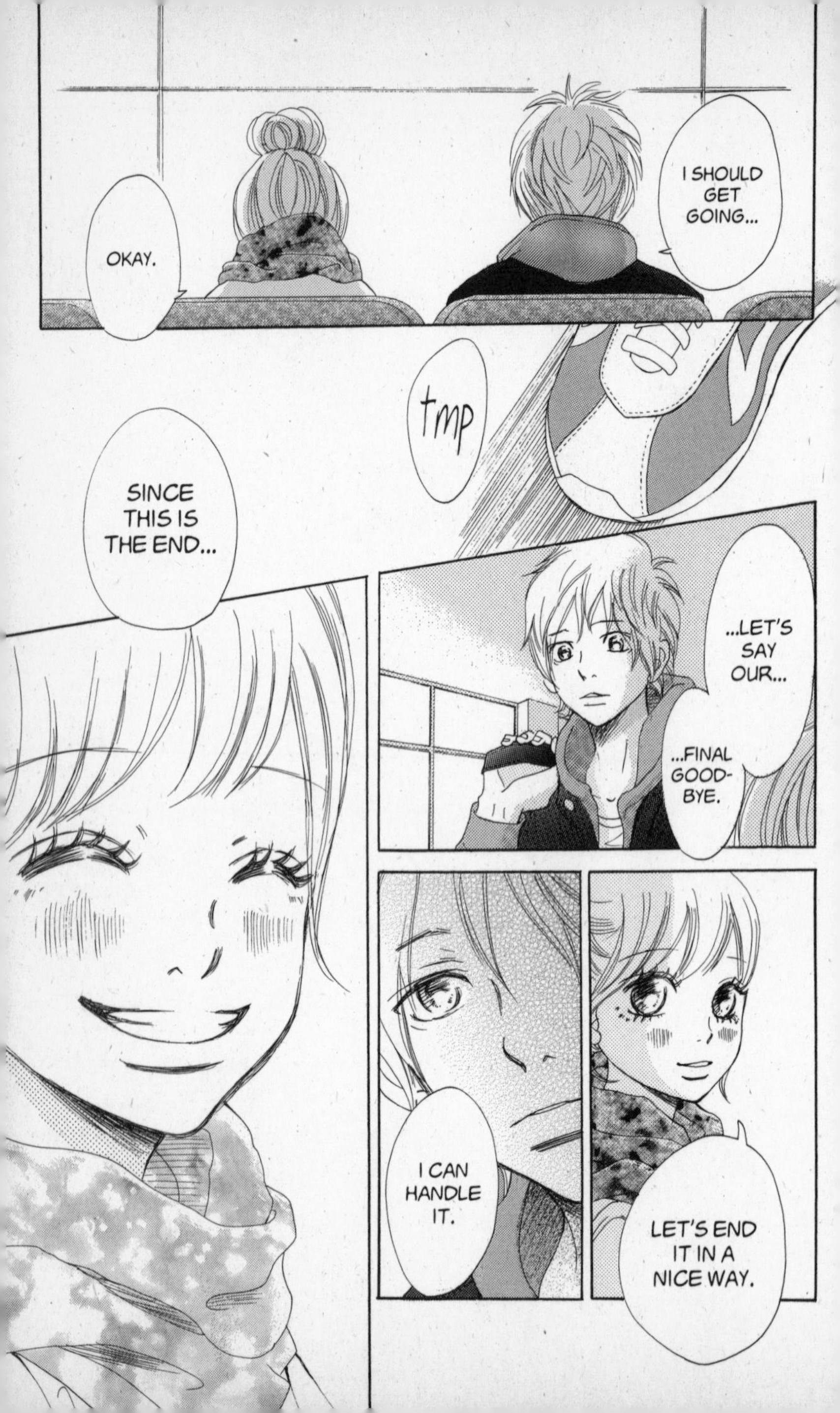
I SHOULD GET GOING...
OKAY.
tmp
SINCE THIS IS THE END...
...LET'S SAY OUR...
...FINAL GOOD-BYE.
LET'S END IT IN A NICE WAY.
I CAN HANDLE IT.

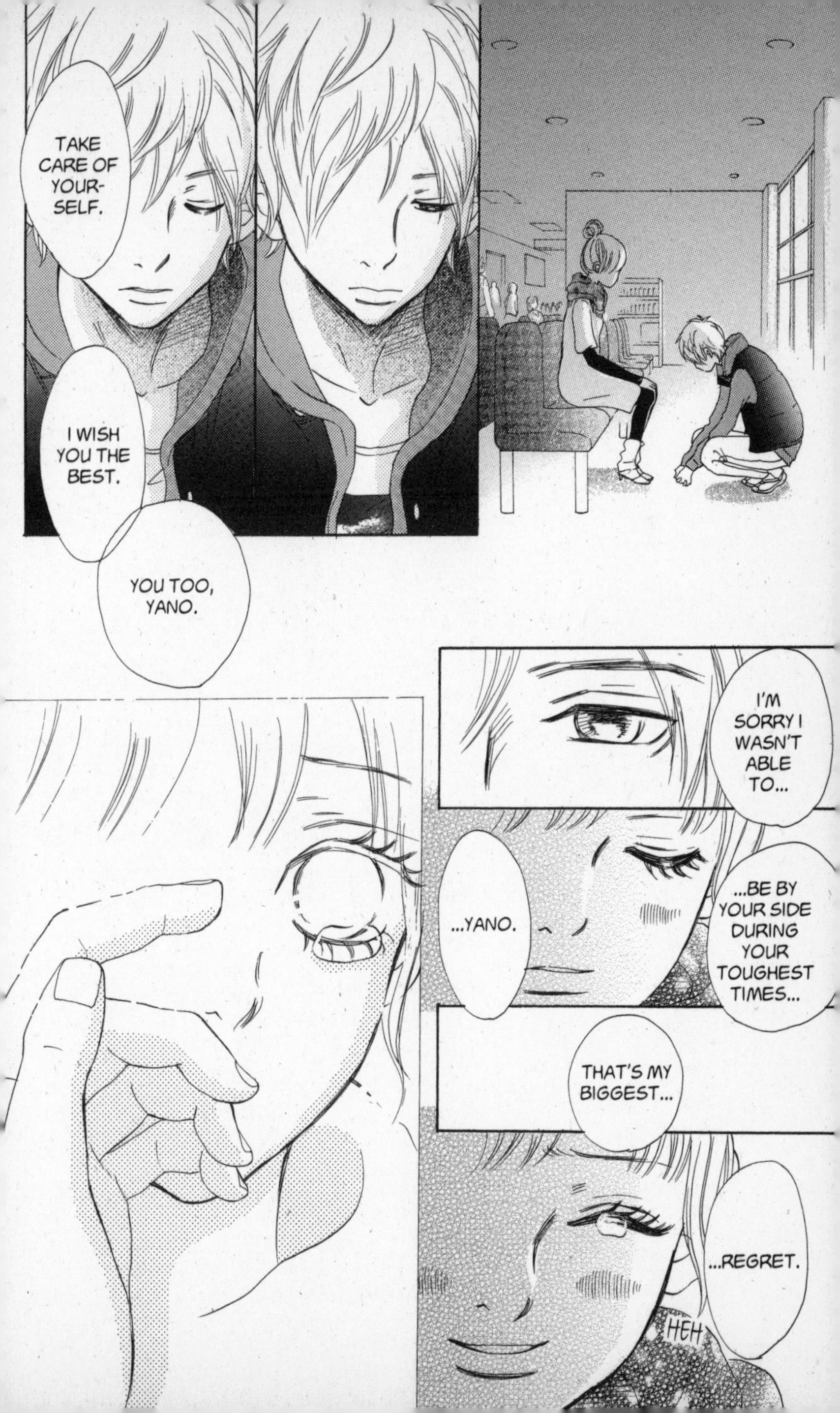
TAKE CARE OF YOUR-SELF.
I WISH YOU THE BEST.
YOU TOO, YANO.
I'M SORRY I WASN'T ABLE TO...
...BE BY YOUR SIDE DURING YOUR TOUGHEST TIMES...
...YANO.
THAT'S MY BIGGEST...
...REGRET.
HEH

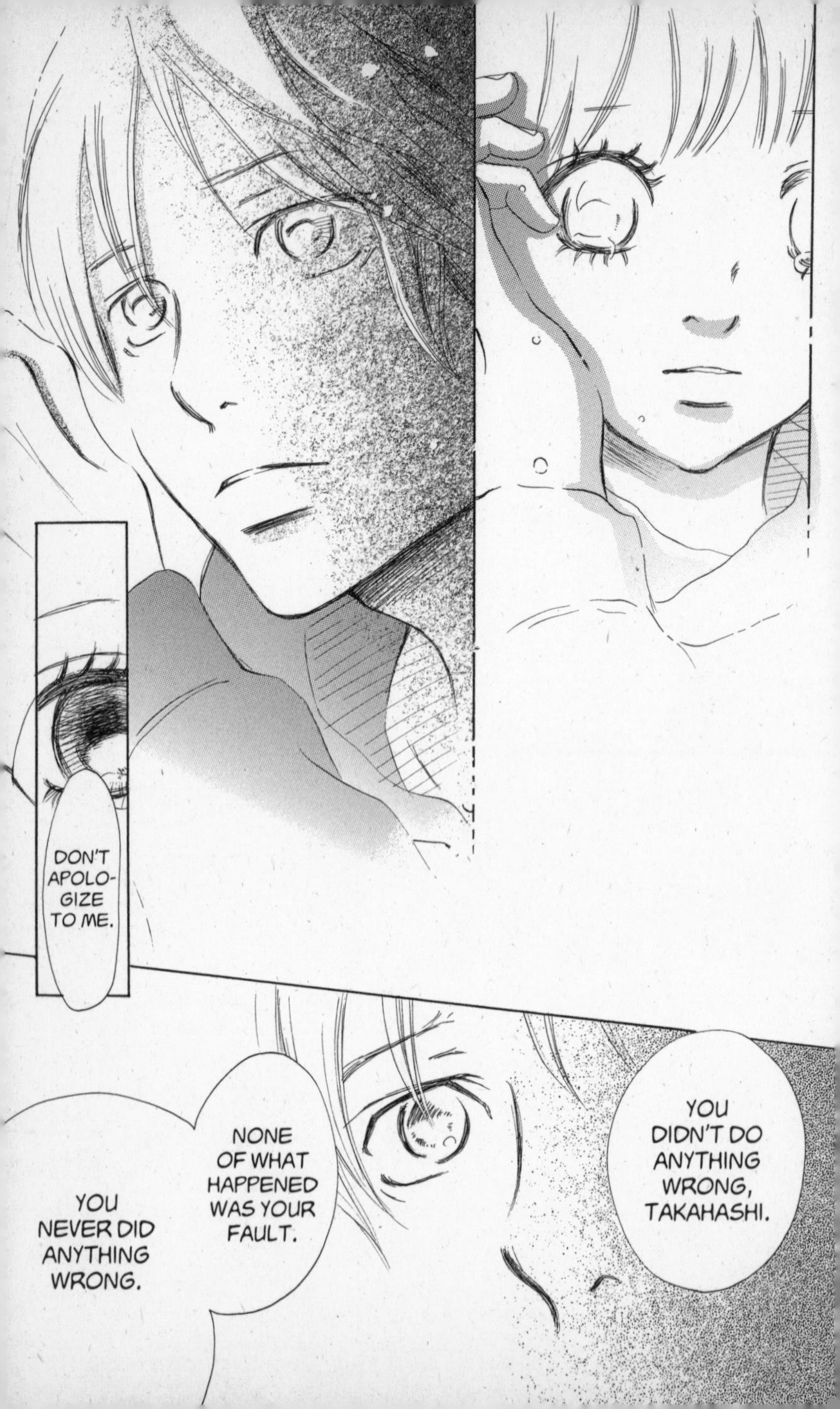
DON'T APOLOGIZE TO ME.
YOU DIDN'T DO ANYTHING WRONG, TAKAHASHI.
NONE OF WHAT HAPPENED WAS YOUR FAULT.
YOU NEVER DID ANYTHING WRONG.

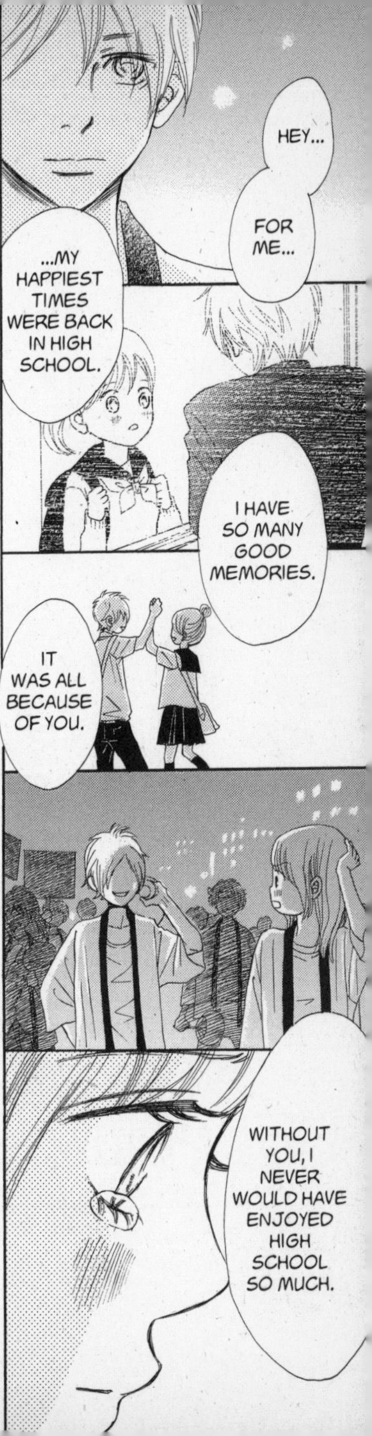
HEY...
FOR ME...
...MY HAPPIEST TIMES WERE BACK IN HIGH SCHOOL.
I HAVE SO MANY GOOD MEMORIES.
IT WAS ALL BECAUSE OF YOU.
WITHOUT YOU, I NEVER WOULD HAVE ENJOYED HIGH SCHOOL SO MUCH.
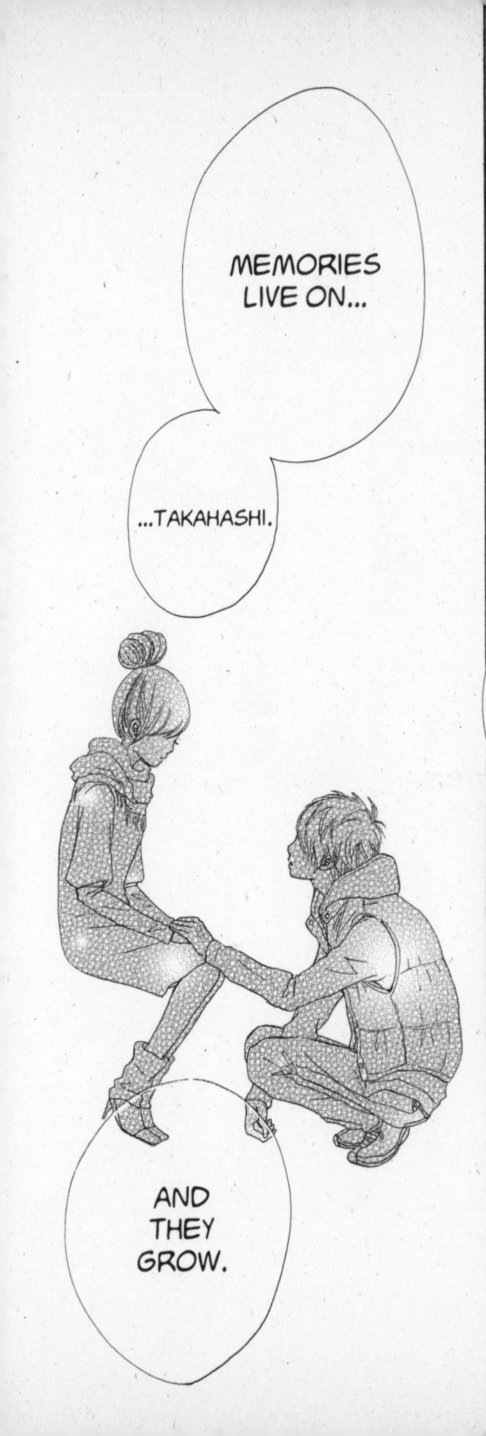
MEMORIES LIVE ON...
...TAKAHASHI.
AND THEY GROW.

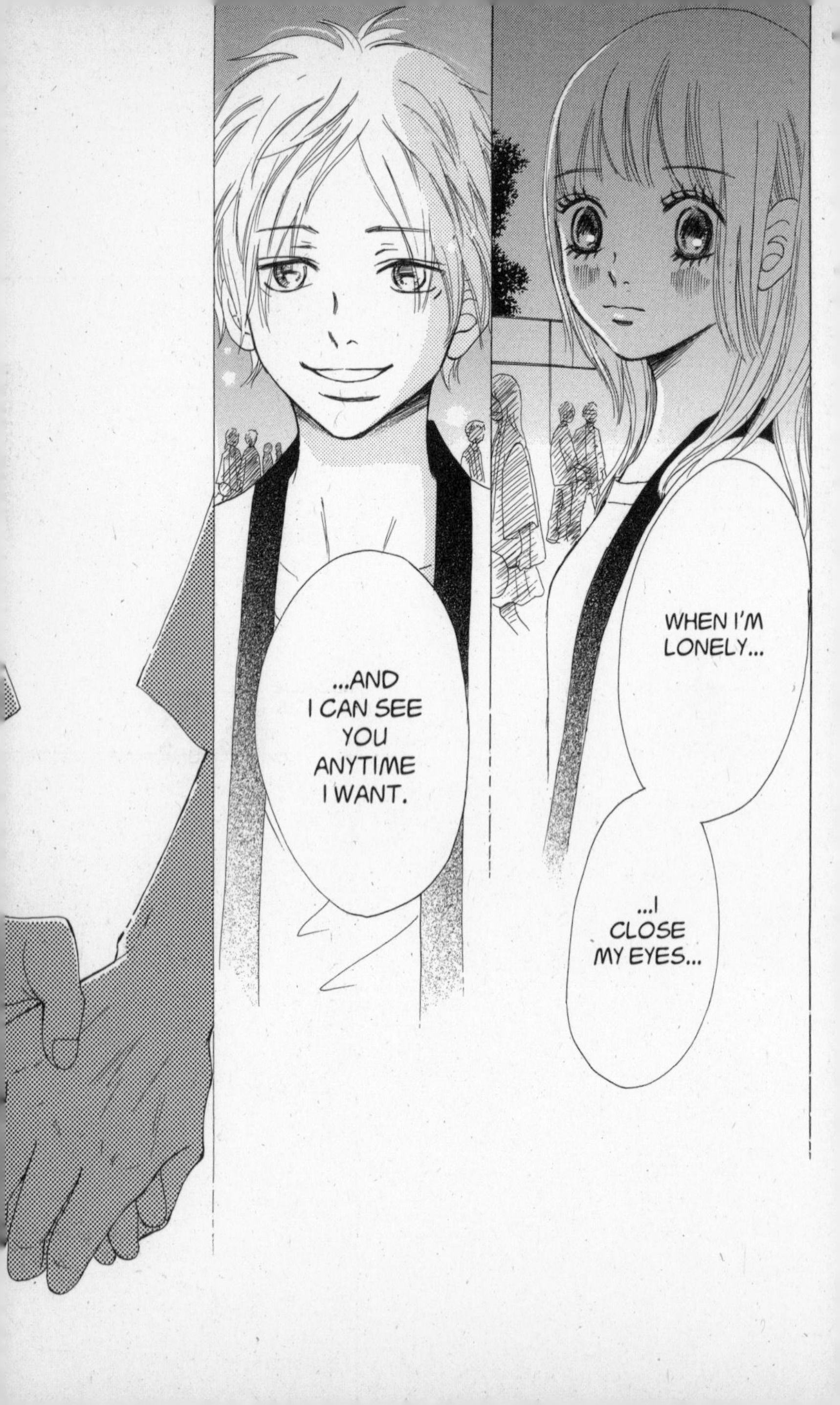
WHEN I'M LONELY...
...I CLOSE MY EYES...
...AND I CAN SEE YOU ANYTIME I WANT.

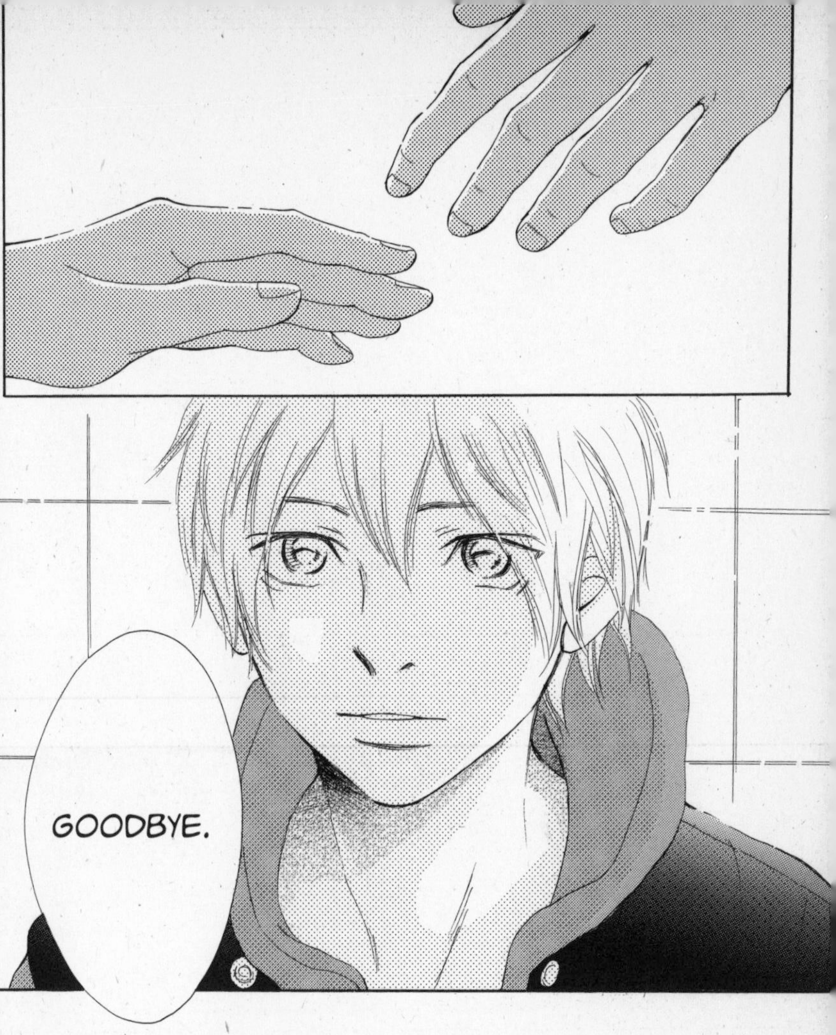
GOODBYE.

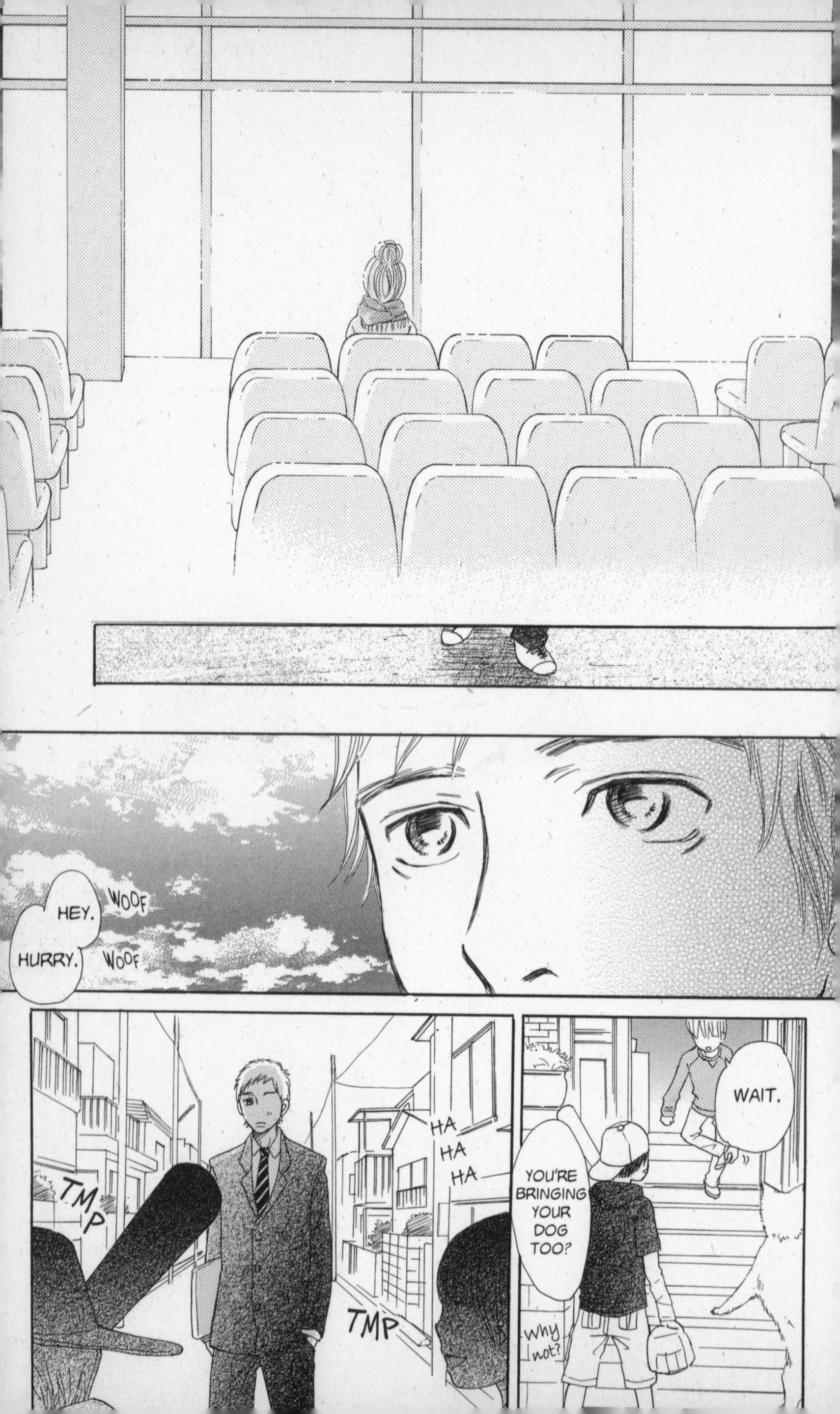
HEY.
WOOF
HURRY.
WOOF
WAIT.
YOU'RE BRINGING YOUR DOG TOO?
Why not?
HA HA HA
TMP
TMP

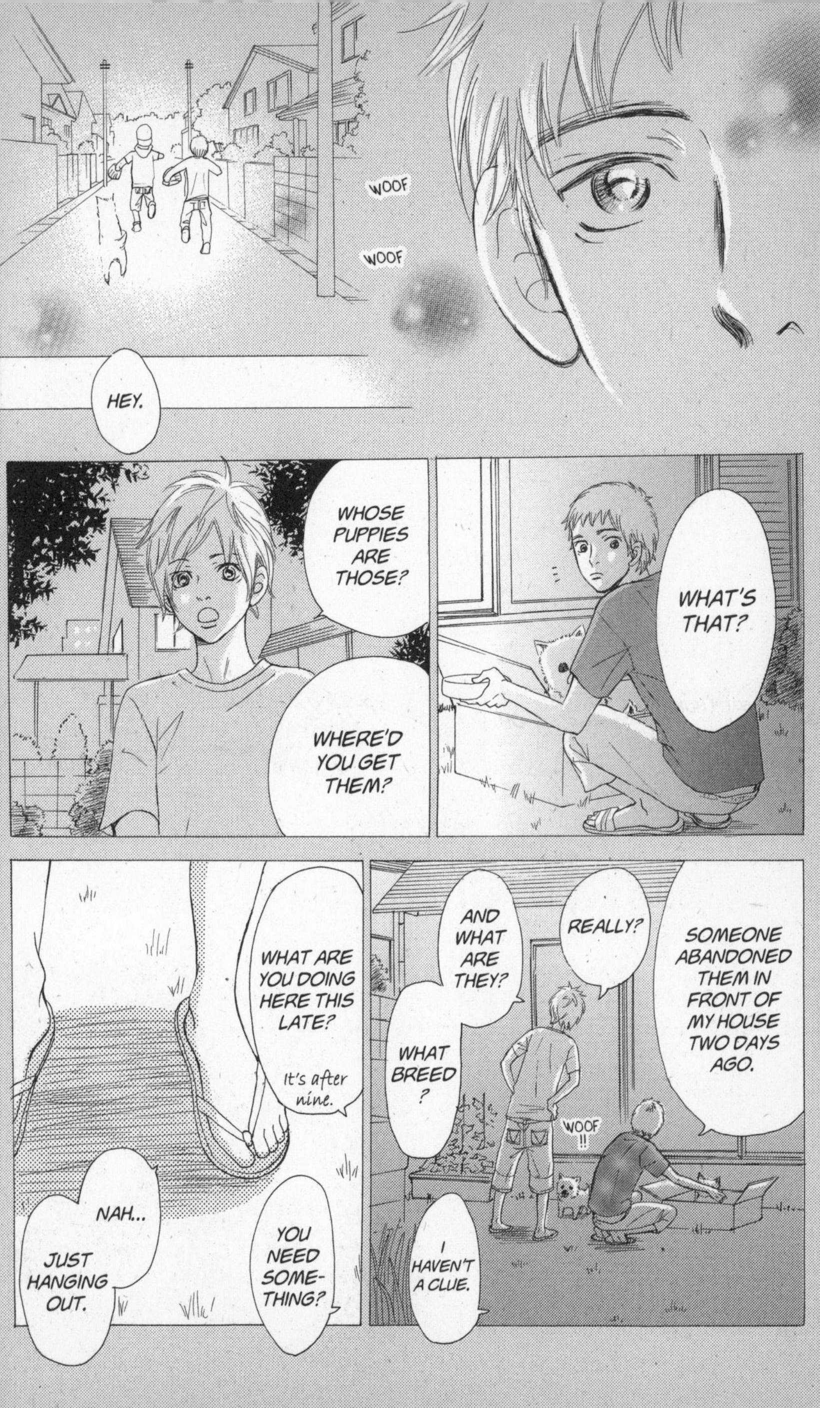
WOOF
WOOF
HEY.
WHAT'S THAT?
WHOSE PUPPIES ARE THOSE?
WHERE'D YOU GET THEM?
SOMEONE ABANDONED THEM IN FRONT OF MY HOUSE TWO DAYS AGO.
REALLY?
AND WHAT ARE THEY?
WHAT BREED?
WOOF !!
I HAVEN'T A CLUE.
WHAT ARE YOU DOING HERE THIS LATE?
It's after nine.
YOU NEED SOME-THING?
NAH...
JUST HANGING OUT.

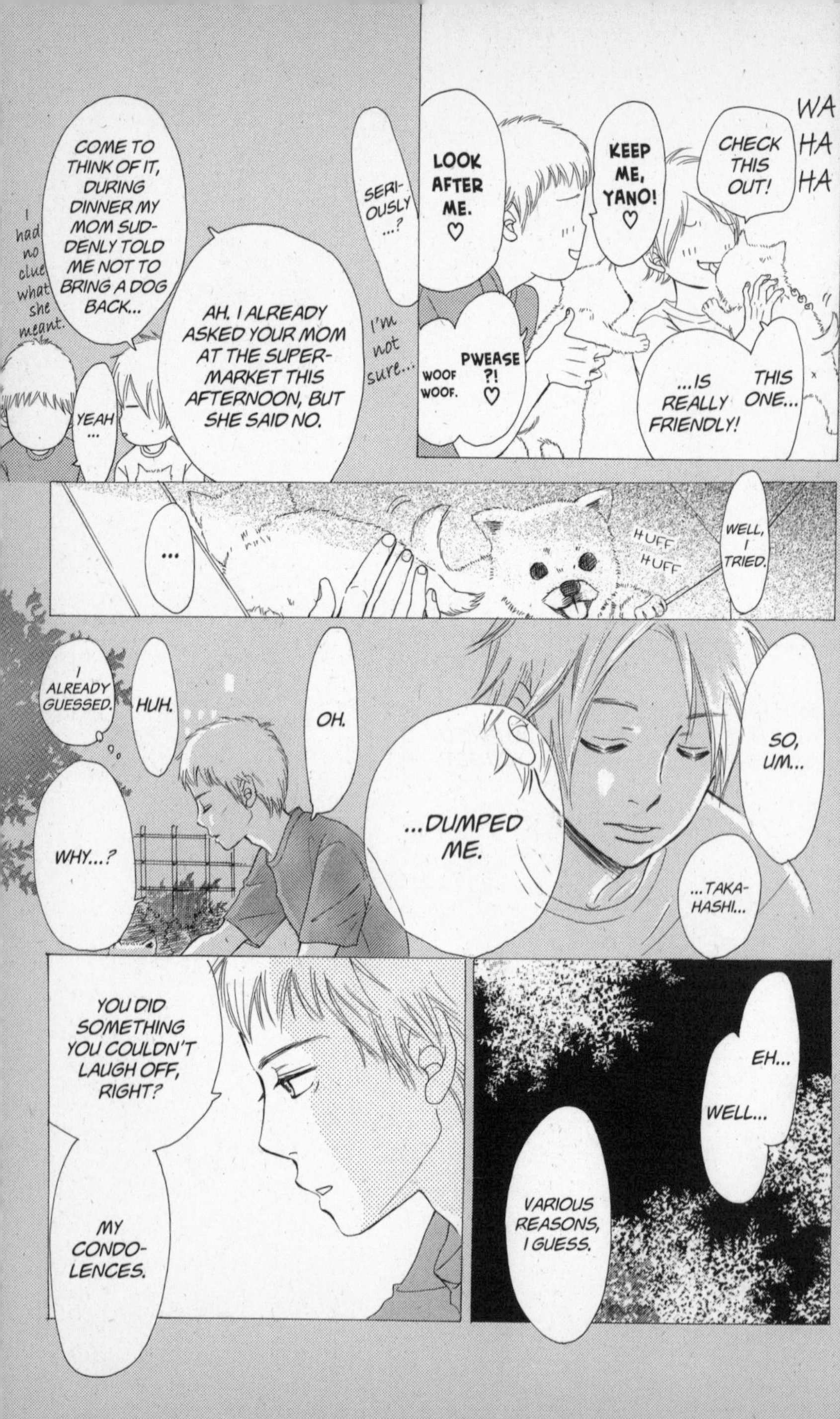
WA HA HA
CHECK THIS OUT!
KEEP ME, YANO! ♡
LOOK AFTER ME. ♡
THIS ONE...
...IS REALLY FRIENDLY!
PWEASE?! ♡
WOOF WOOF.
SERI-OUSLY...?
COME TO THINK OF IT, DURING DINNER MY MOM SUD-DENLY TOLD ME NOT TO BRING A DOG BACK...
I had no clue what she meant.
AH. I ALREADY ASKED YOUR MOM AT THE SUPER-MARKET THIS AFTERNOON, BUT SHE SAID NO.
I'm not sure...
YEAH...
WELL, I TRIED.
HUFF HUFF
...
SO, UM...
...TAKA-HASHI...
...DUMPED ME.
OH.
HUH.
I ALREADY GUESSED.
WHY...?
EH...
WELL...
VARIOUS REASONS, I GUESS.
YOU DID SOMETHING YOU COULDN'T LAUGH OFF, RIGHT?
MY CONDO-LENCES.

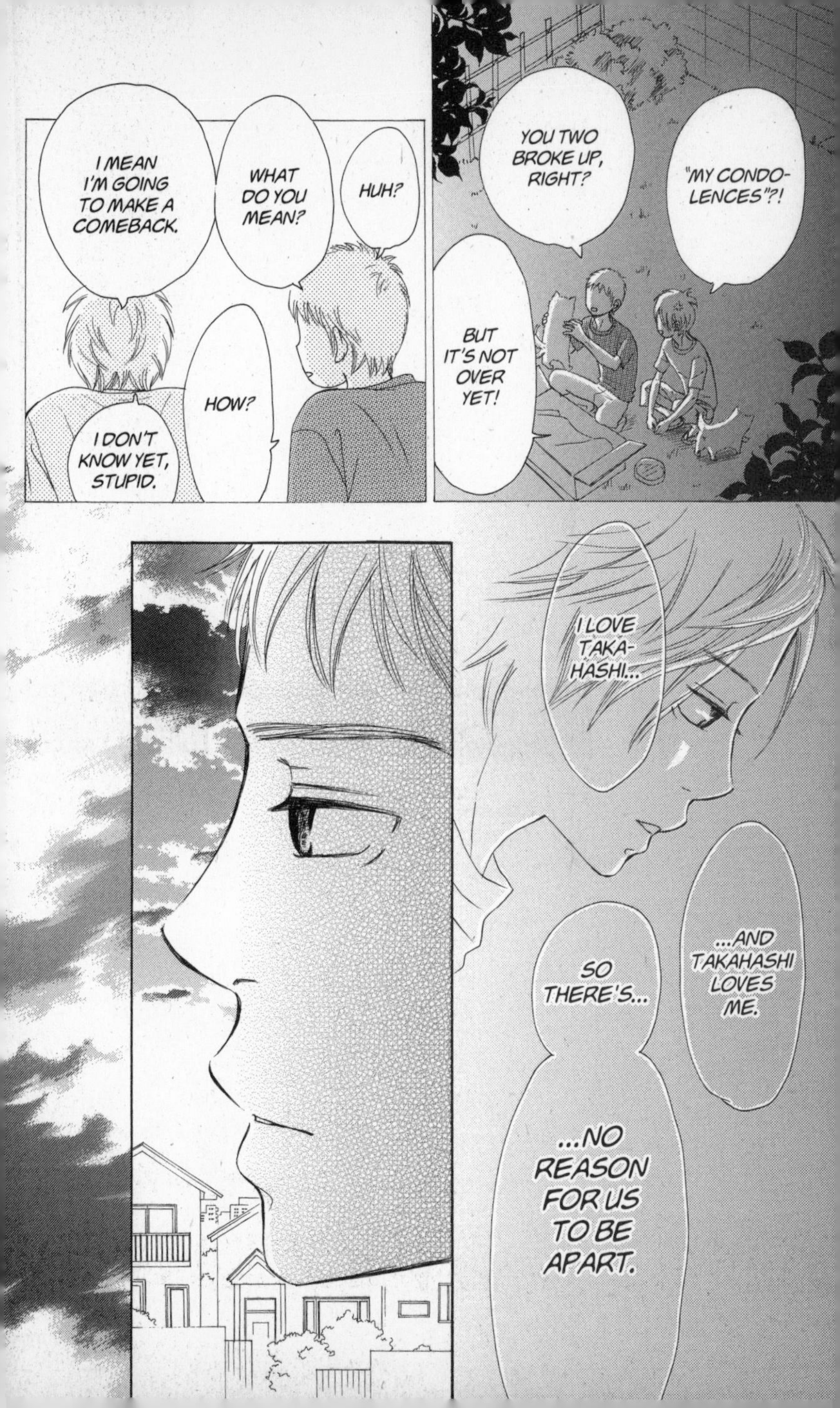
"MY CONDOLENCES"?!
YOU TWO BROKE UP, RIGHT?
BUT IT'S NOT OVER YET!
HUH?
WHAT DO YOU MEAN?
I MEAN I'M GOING TO MAKE A COMEBACK.
HOW?
I DON'T KNOW YET, STUPID.
I LOVE TAKAHASHI...
...AND TAKAHASHI LOVES ME.
SO THERE'S...
...NO REASON FOR US TO BE APART.

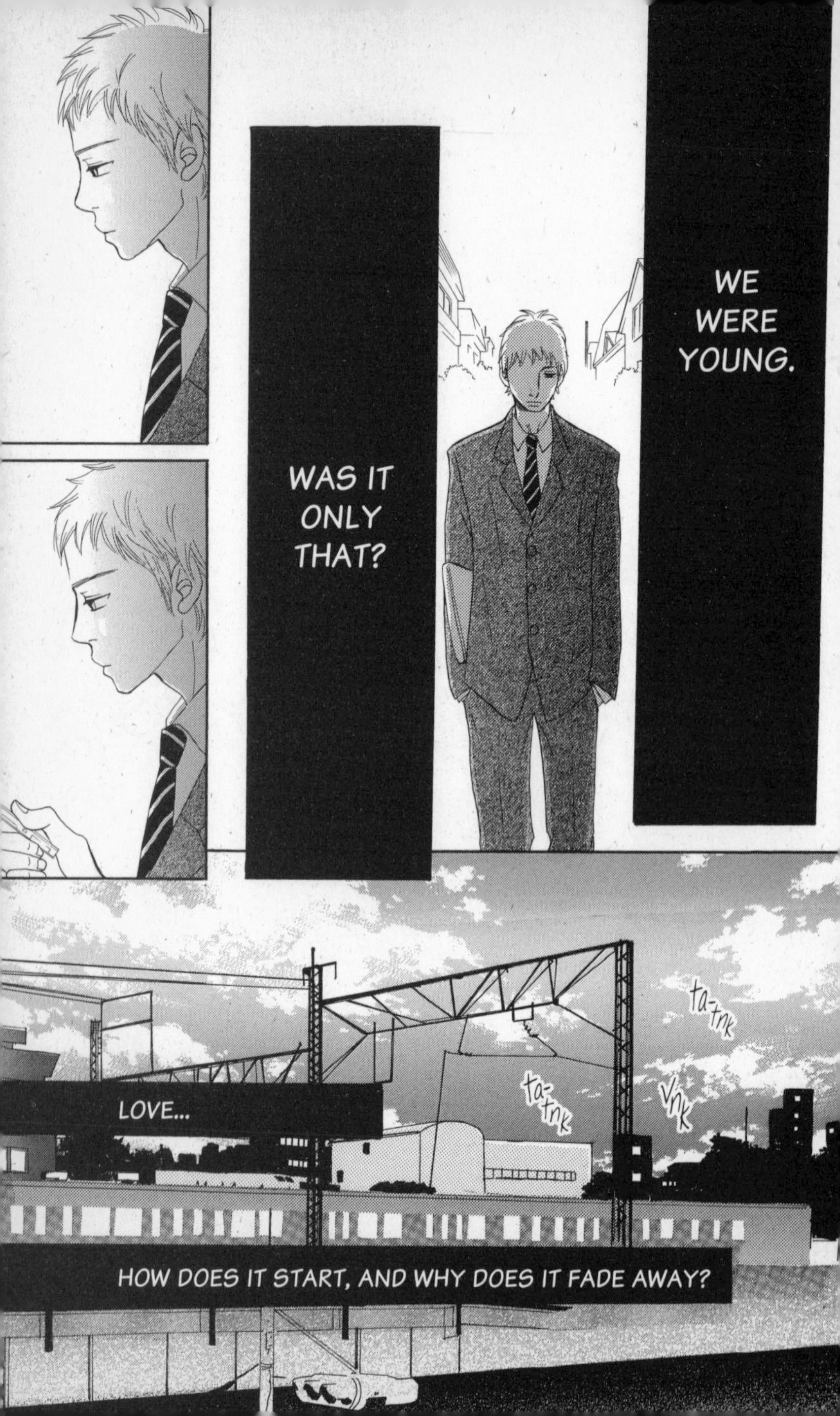
WE WERE YOUNG.
WAS IT ONLY THAT?
ta-tnk
ta-tnk
vnk
LOVE...
HOW DOES IT START, AND WHY DOES IT FADE AWAY?

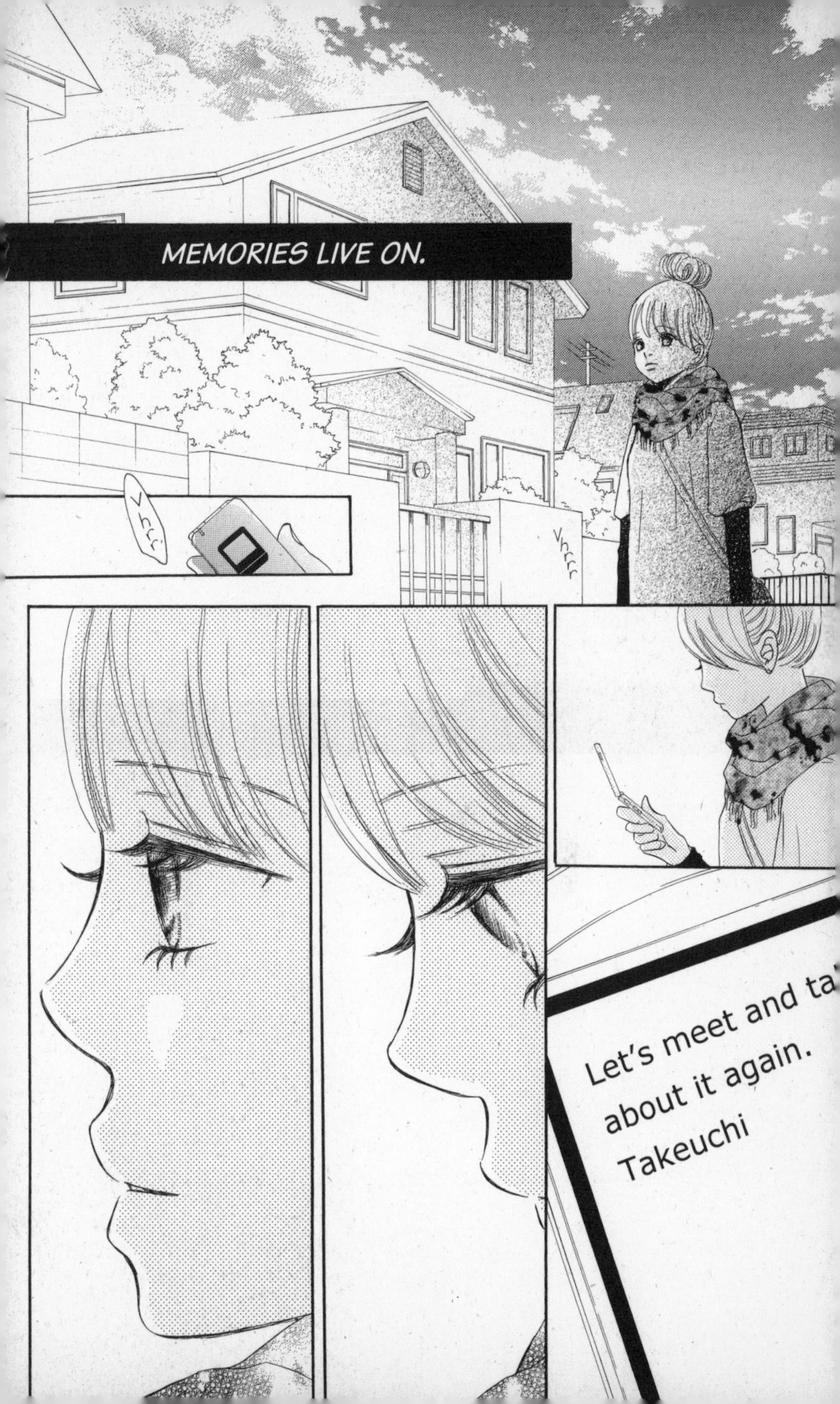
MEMORIES LIVE ON.
Vhrrr
Vhrr
Let's meet and ta
about it again.
Takeuchi

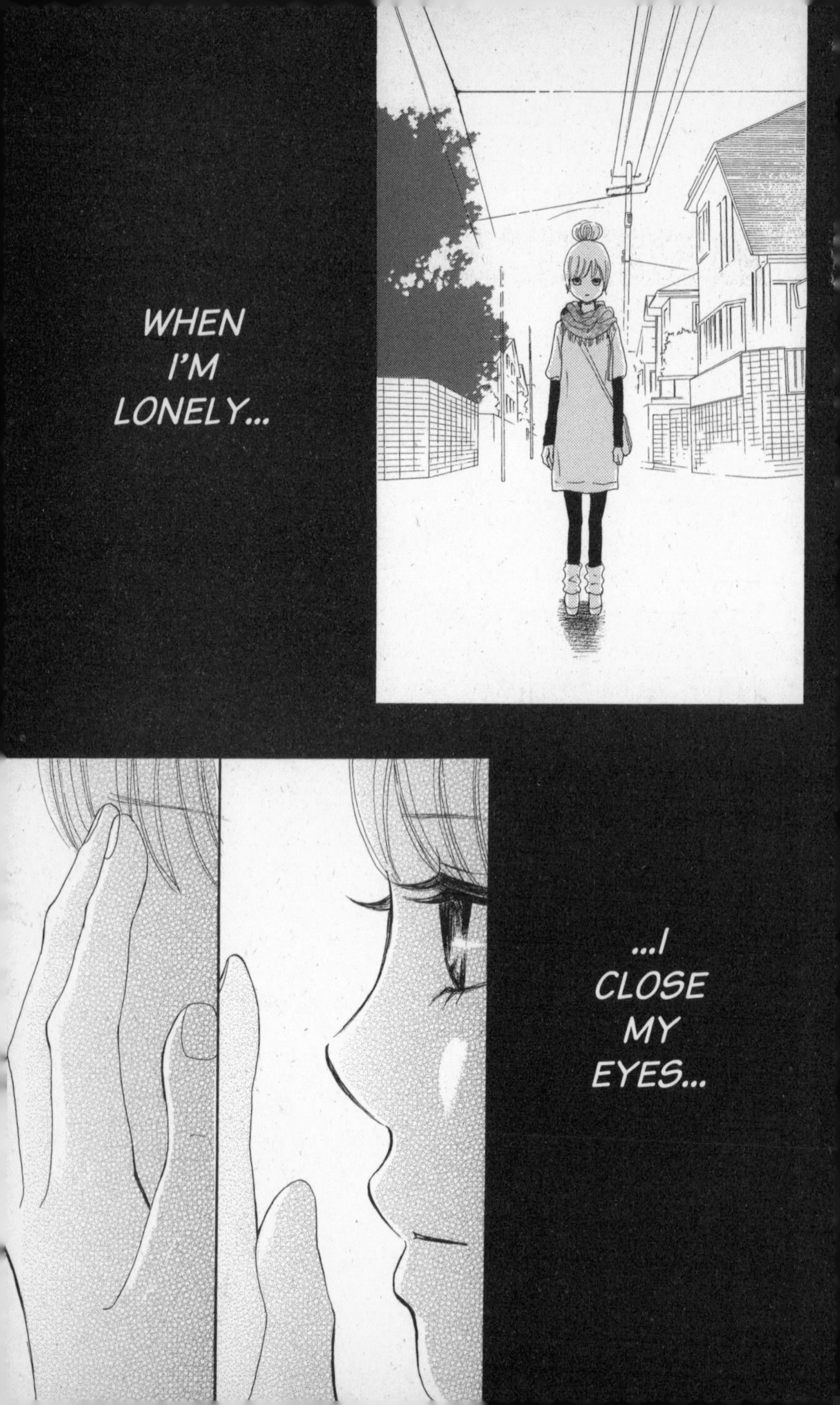
WHEN I'M LONELY...
...I CLOSE MY EYES...

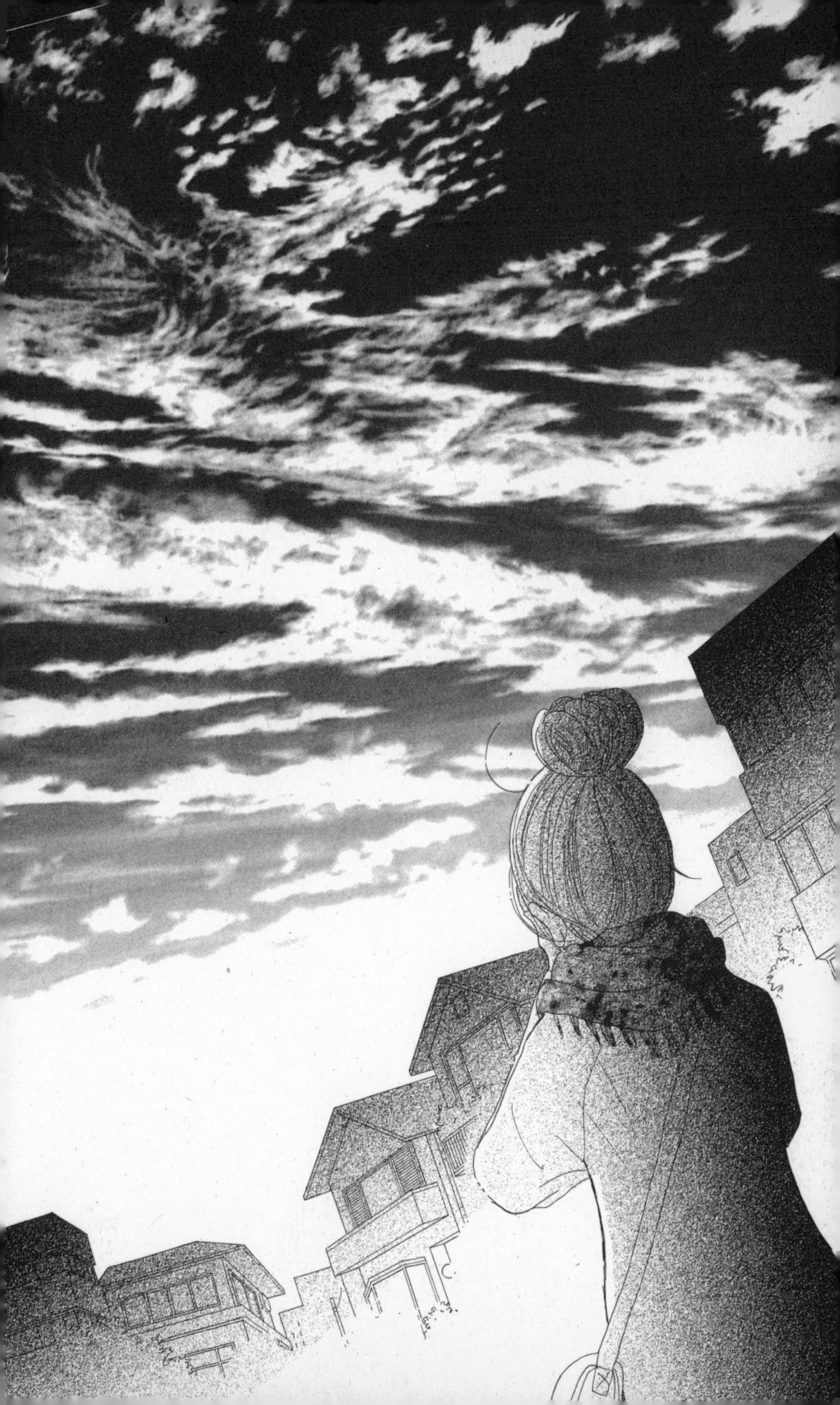

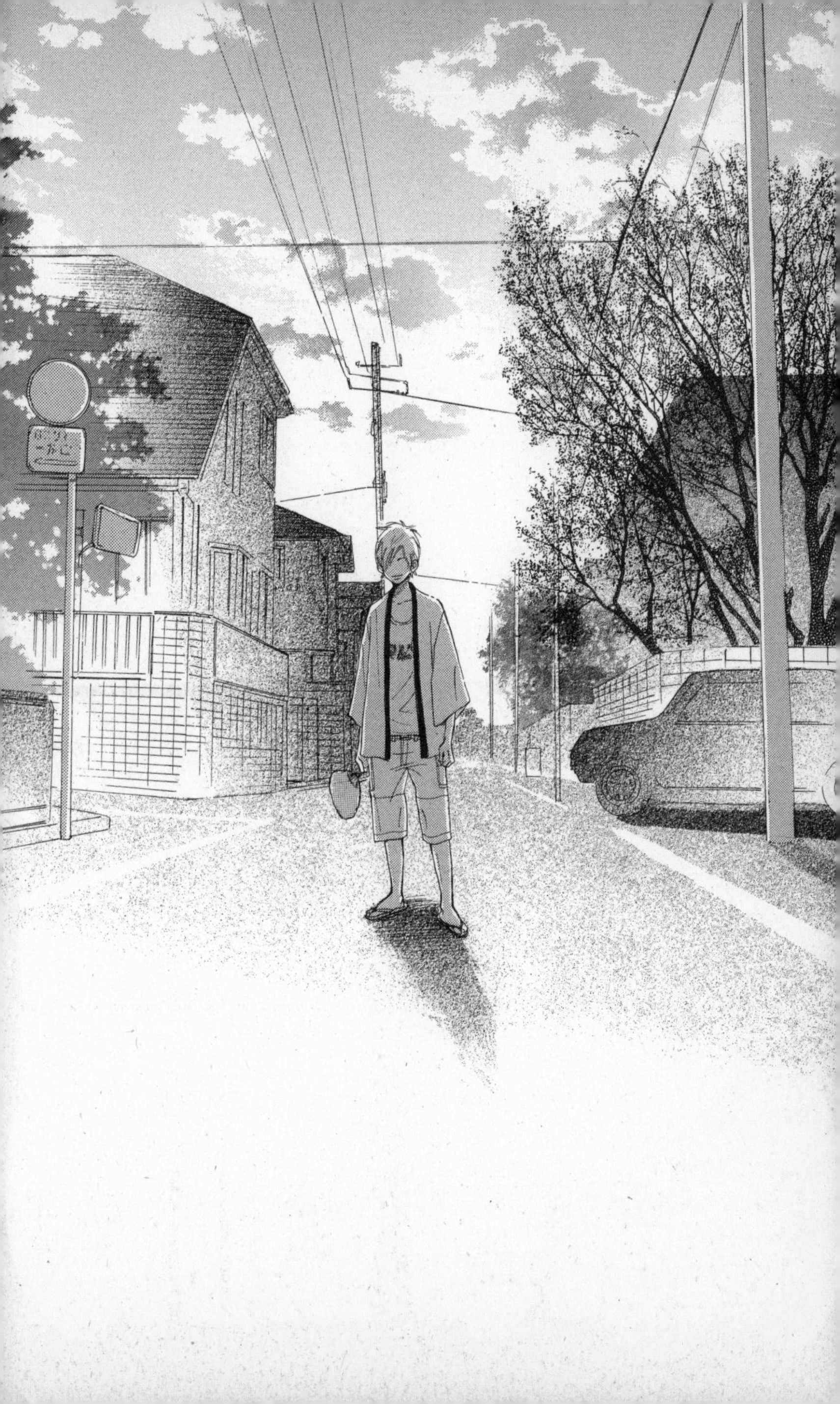

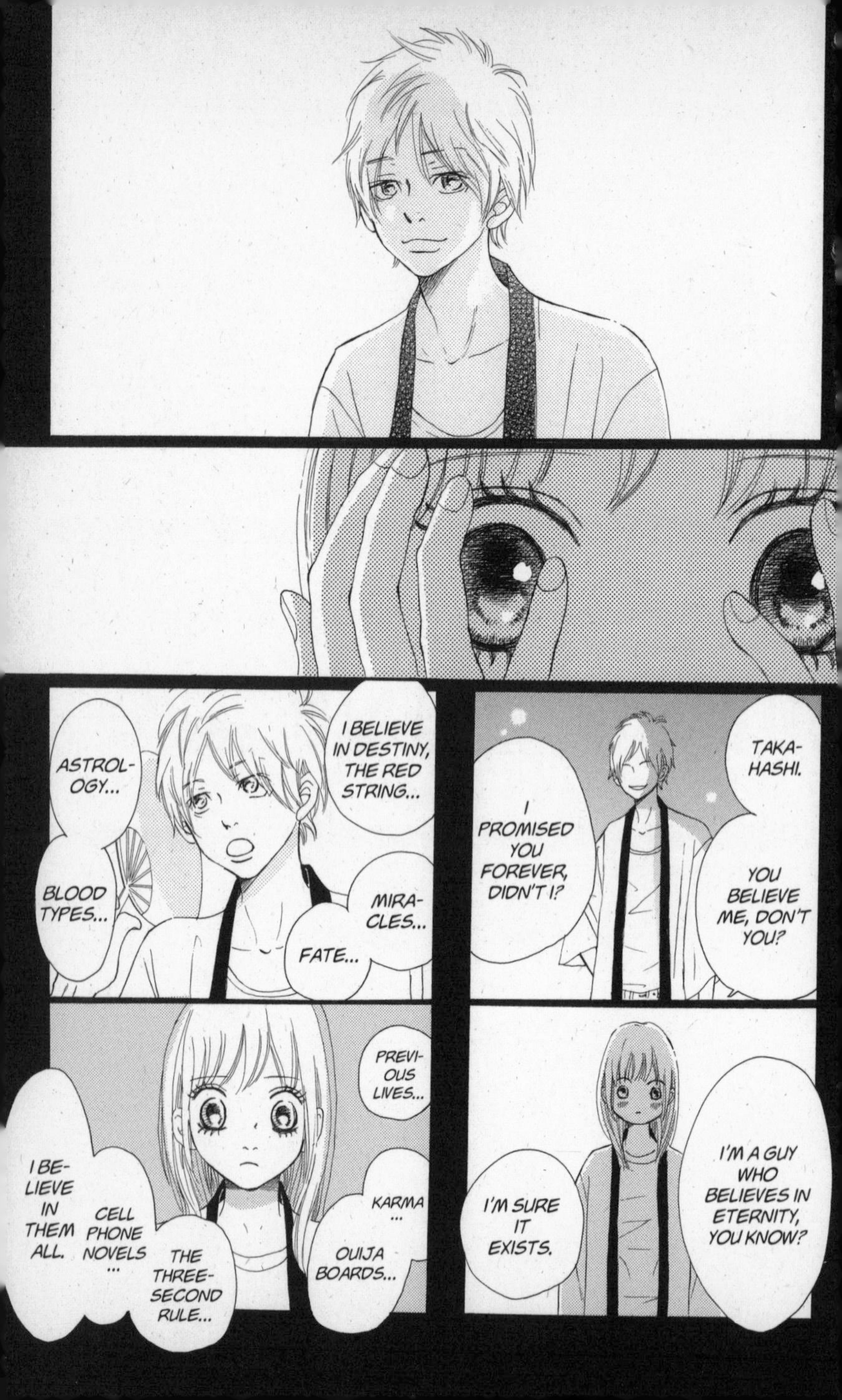
TAKA-HASHI.
I PROMISED YOU FOREVER, DIDN'T I?
YOU BELIEVE ME, DON'T YOU?
I BELIEVE IN DESTINY, THE RED STRING...
ASTROL-OGY...
MIRA-CLES...
BLOOD TYPES...
FATE...
I'M A GUY WHO BELIEVES IN ETERNITY, YOU KNOW?
I'M SURE IT EXISTS.
PREVI-OUS LIVES...
KARMA ...
OUIJA BOARDS...
CELL PHONE NOVELS ...
THE THREE-SECOND RULE...
I BE-LIEVE IN THEM ALL.

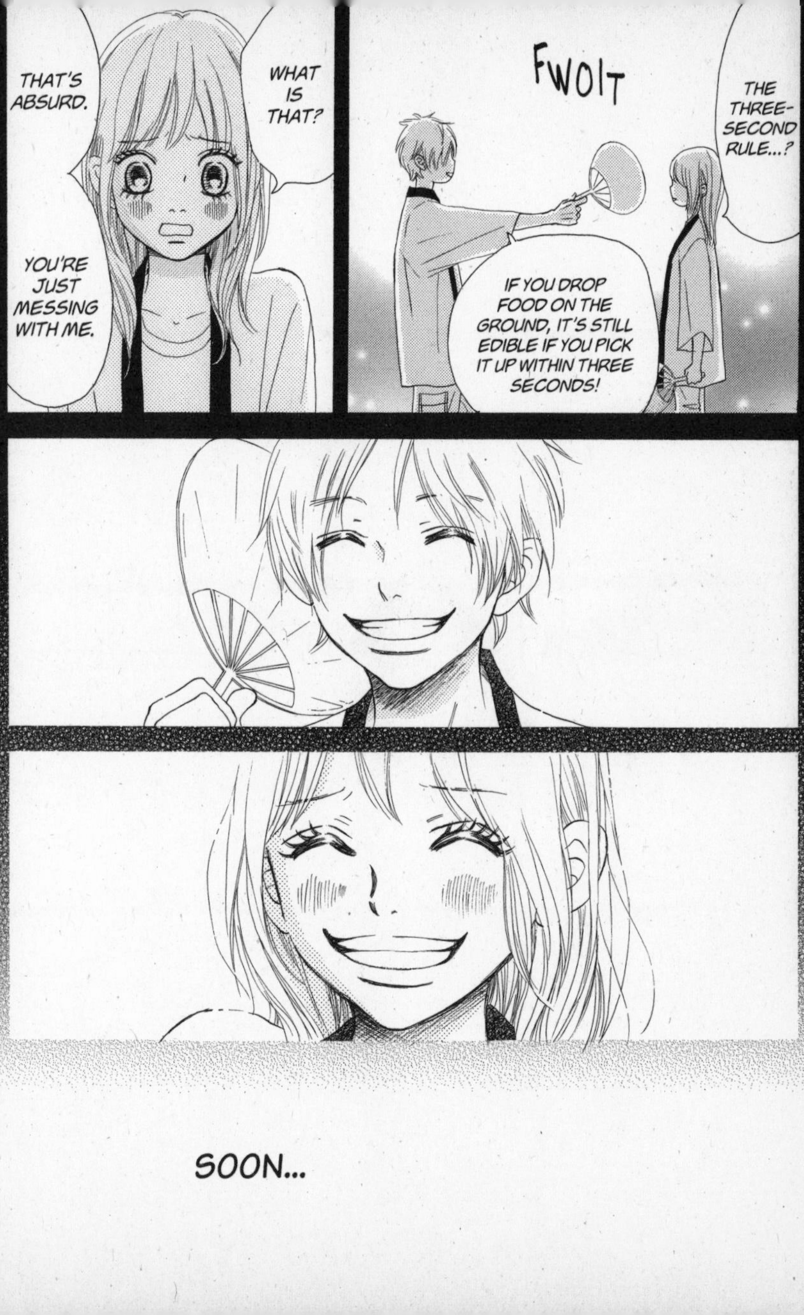
FWOIT
THE THREE-SECOND RULE...?
IF YOU DROP FOOD ON THE GROUND, IT'S STILL EDIBLE IF YOU PICK IT UP WITHIN THREE SECONDS!
WHAT IS THAT?
THAT'S ABSURD.
YOU'RE JUST MESSING WITH ME.
SOON...

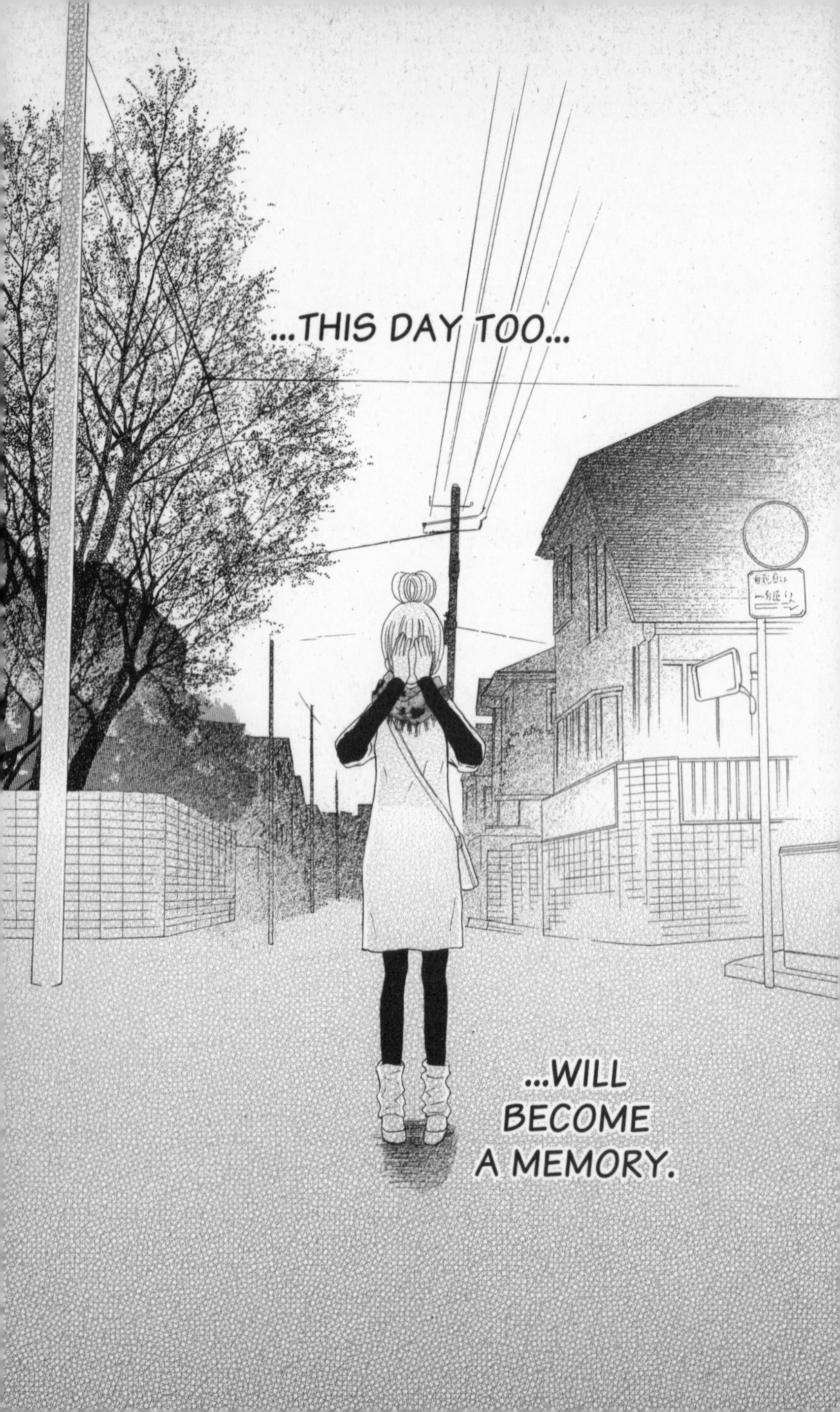
...THIS DAY TOO...
...WILL BECOME A MEMORY.

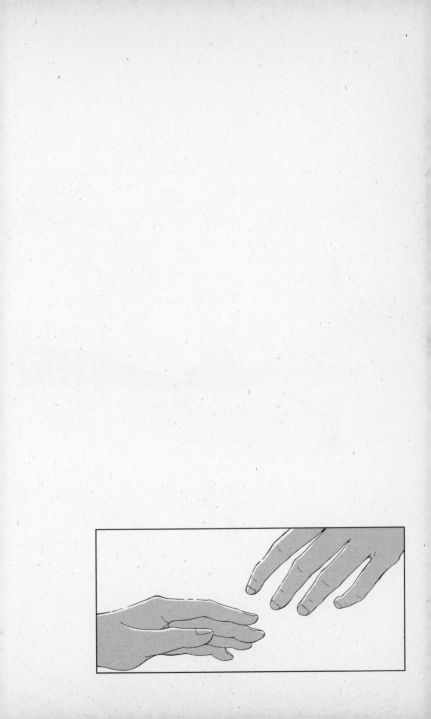

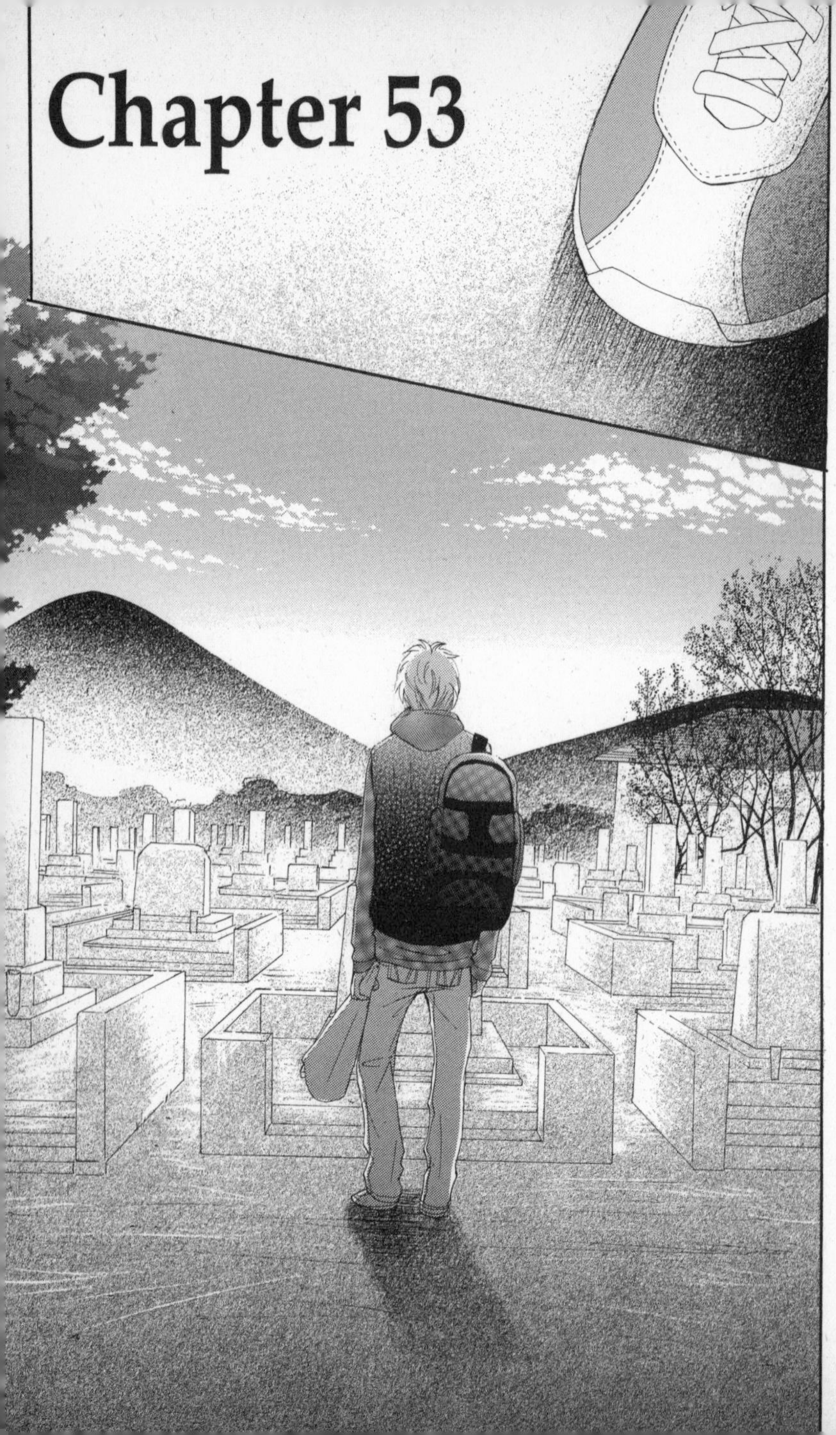
Chapter 53

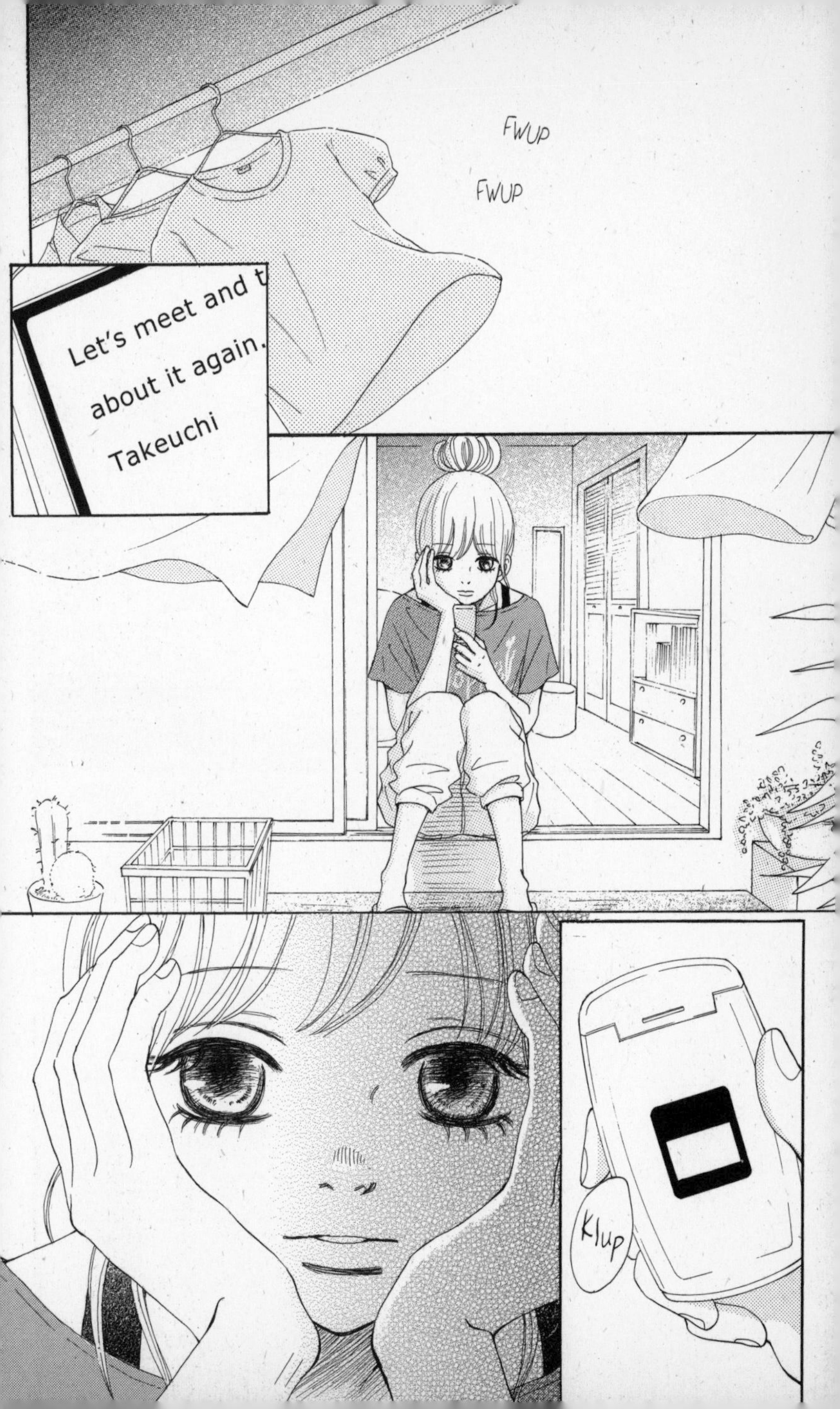
FWUP
FWUP
Let's meet and t
about it again.
Takeuchi
Klup

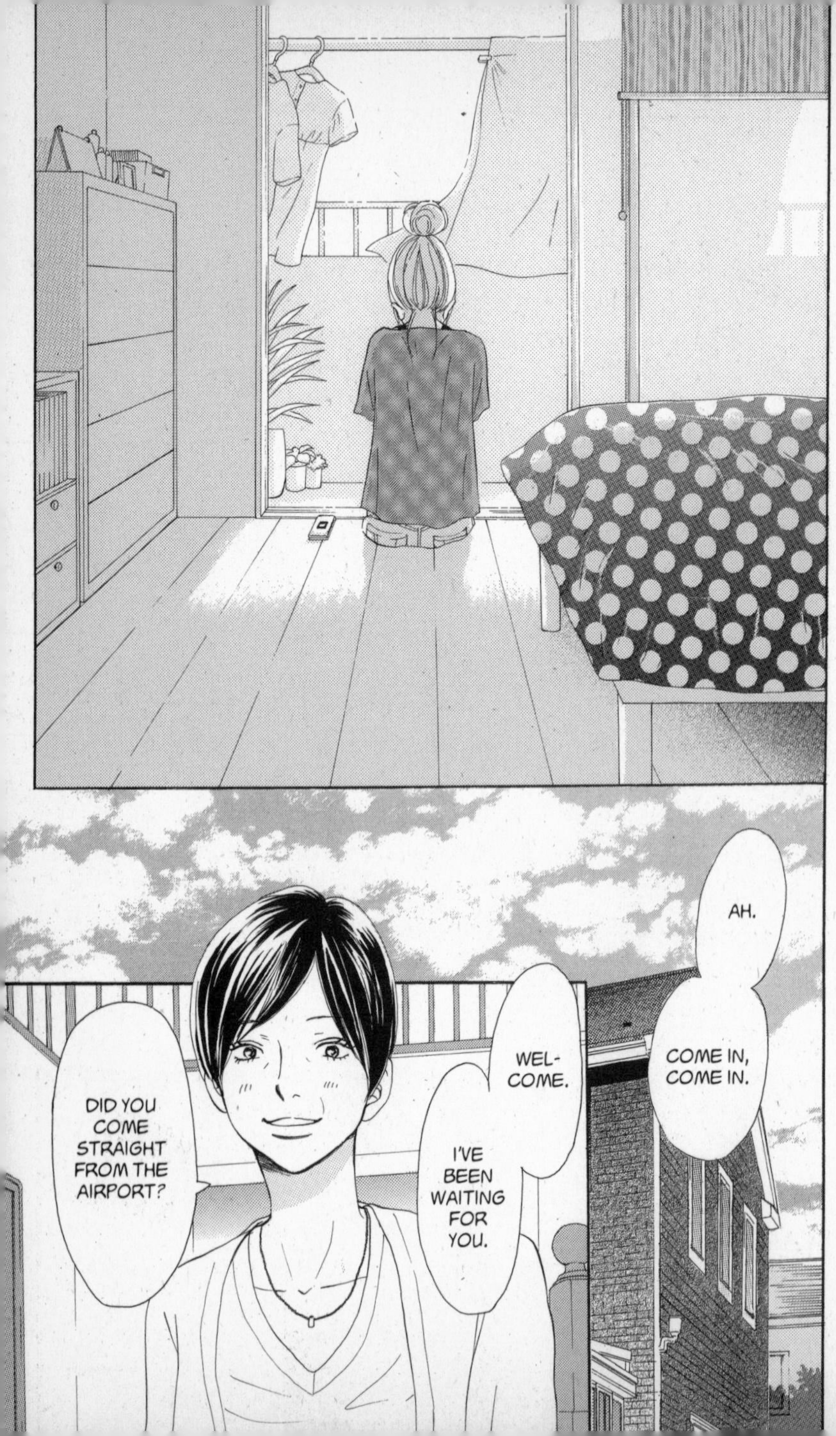
AH.
COME IN, COME IN.
WEL-COME.
I'VE BEEN WAITING FOR YOU.
DID YOU COME STRAIGHT FROM THE AIRPORT?

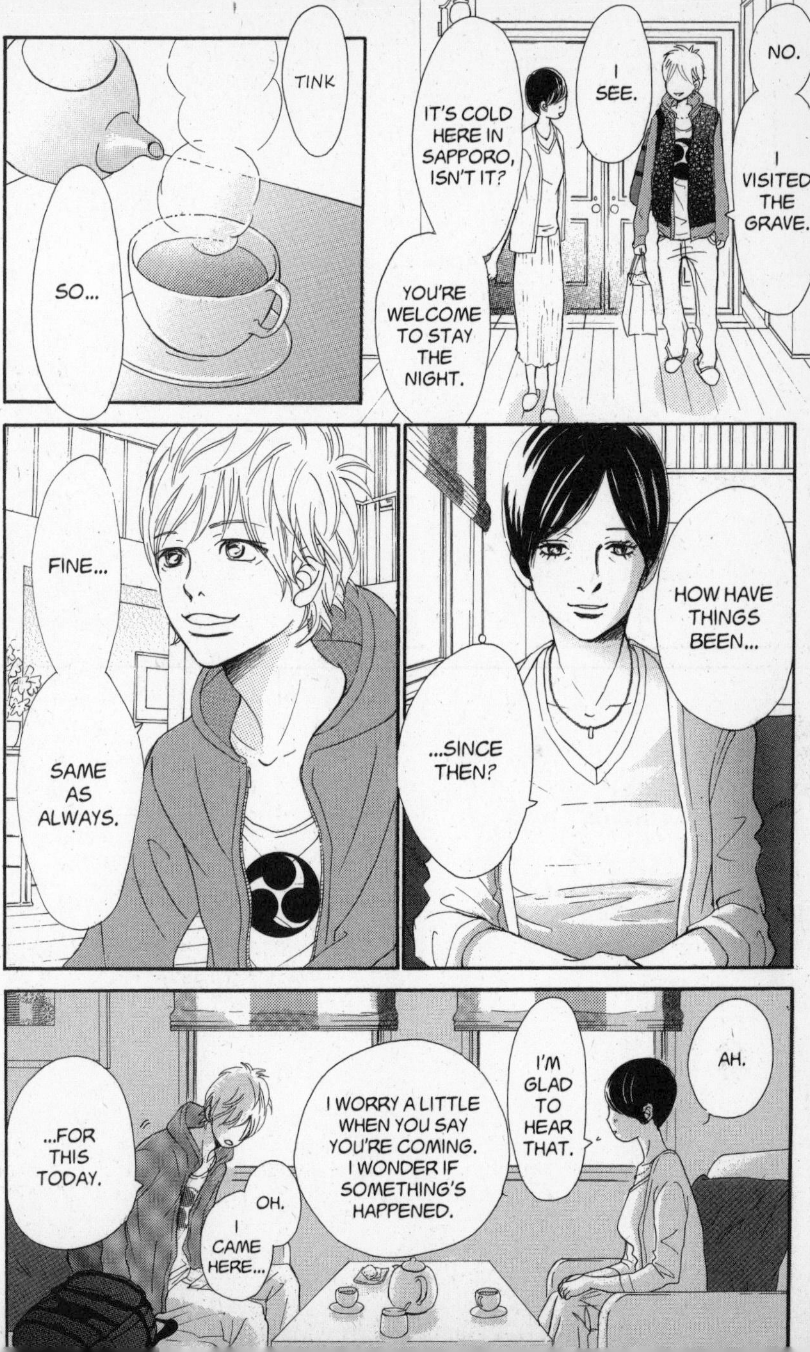
NO.
I VISITED THE GRAVE.
I SEE.
IT'S COLD HERE IN SAPPORO, ISN'T IT?
YOU'RE WELCOME TO STAY THE NIGHT.
TINK
SO...
HOW HAVE THINGS BEEN...
...SINCE THEN?
FINE...
SAME AS ALWAYS.
AH.
I'M GLAD TO HEAR THAT.
I WORRY A LITTLE WHEN YOU SAY YOU'RE COMING. I WONDER IF SOMETHING'S HAPPENED.
OH.
I CAME HERE...
...FOR THIS TODAY.

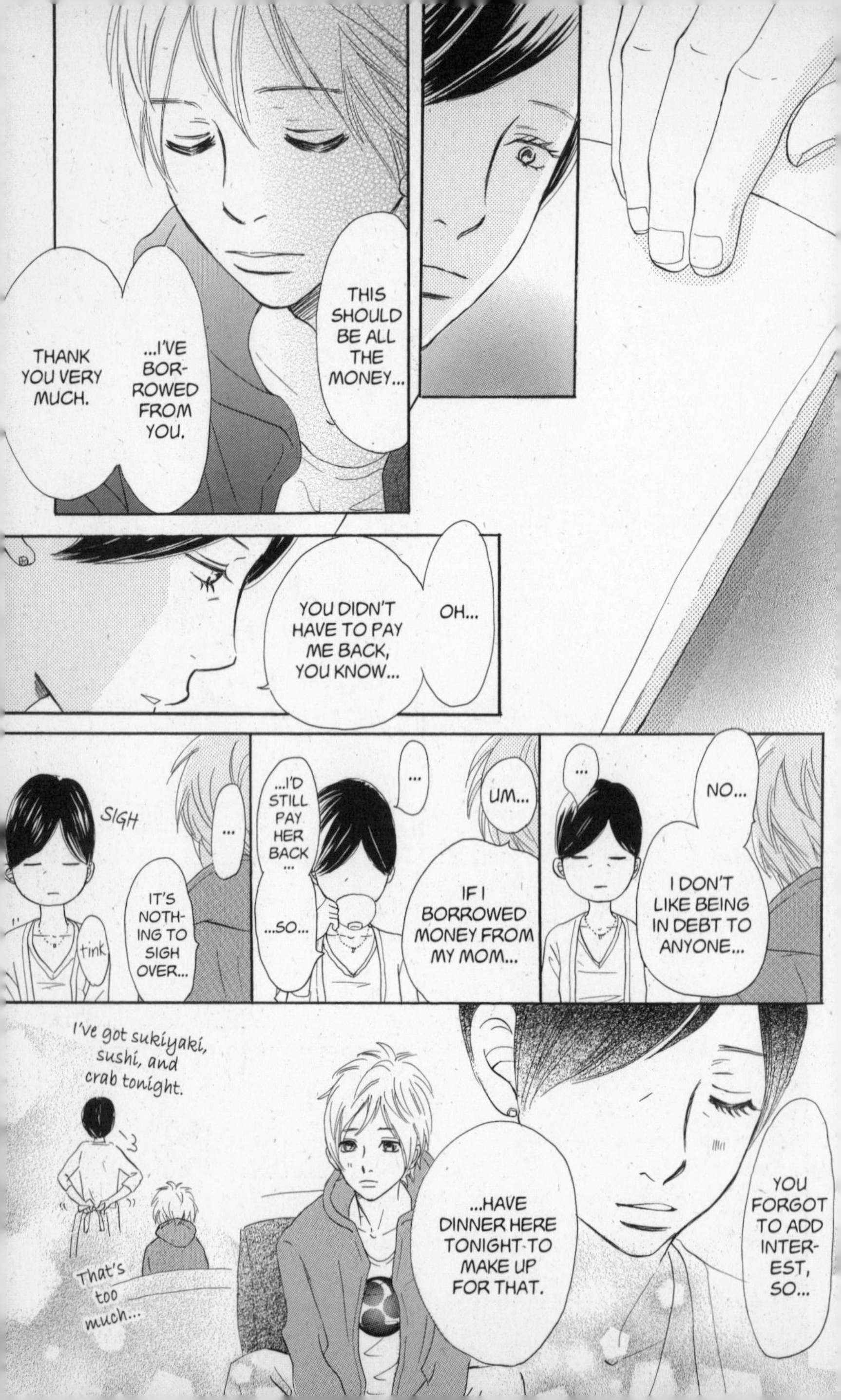
THIS SHOULD BE ALL THE MONEY...
...I'VE BORROWED FROM YOU.
THANK YOU VERY MUCH.
OH...
YOU DIDN'T HAVE TO PAY ME BACK, YOU KNOW...
NO...
...
I DON'T LIKE BEING IN DEBT TO ANYONE...
UM...
IF I BORROWED MONEY FROM MY MOM...
...
...I'D STILL PAY HER BACK...
...SO...
...
SIGH
IT'S NOTHING TO SIGH OVER...
tink
YOU FORGOT TO ADD INTEREST, SO...
...HAVE DINNER HERE TONIGHT TO MAKE UP FOR THAT.
I've got sukiyaki, sushi, and crab tonight.
That's too much...

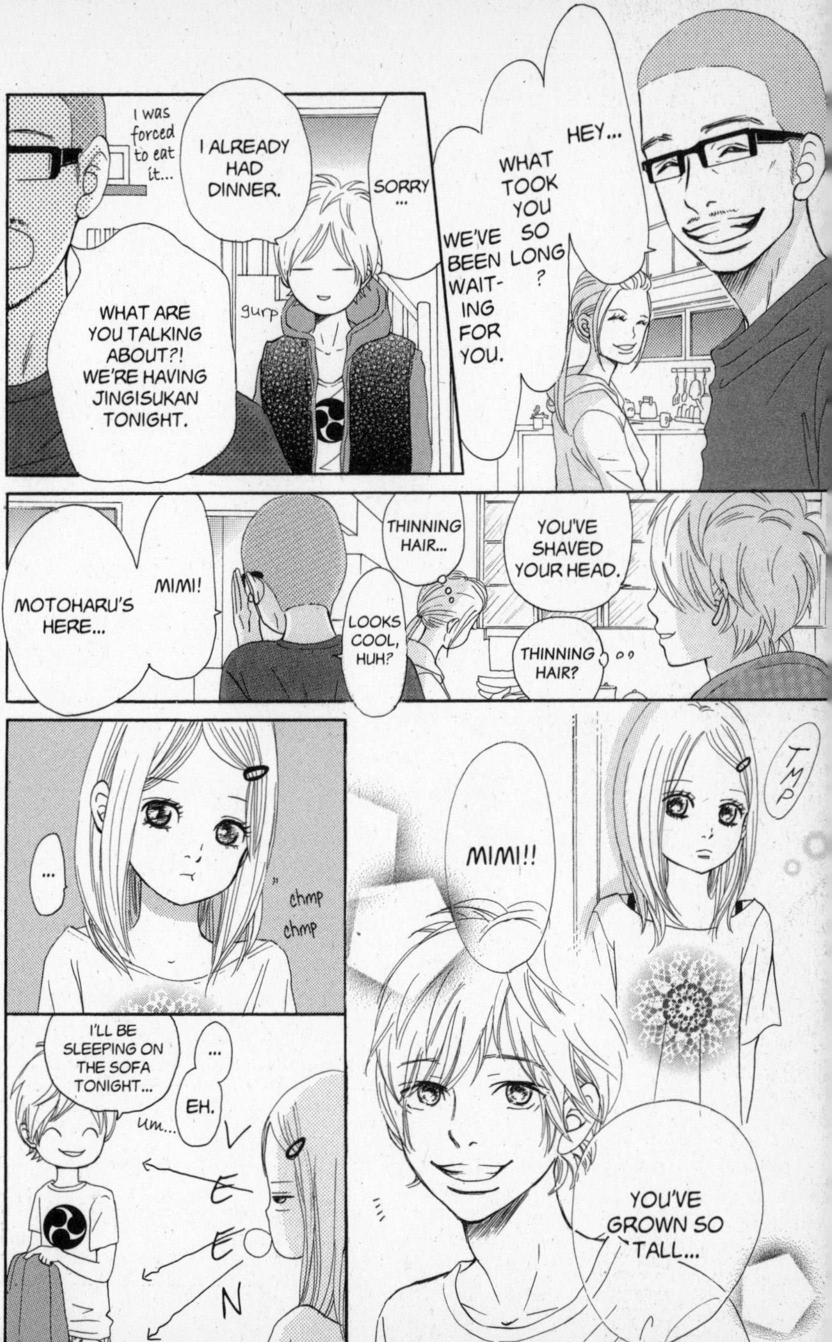
HEY...
WHAT TOOK YOU SO LONG?
WE'VE BEEN WAIT-ING FOR YOU.
SORRY...
I ALREADY HAD DINNER.
I was forced to eat it...
gurp
WHAT ARE YOU TALKING ABOUT?! WE'RE HAVING JINGISUKAN TONIGHT.
YOU'VE SHAVED YOUR HEAD.
THINNING HAIR?
THINNING HAIR...
LOOKS COOL, HUH?
MIMI!
MOTOHARU'S HERE...
TMP
MIMI!!
YOU'VE GROWN SO TALL...
...
chmp chmp
...
EH.
I'LL BE SLEEPING ON THE SOFA TONIGHT...
um...
VEEN

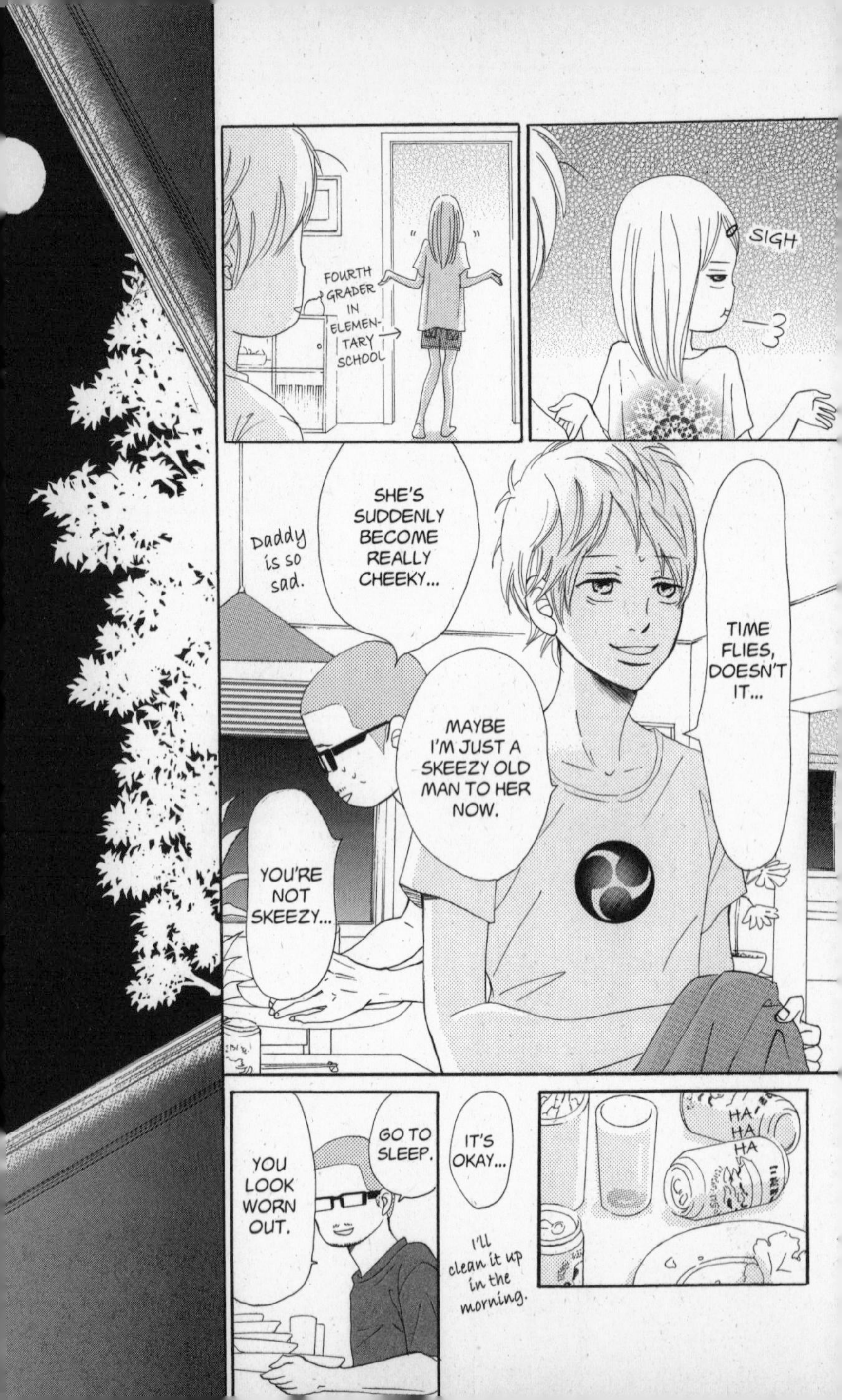
SIGH
FOURTH GRADER IN ELEMENTARY SCHOOL
" "
TIME FLIES, DOESN'T IT...
SHE'S SUDDENLY BECOME REALLY CHEEKY...
Daddy is so sad.
MAYBE I'M JUST A SKEEZY OLD MAN TO HER NOW.
YOU'RE NOT SKEEZY...
HA HA HA
IT'S OKAY...
I'll clean it up in the morning.
GO TO SLEEP.
YOU LOOK WORN OUT.

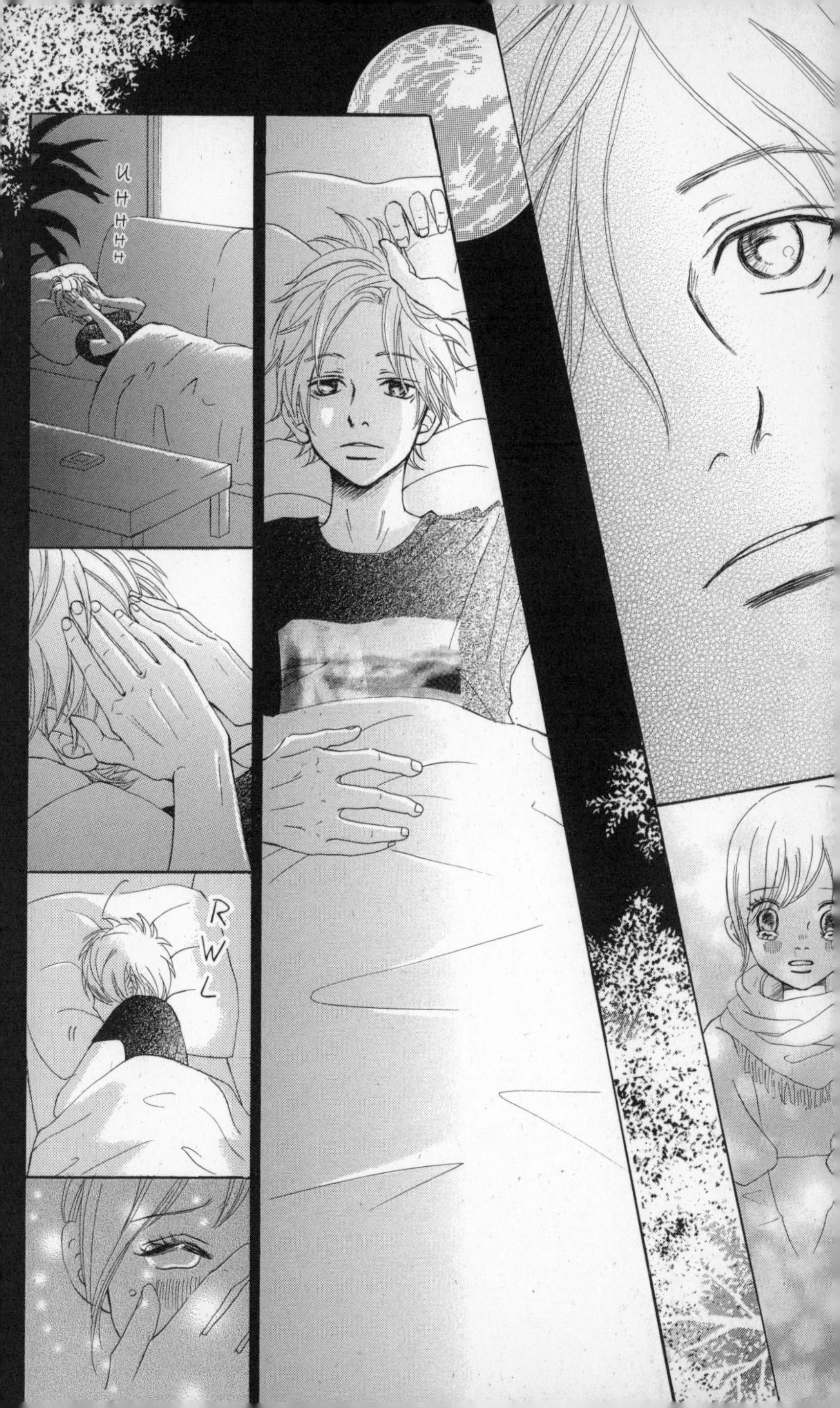

UHHHHH
RWL

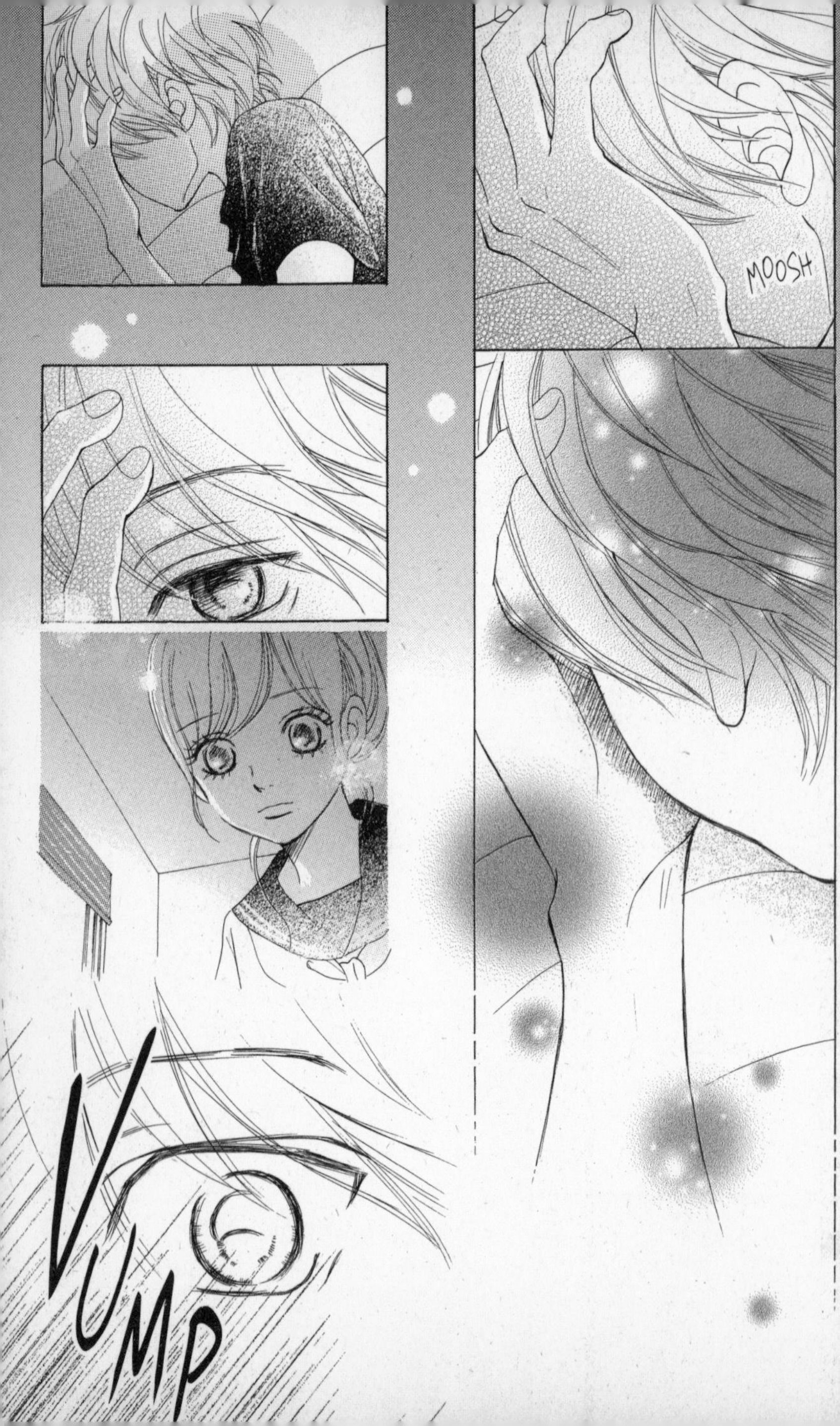
MOOSH
VUMP

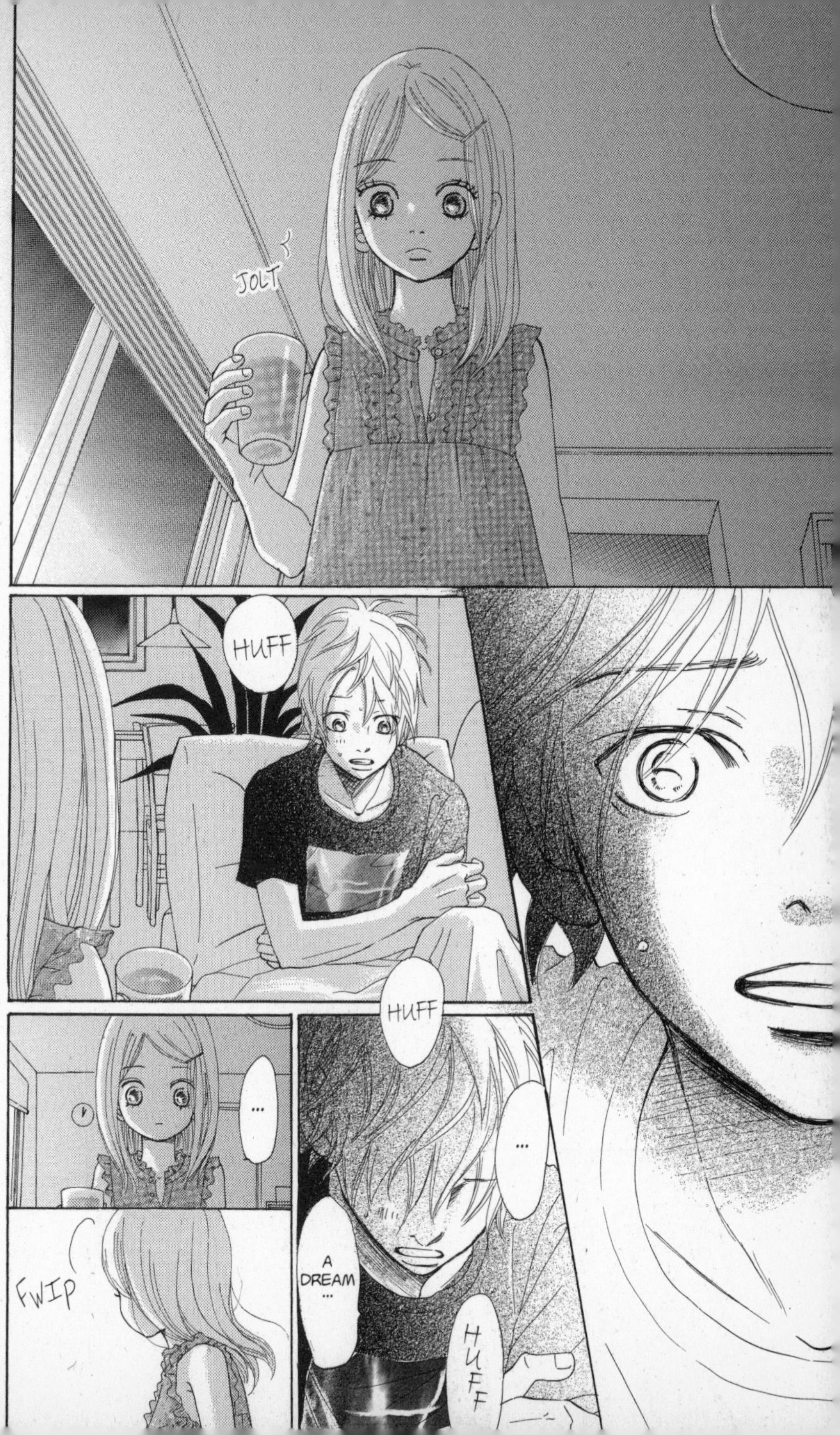
JOLT
HUFF
HUFF
...
A DREAM ...
HUFF
...
FWIP

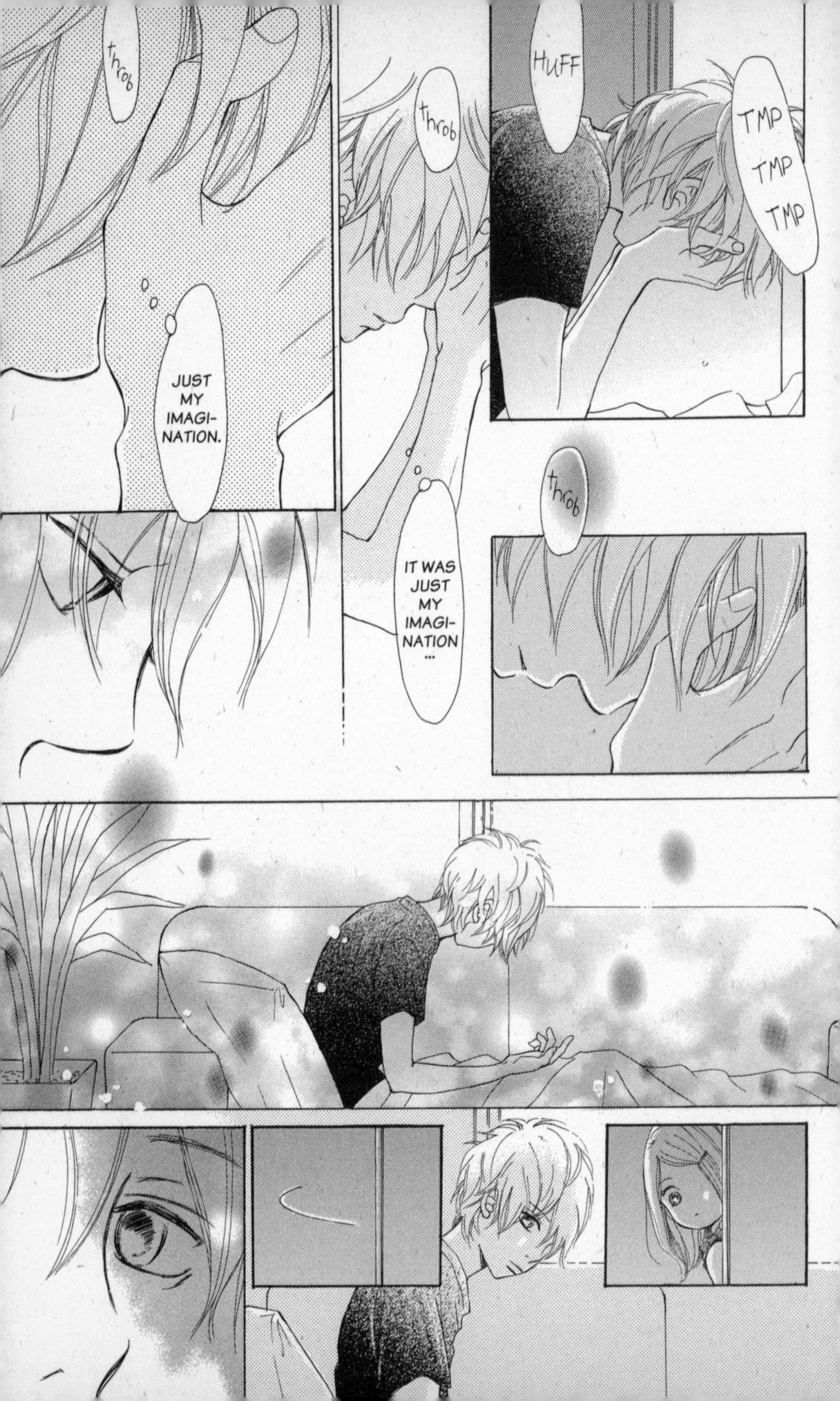
HUFF
TMP TMP TMP
throb
throb
IT WAS JUST MY IMAGINATION...
throb
JUST MY IMAGINATION.

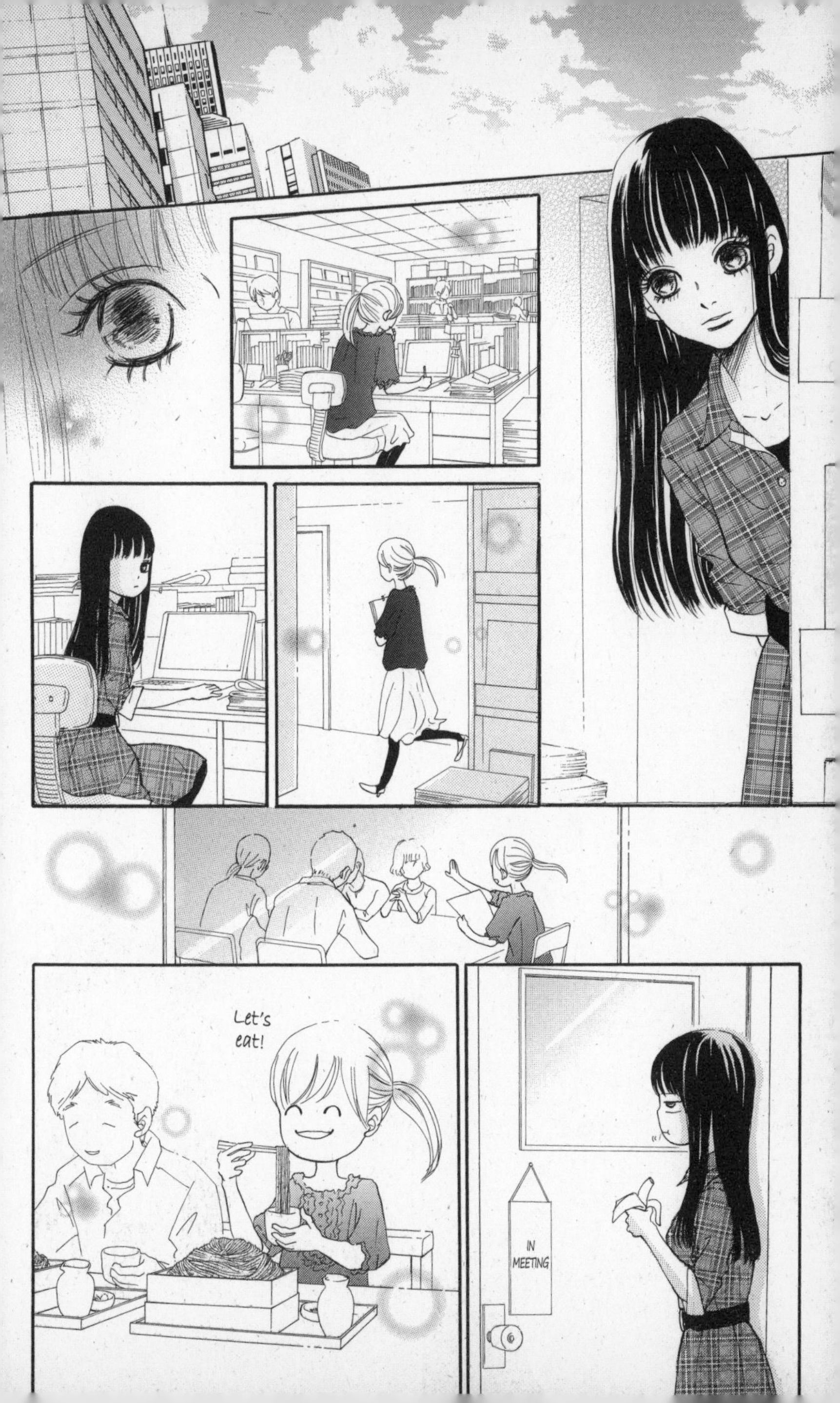
Let's eat!
IN MEETING

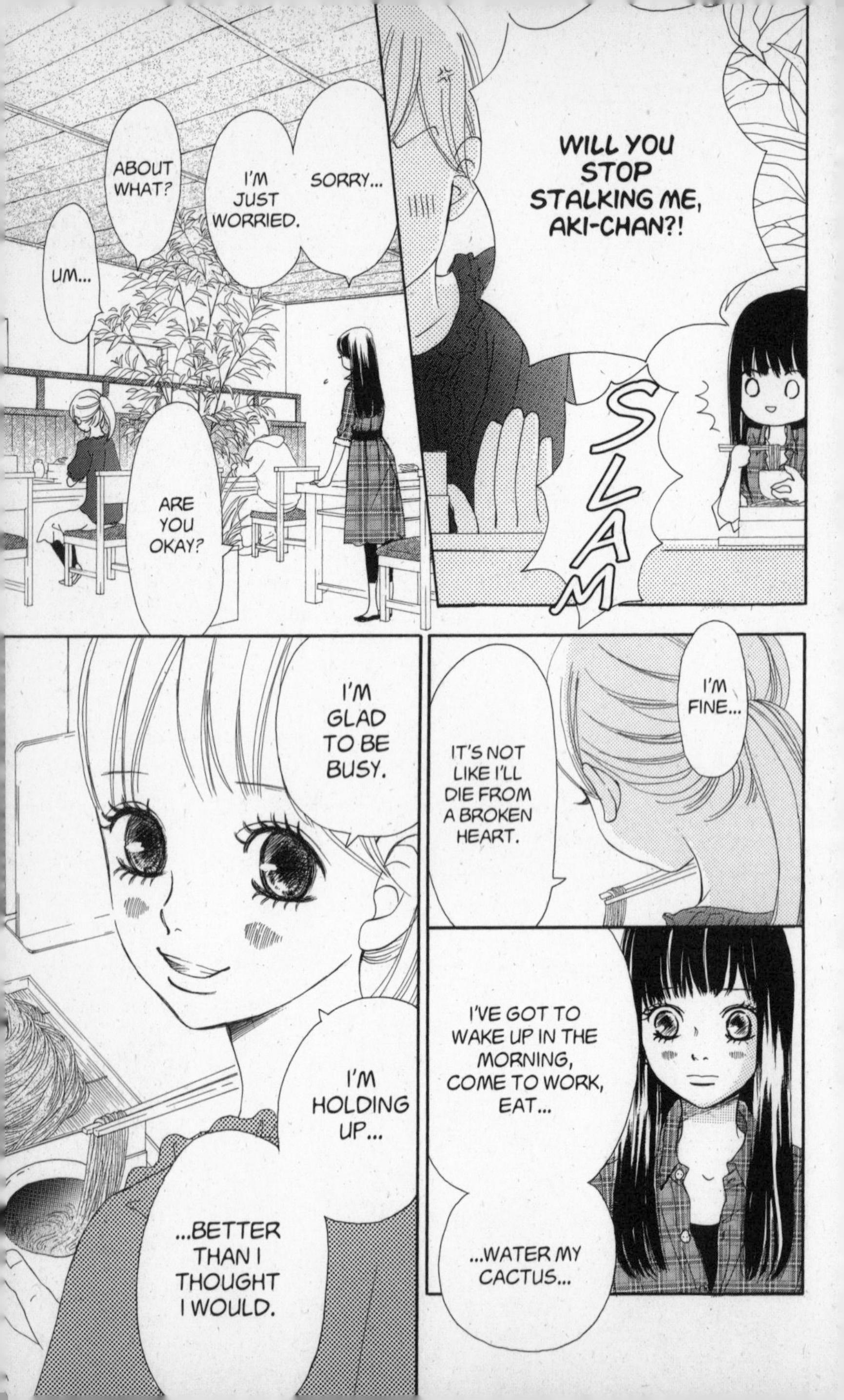
WILL YOU STOP STALKING ME, AKI-CHAN?!
SLAM
SORRY...
I'M JUST WORRIED.
ABOUT WHAT?
UM...
ARE YOU OKAY?
I'M FINE...
IT'S NOT LIKE I'LL DIE FROM A BROKEN HEART.
I'VE GOT TO WAKE UP IN THE MORNING, COME TO WORK, EAT...
...WATER MY CACTUS...
I'M GLAD TO BE BUSY.
I'M HOLDING UP...
...BETTER THAN I THOUGHT I WOULD.

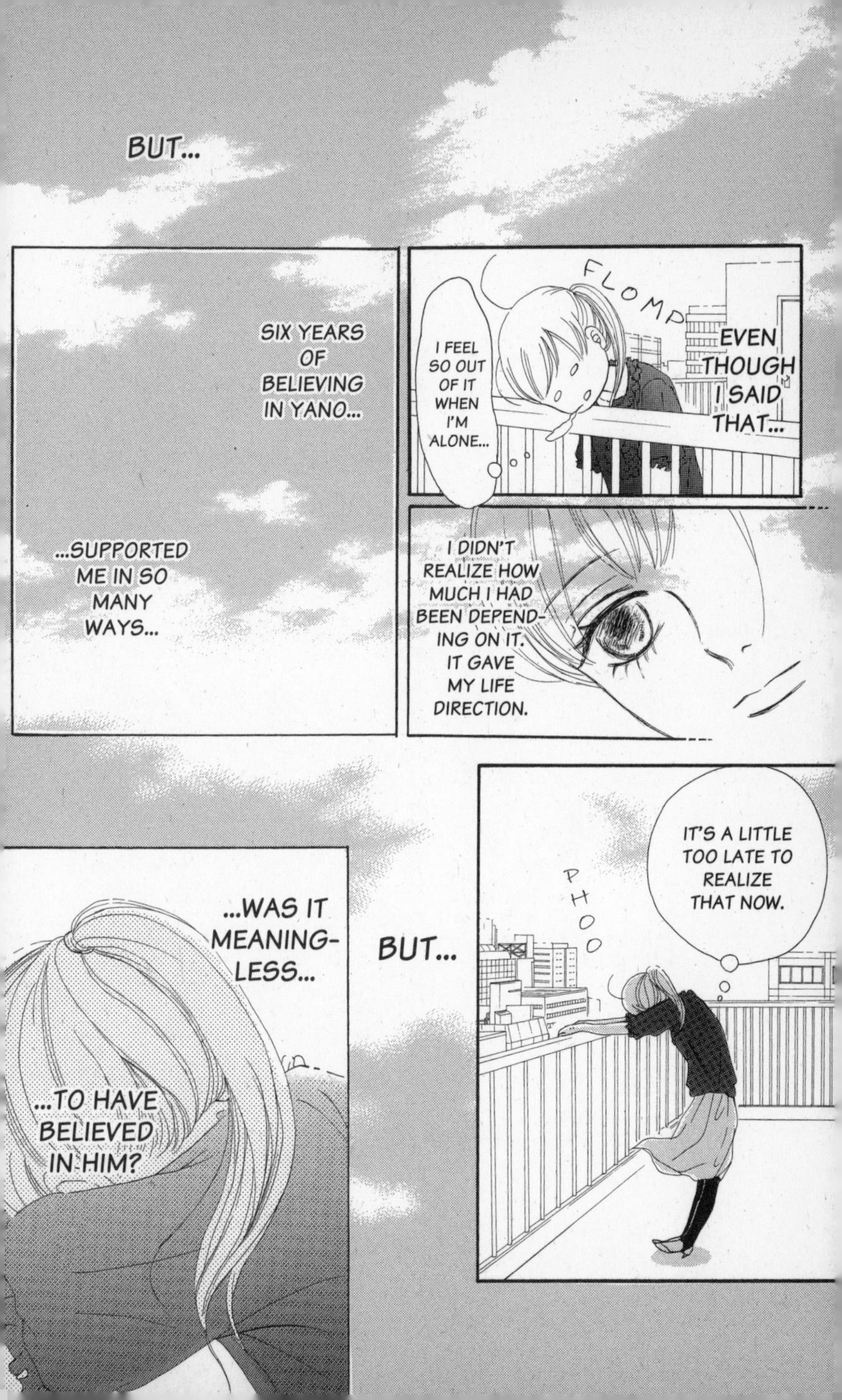
BUT...
EVEN THOUGH I SAID THAT...
FLOMP
I FEEL SO OUT OF IT WHEN I'M ALONE...
I DIDN'T REALIZE HOW MUCH I HAD BEEN DEPENDING ON IT. IT GAVE MY LIFE DIRECTION.
SIX YEARS OF BELIEVING IN YANO...
...SUPPORTED ME IN SO MANY WAYS...
IT'S A LITTLE TOO LATE TO REALIZE THAT NOW.
PHOO
BUT...
...WAS IT MEANINGLESS...
...TO HAVE BELIEVED IN HIM?

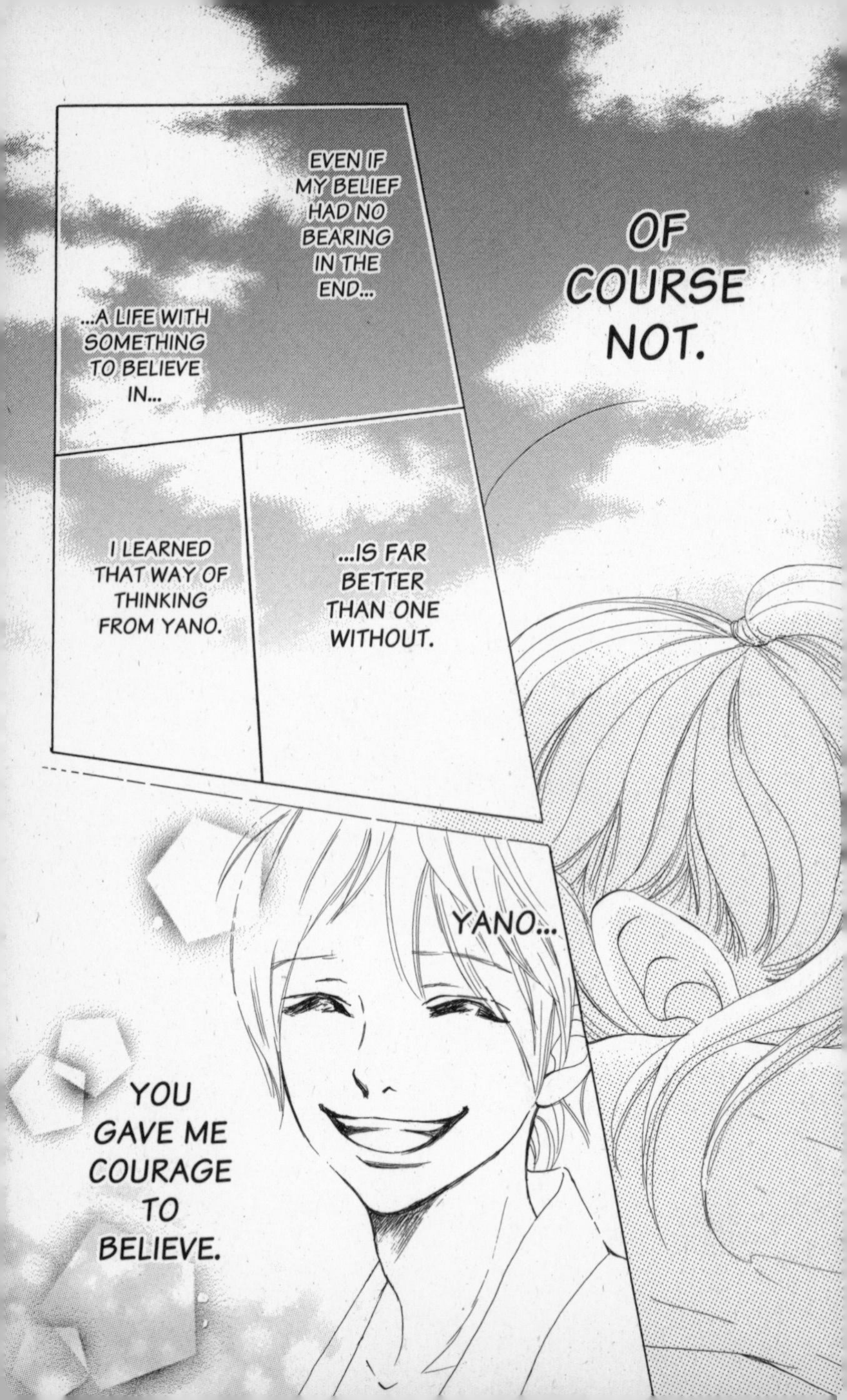
OF COURSE NOT.
EVEN IF MY BELIEF HAD NO BEARING IN THE END...
...A LIFE WITH SOMETHING TO BELIEVE IN...
...IS FAR BETTER THAN ONE WITHOUT.
I LEARNED THAT WAY OF THINKING FROM YANO.
YANO...
YOU GAVE ME COURAGE TO BELIEVE.

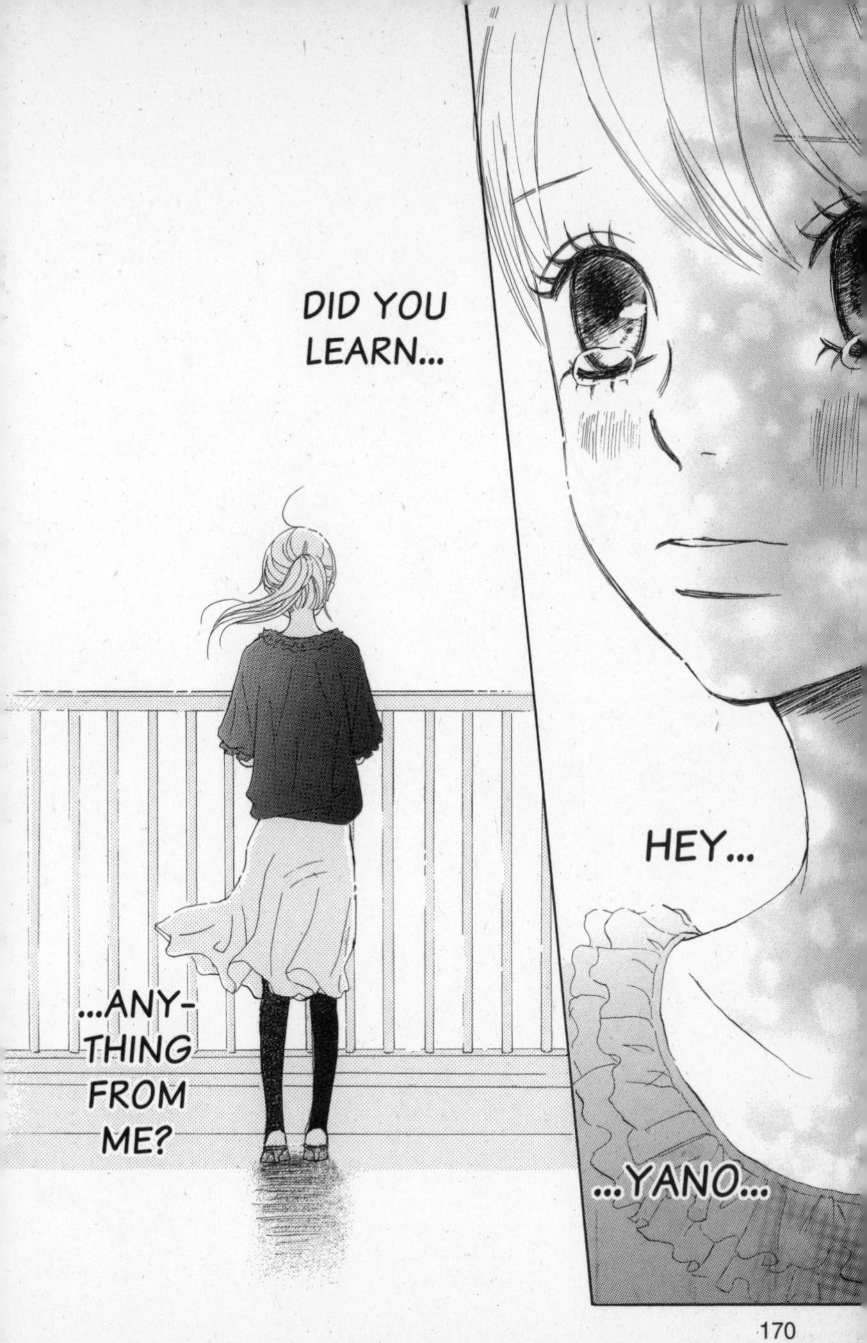
HEY...
...YANO...
DID YOU LEARN...
...ANY-THING FROM ME?

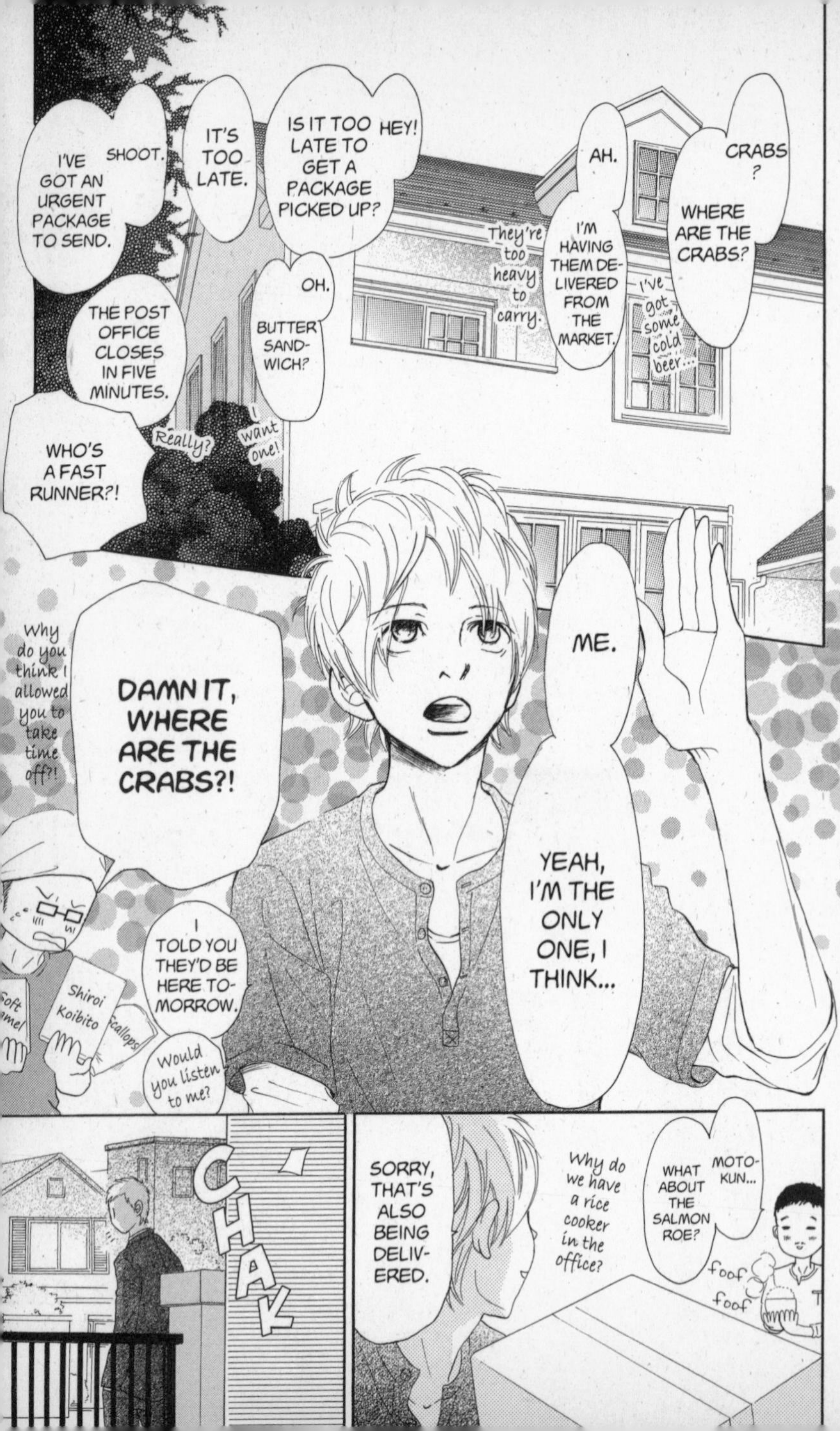
CRABS? WHERE ARE THE CRABS?
I've got some cold beer...
AH. I'M HAVING THEM DELIVERED FROM THE MARKET.
They're too heavy to carry.
HEY! IS IT TOO LATE TO GET A PACKAGE PICKED UP?
IT'S TOO LATE.
SHOOT. I'VE GOT AN URGENT PACKAGE TO SEND.
OH. BUTTER SANDWICH?
I want one!
THE POST OFFICE CLOSES IN FIVE MINUTES.
Really?
WHO'S A FAST RUNNER?!
ME.
YEAH, I'M THE ONLY ONE, I THINK...
DAMN IT, WHERE ARE THE CRABS?!
Why do you think I allowed you to take time off?!
I TOLD YOU THEY'D BE HERE TOMORROW.
Would you listen to me?
Scallops
Shiroi Koibito
MOTO-KUN... WHAT ABOUT THE SALMON ROE?
foof foof
Why do we have a rice cooker in the office?
SORRY, THAT'S ALSO BEING DELIVERED.
CHAK

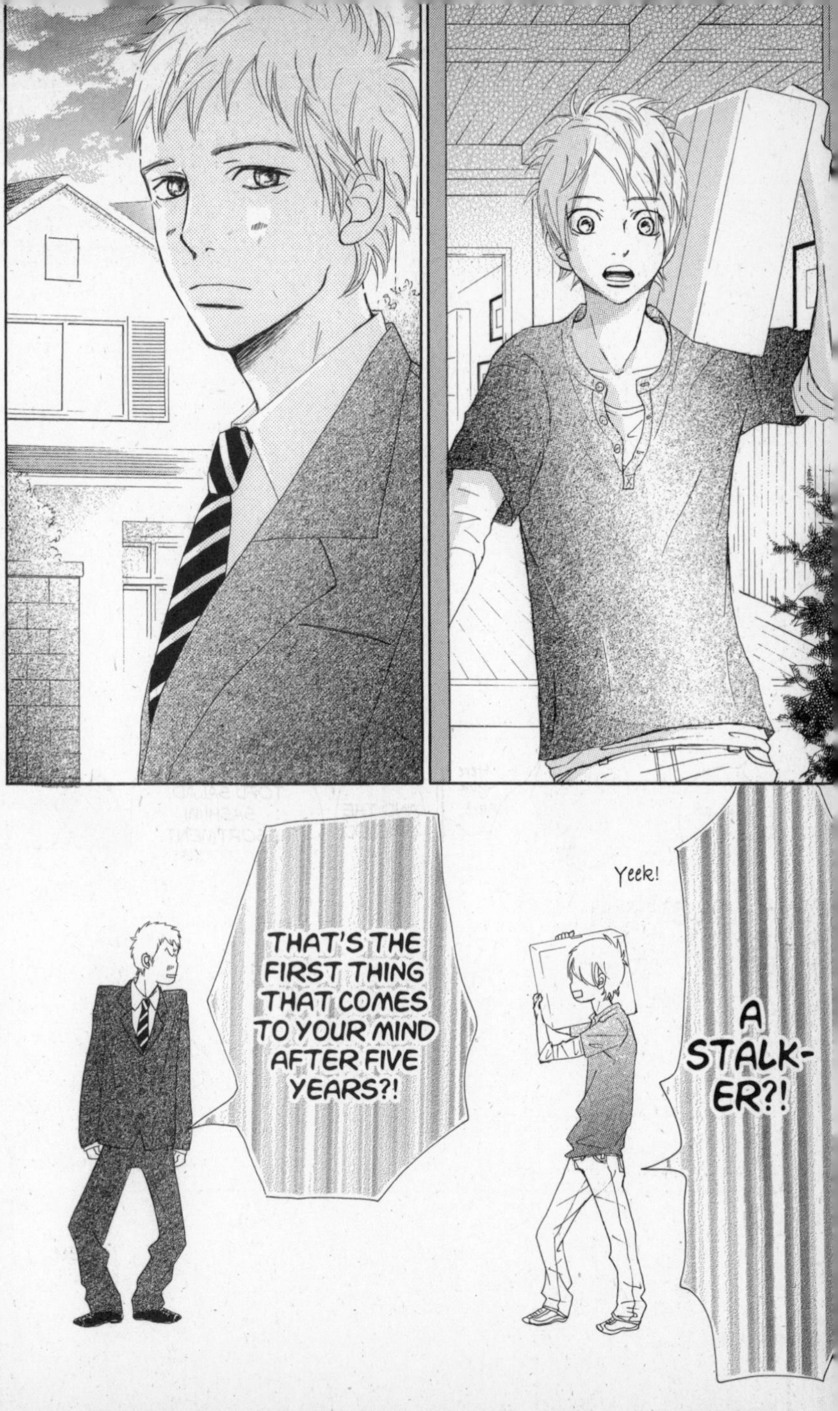
Yeek!
A STALK-ER?!
THAT'S THE FIRST THING THAT COMES TO YOUR MIND AFTER FIVE YEARS?!

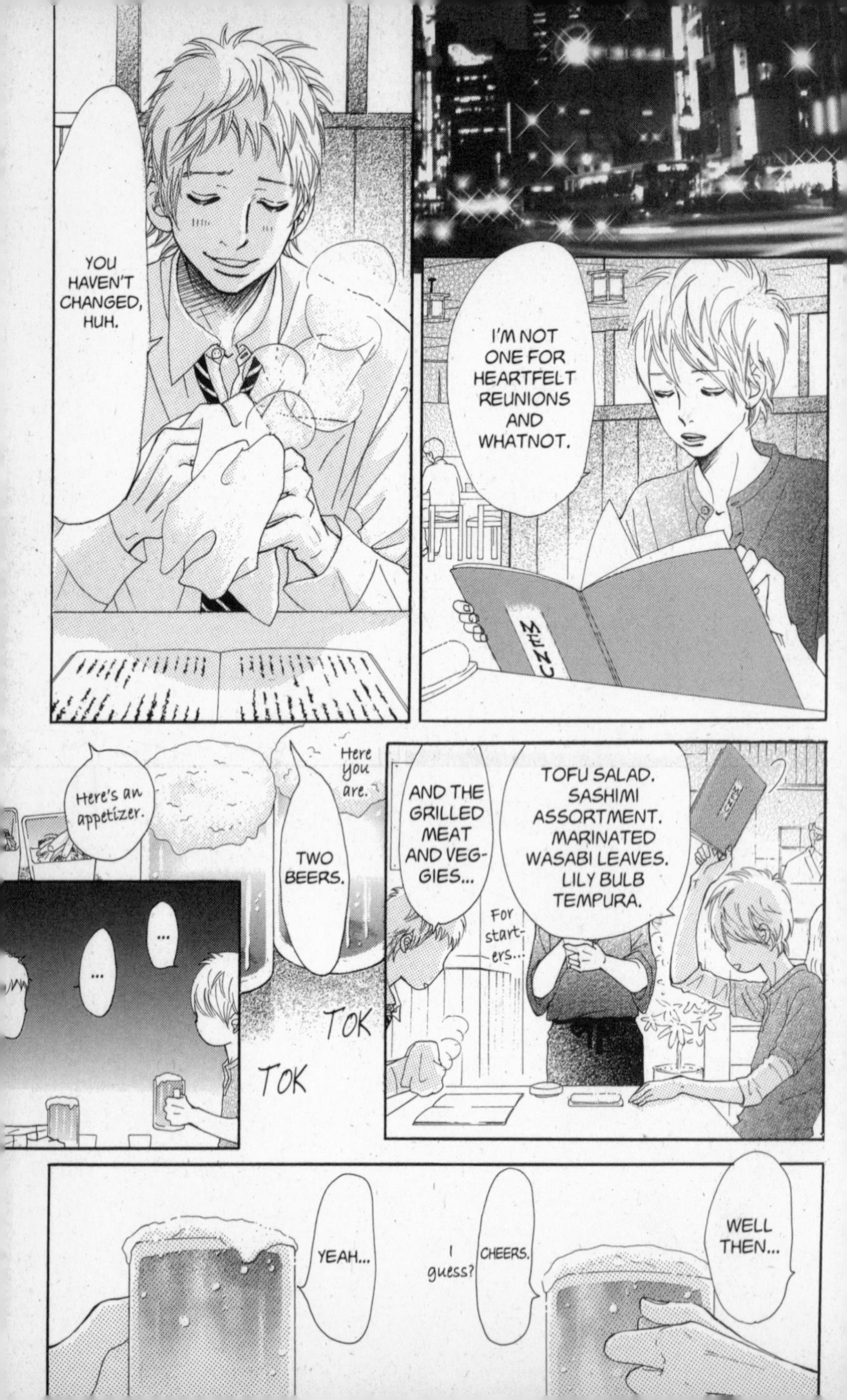
I'M NOT ONE FOR HEARTFELT REUNIONS AND WHATNOT.
YOU HAVEN'T CHANGED, HUH.
TOFU SALAD. SASHIMI ASSORTMENT. MARINATED WASABI LEAVES. LILY BULB TEMPURA.
For starters...
AND THE GRILLED MEAT AND VEG-GIES...
Here you are.
TWO BEERS.
Here's an appetizer.
TOK
TOK
...
...
WELL THEN...
CHEERS.
I guess?
YEAH...

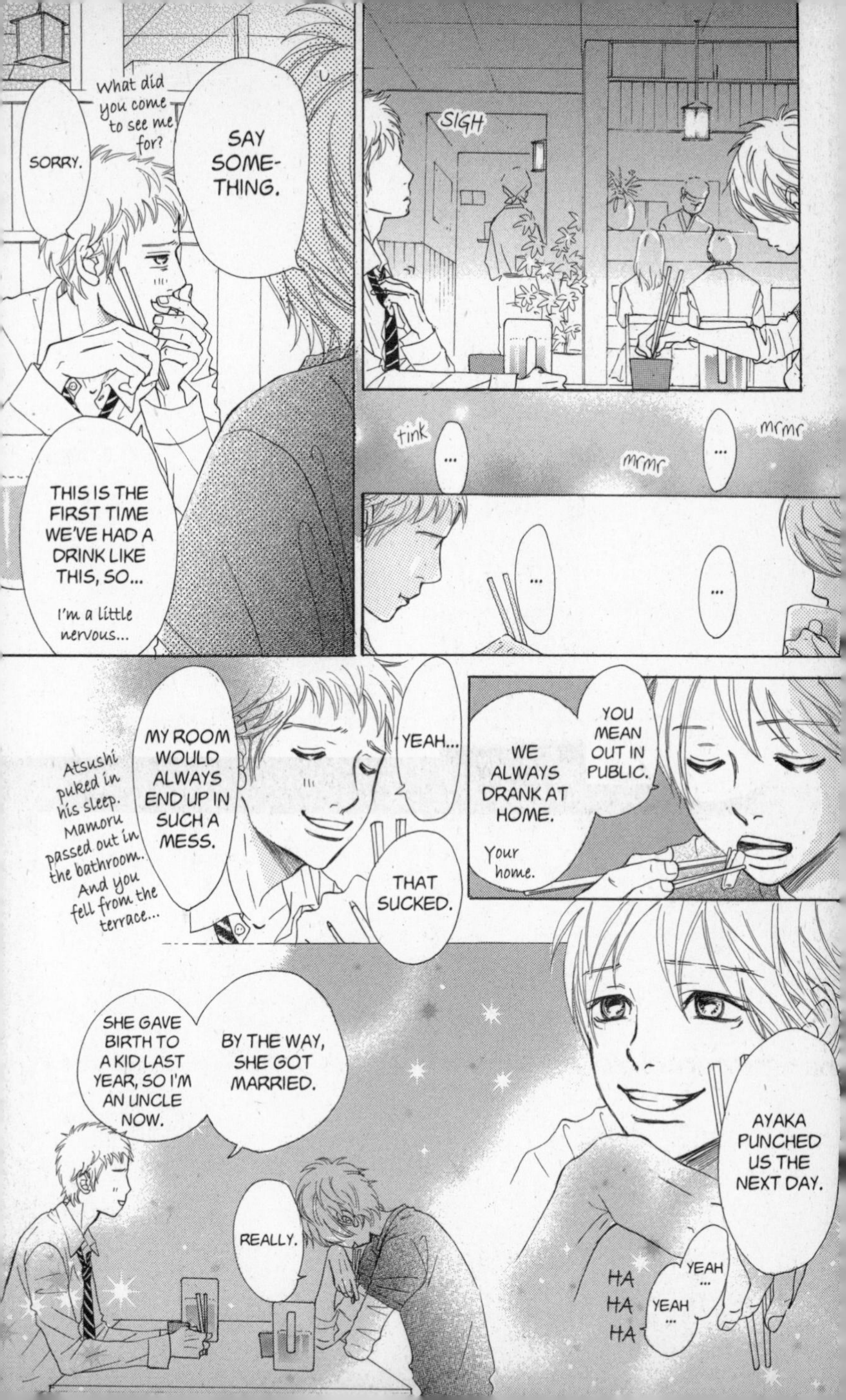
SIGH
mrmr
...
mrmr
...
tink
...
...
SAY SOME-THING.
What did you come to see me for?
SORRY.
THIS IS THE FIRST TIME WE'VE HAD A DRINK LIKE THIS, SO...
I'm a little nervous...
YOU MEAN OUT IN PUBLIC.
WE ALWAYS DRANK AT HOME.
Your home.
YEAH...
MY ROOM WOULD ALWAYS END UP IN SUCH A MESS.
Atsushi puked in his sleep. Mamoru passed out in the bathroom. And you fell from the terrace...
THAT SUCKED.
AYAKA PUNCHED US THE NEXT DAY.
YEAH...
YEAH...
HA HA HA
BY THE WAY, SHE GOT MARRIED.
SHE GAVE BIRTH TO A KID LAST YEAR, SO I'M AN UNCLE NOW.
REALLY.

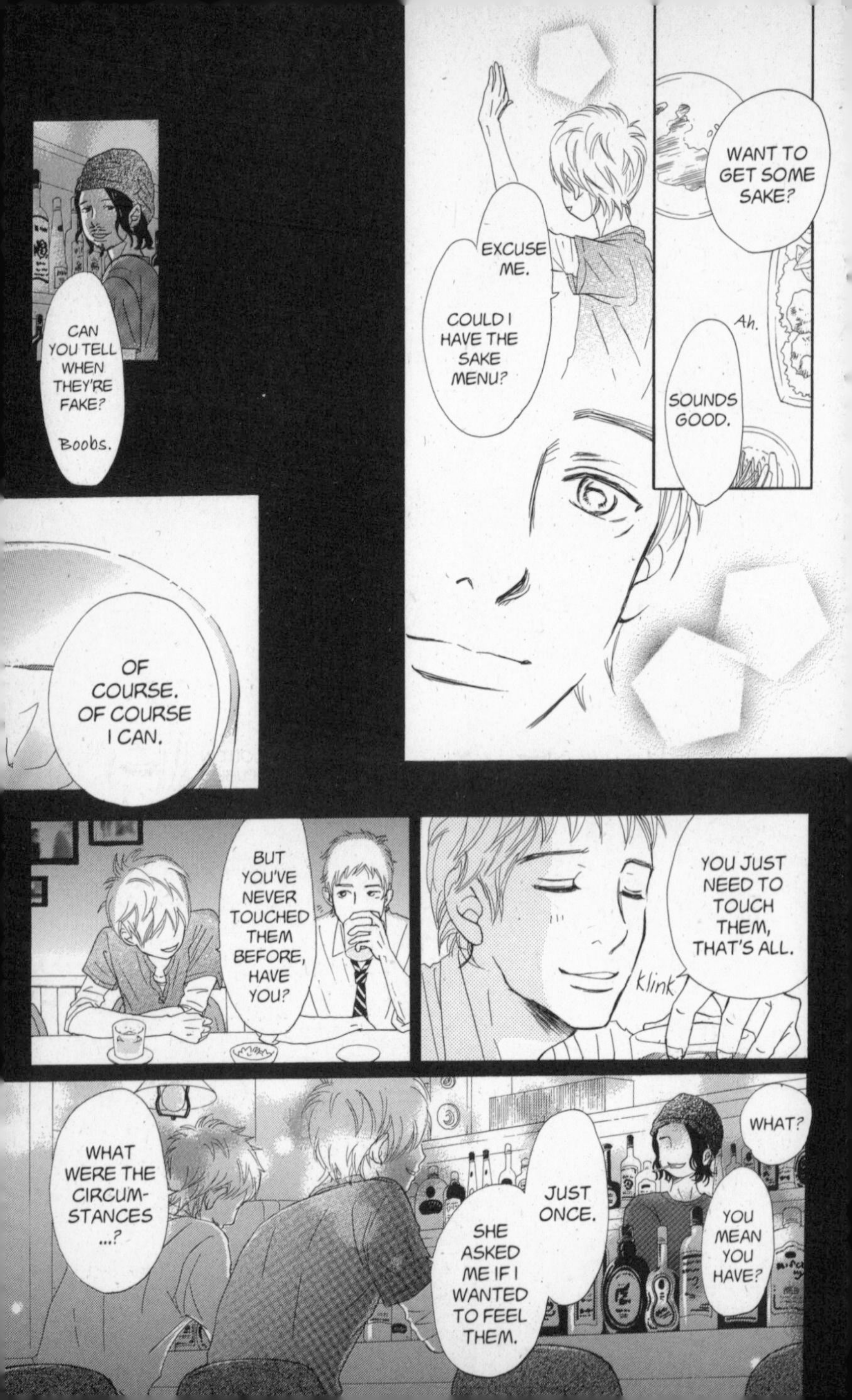
WANT TO GET SOME SAKE?
Ah.
SOUNDS GOOD.
EXCUSE ME.
COULD I HAVE THE SAKE MENU?
CAN YOU TELL WHEN THEY'RE FAKE?
Boobs.
OF COURSE. OF COURSE I CAN.
YOU JUST NEED TO TOUCH THEM, THAT'S ALL.
klink
BUT YOU'VE NEVER TOUCHED THEM BEFORE, HAVE YOU?
WHAT?
YOU MEAN YOU HAVE?
JUST ONCE.
SHE ASKED ME IF I WANTED TO FEEL THEM.
WHAT WERE THE CIRCUMSTANCES ...?

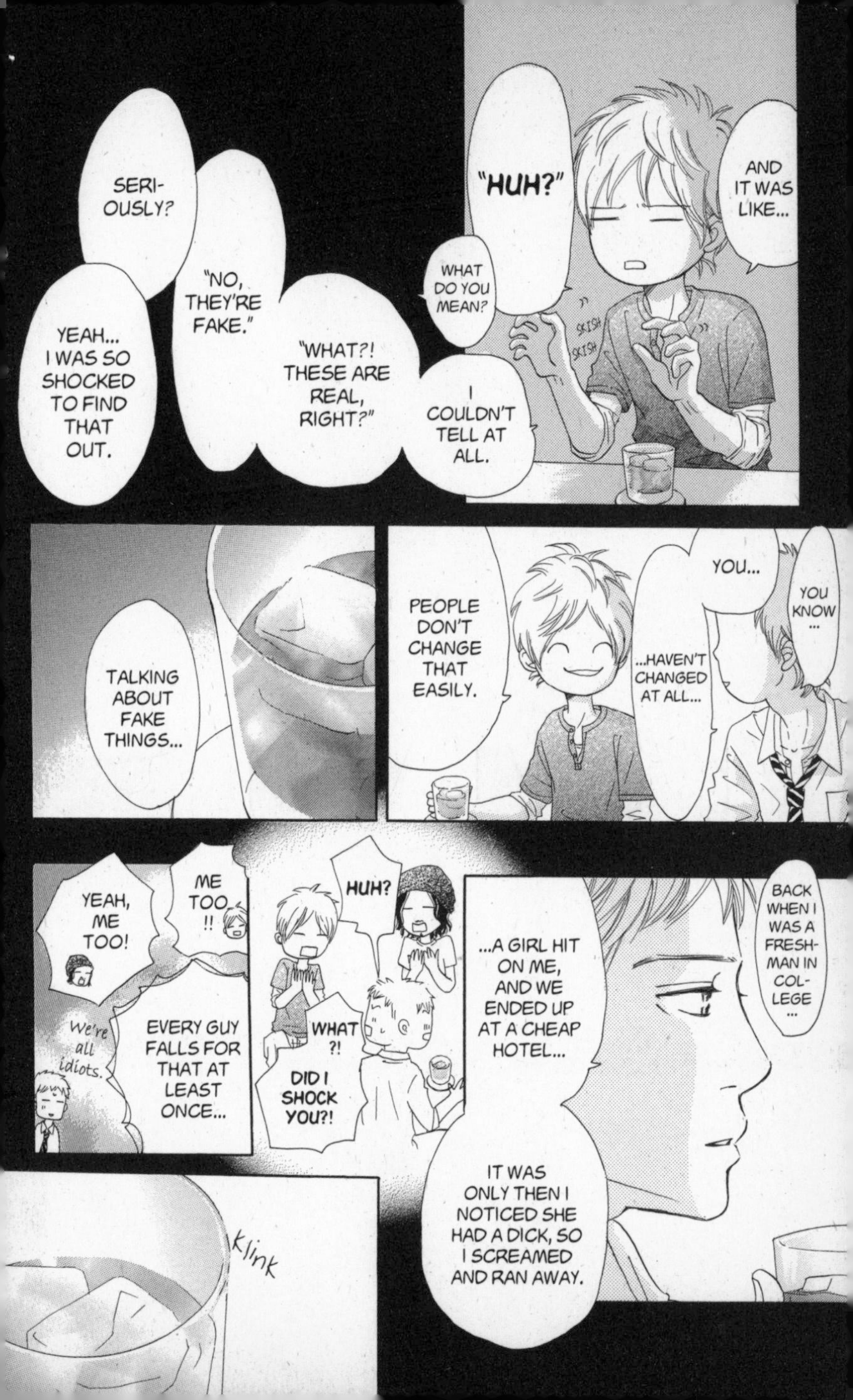
AND IT WAS LIKE...
"HUH?"
WHAT DO YOU MEAN?
SKISH SKISH
I COULDN'T TELL AT ALL.
"WHAT?! THESE ARE REAL, RIGHT?"
"NO, THEY'RE FAKE."
SERI-OUSLY?
YEAH... I WAS SO SHOCKED TO FIND THAT OUT.
YOU KNOW...
YOU...
...HAVEN'T CHANGED AT ALL...
PEOPLE DON'T CHANGE THAT EASILY.
TALKING ABOUT FAKE THINGS...
BACK WHEN I WAS A FRESH-MAN IN COL-LEGE...
...A GIRL HIT ON ME, AND WE ENDED UP AT A CHEAP HOTEL...
IT WAS ONLY THEN I NOTICED SHE HAD A DICK, SO I SCREAMED AND RAN AWAY.
HUH?
WHAT?!
DID I SHOCK YOU?!
ME TOO!!
YEAH, ME TOO!
EVERY GUY FALLS FOR THAT AT LEAST ONCE...
We're all idiots.
klink

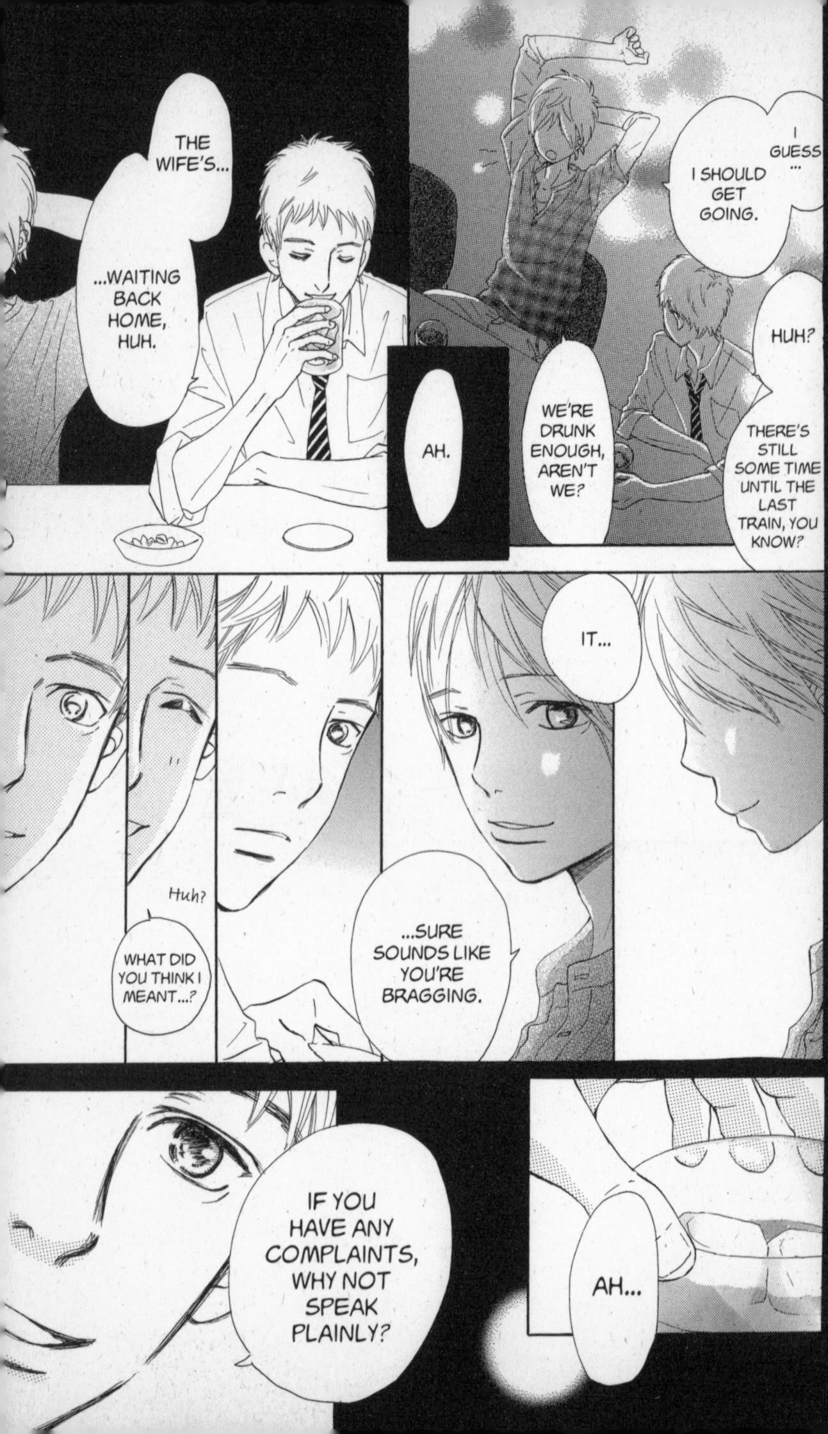
I GUESS... I SHOULD GET GOING.
HUH?
THERE'S STILL SOME TIME UNTIL THE LAST TRAIN, YOU KNOW?
WE'RE DRUNK ENOUGH, AREN'T WE?
AH.
THE WIFE'S...
...WAITING BACK HOME, HUH.
IT...
...SURE SOUNDS LIKE YOU'RE BRAGGING.
Huh?
WHAT DID YOU THINK I MEANT...?
AH...
IF YOU HAVE ANY COMPLAINTS, WHY NOT SPEAK PLAINLY?

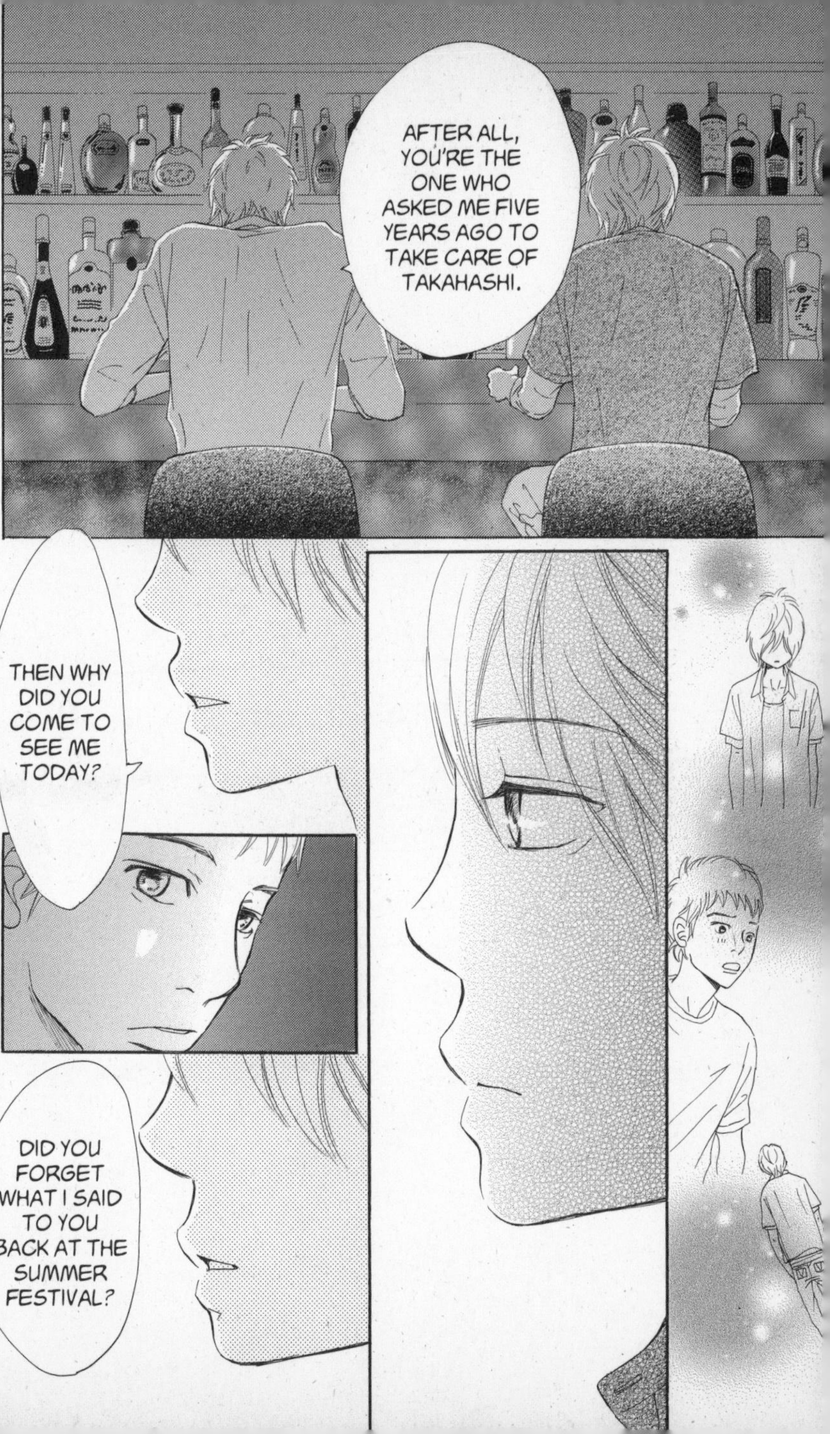
AFTER ALL, YOU'RE THE ONE WHO ASKED ME FIVE YEARS AGO TO TAKE CARE OF TAKAHASHI.
THEN WHY DID YOU COME TO SEE ME TODAY?
DID YOU FORGET WHAT I SAID TO YOU BACK AT THE SUMMER FESTIVAL?

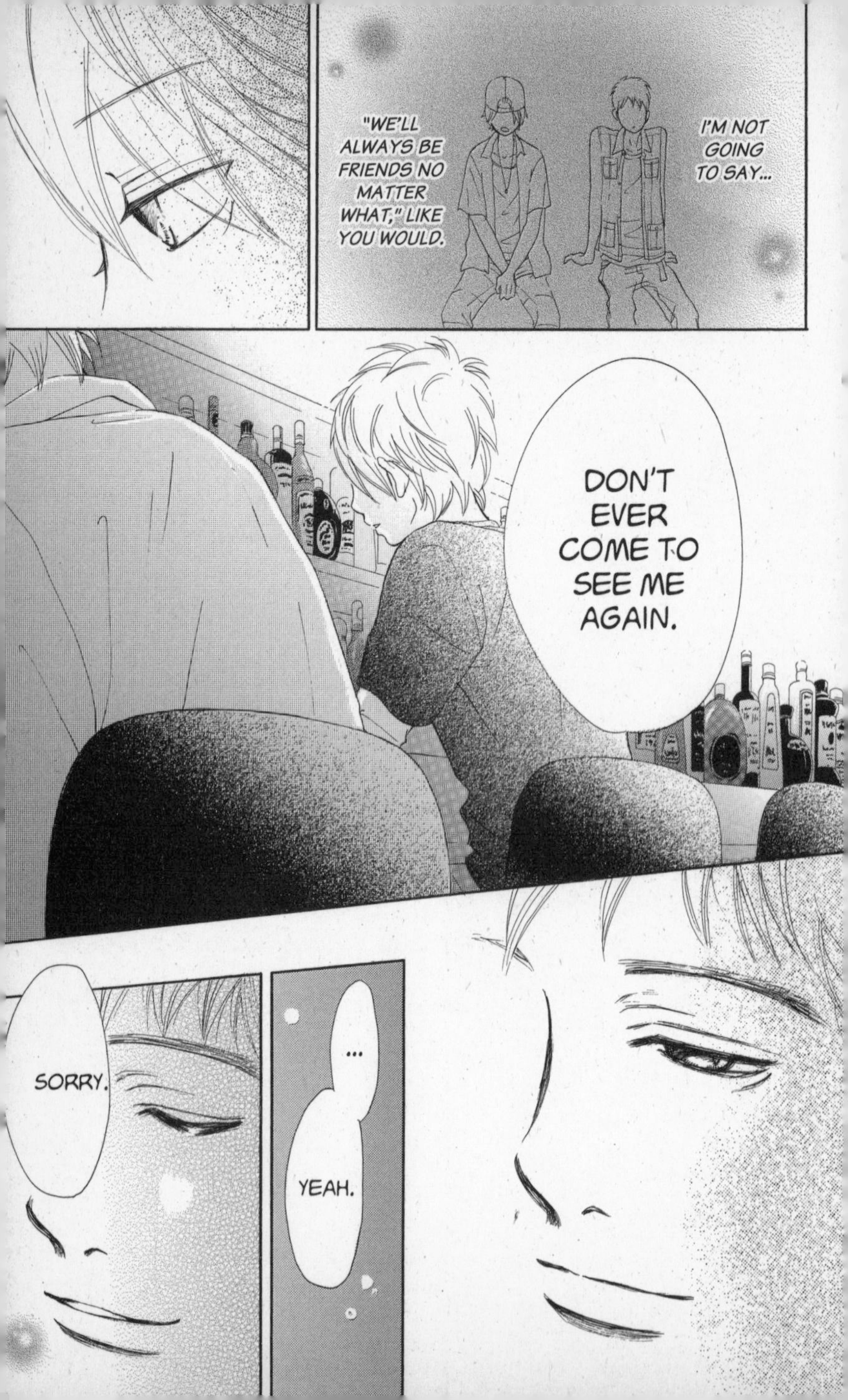
I'M NOT GOING TO SAY...
"WE'LL ALWAYS BE FRIENDS NO MATTER WHAT," LIKE YOU WOULD.
DON'T EVER COME TO SEE ME AGAIN.
...
YEAH.
SORRY.

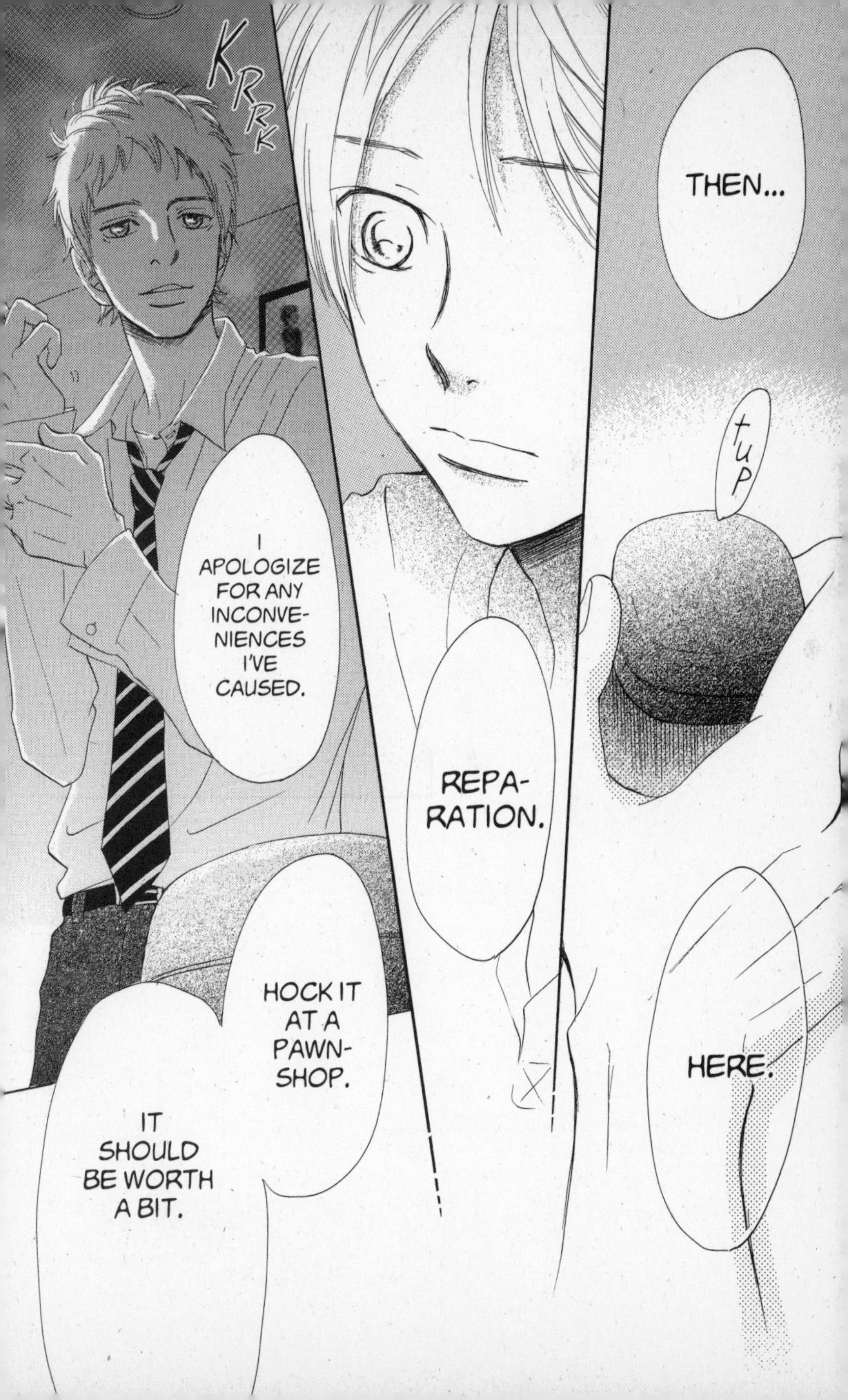
THEN...
tup
HERE.
REPA-RATION.
KRRK
I APOLOGIZE FOR ANY INCONVE-NIENCES I'VE CAUSED.
HOCK IT AT A PAWN-SHOP.
IT SHOULD BE WORTH A BIT.

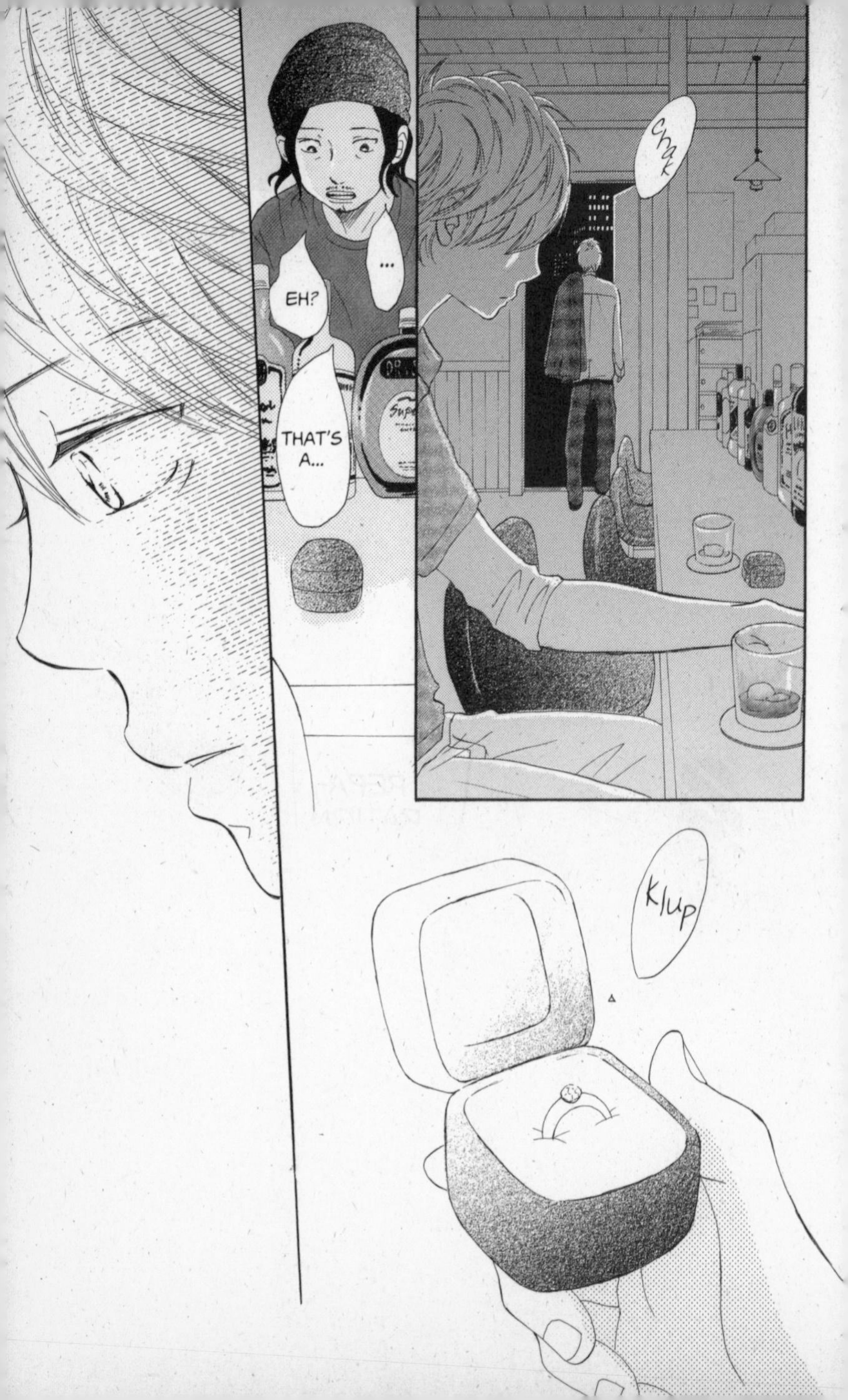
Chak
...
EH?
THAT'S A...
Klup

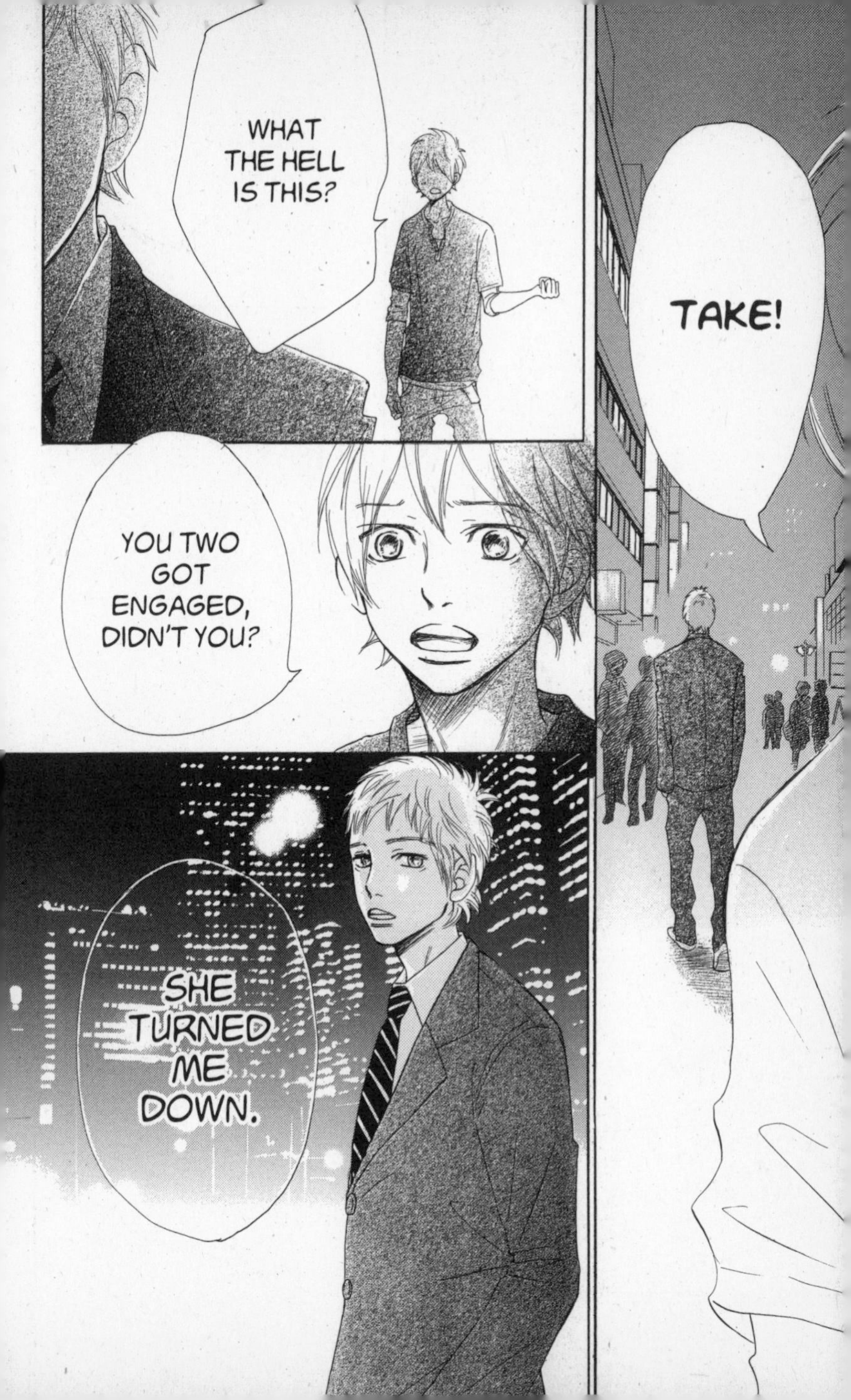
TAKE!
WHAT THE HELL IS THIS?
YOU TWO GOT ENGAGED, DIDN'T YOU?
SHE TURNED ME DOWN.

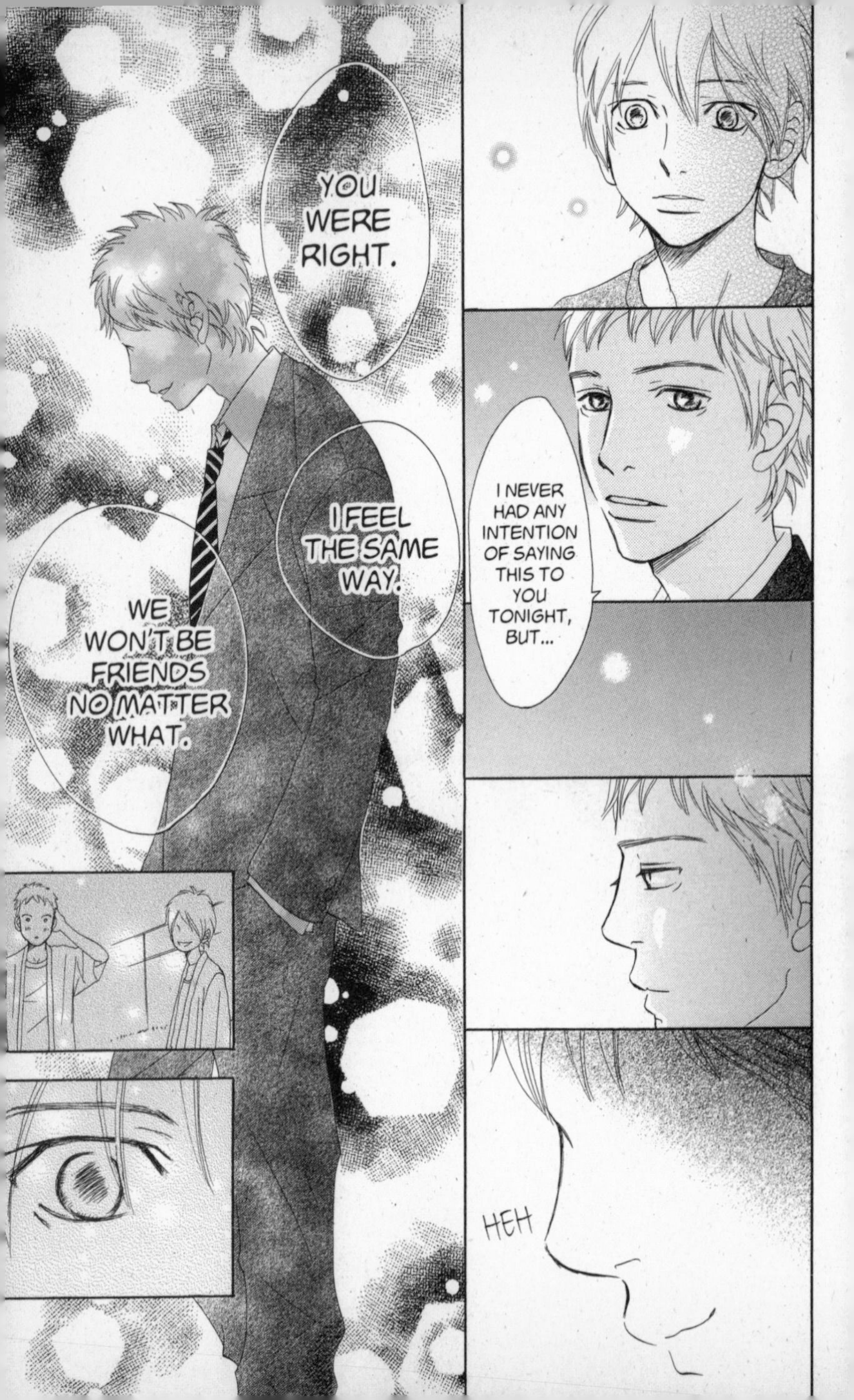
I NEVER HAD ANY INTENTION OF SAYING THIS TO YOU TONIGHT, BUT...
HEH
YOU WERE RIGHT.
I FEEL THE SAME WAY.
WE WON'T BE FRIENDS NO MATTER WHAT.

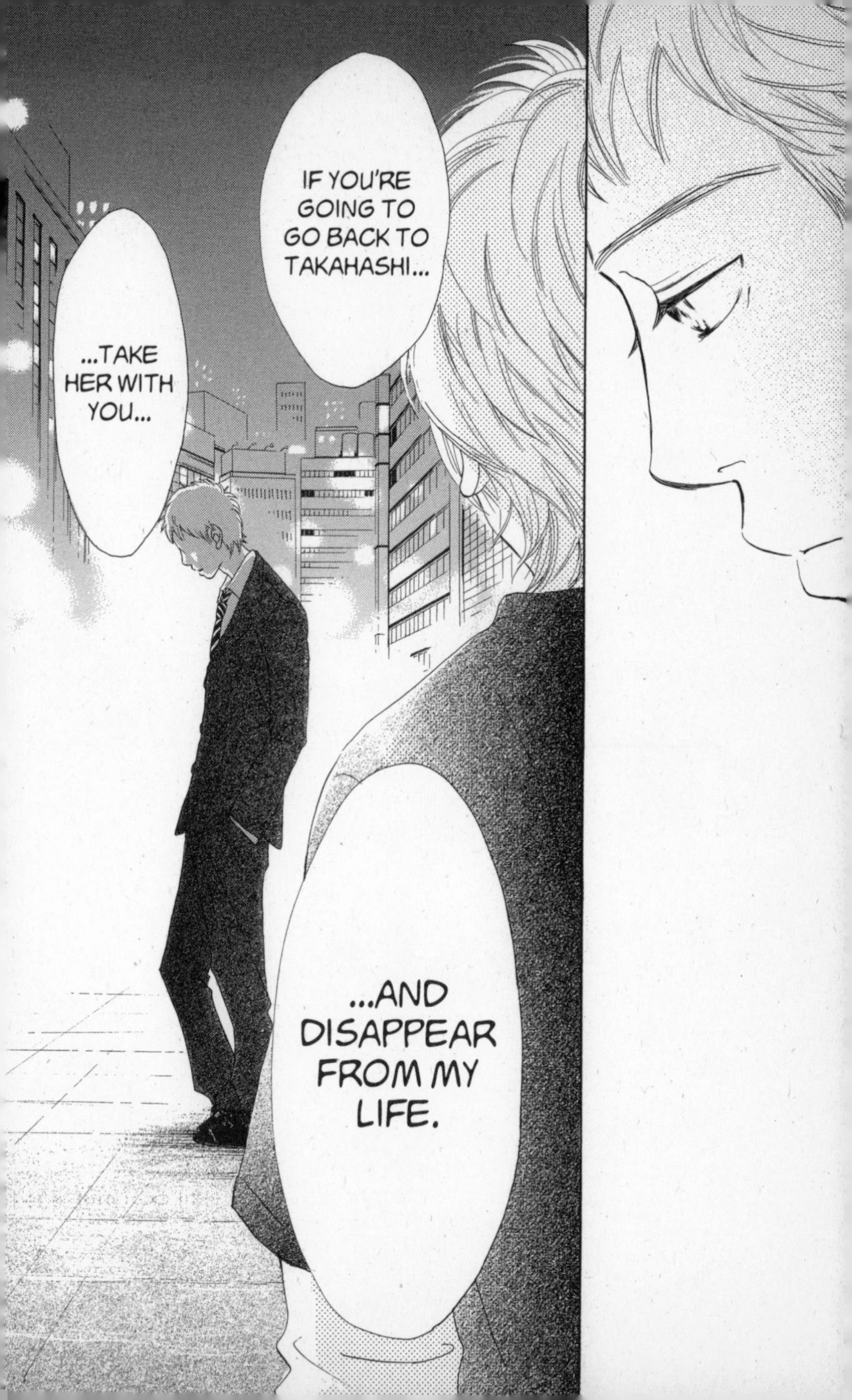
IF YOU'RE GOING TO GO BACK TO TAKAHASHI...
...TAKE HER WITH YOU...
...AND DISAPPEAR FROM MY LIFE.

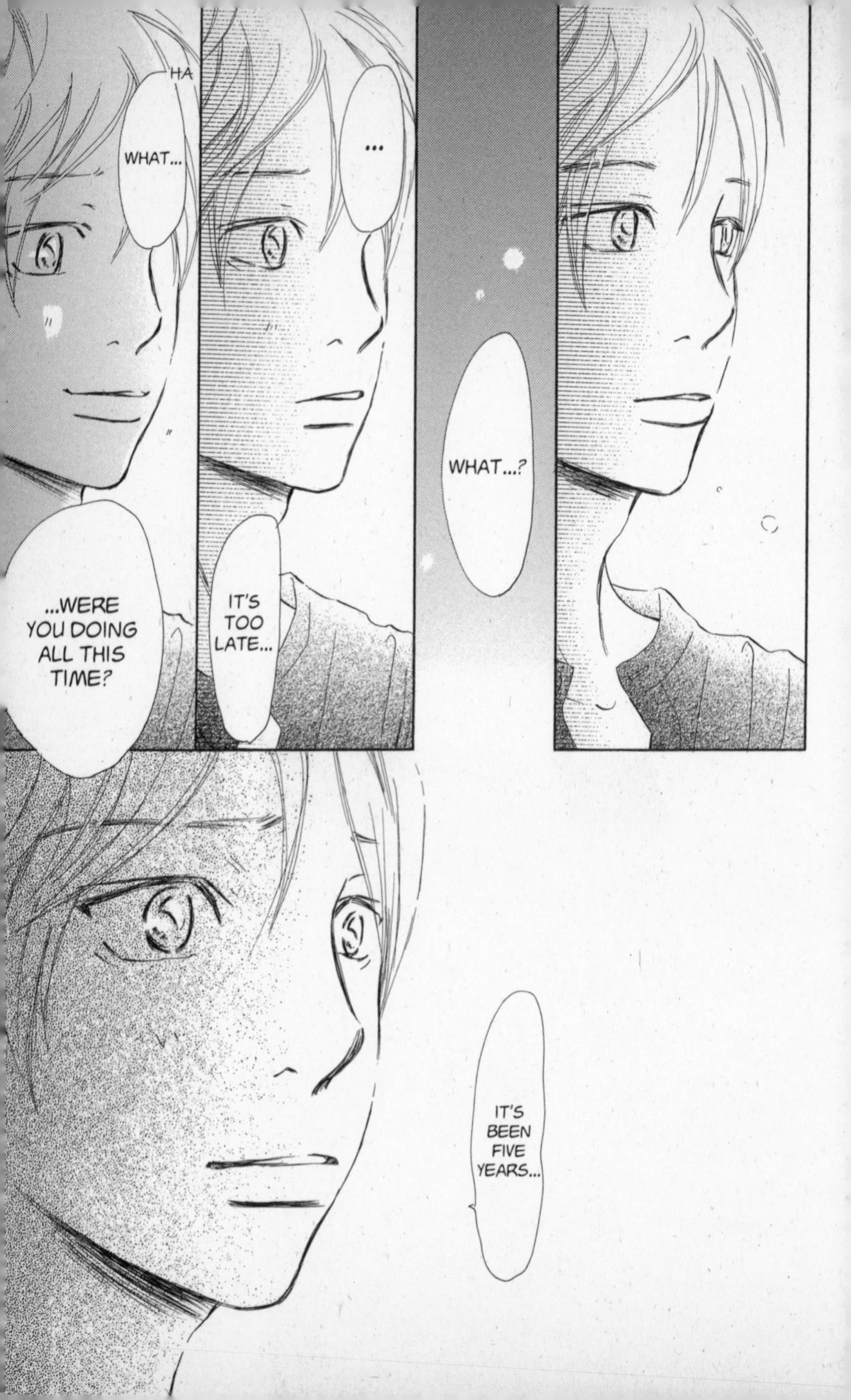
WHAT...?
...
IT'S TOO LATE...
HA
WHAT...
...WERE YOU DOING ALL THIS TIME?
IT'S BEEN FIVE YEARS...

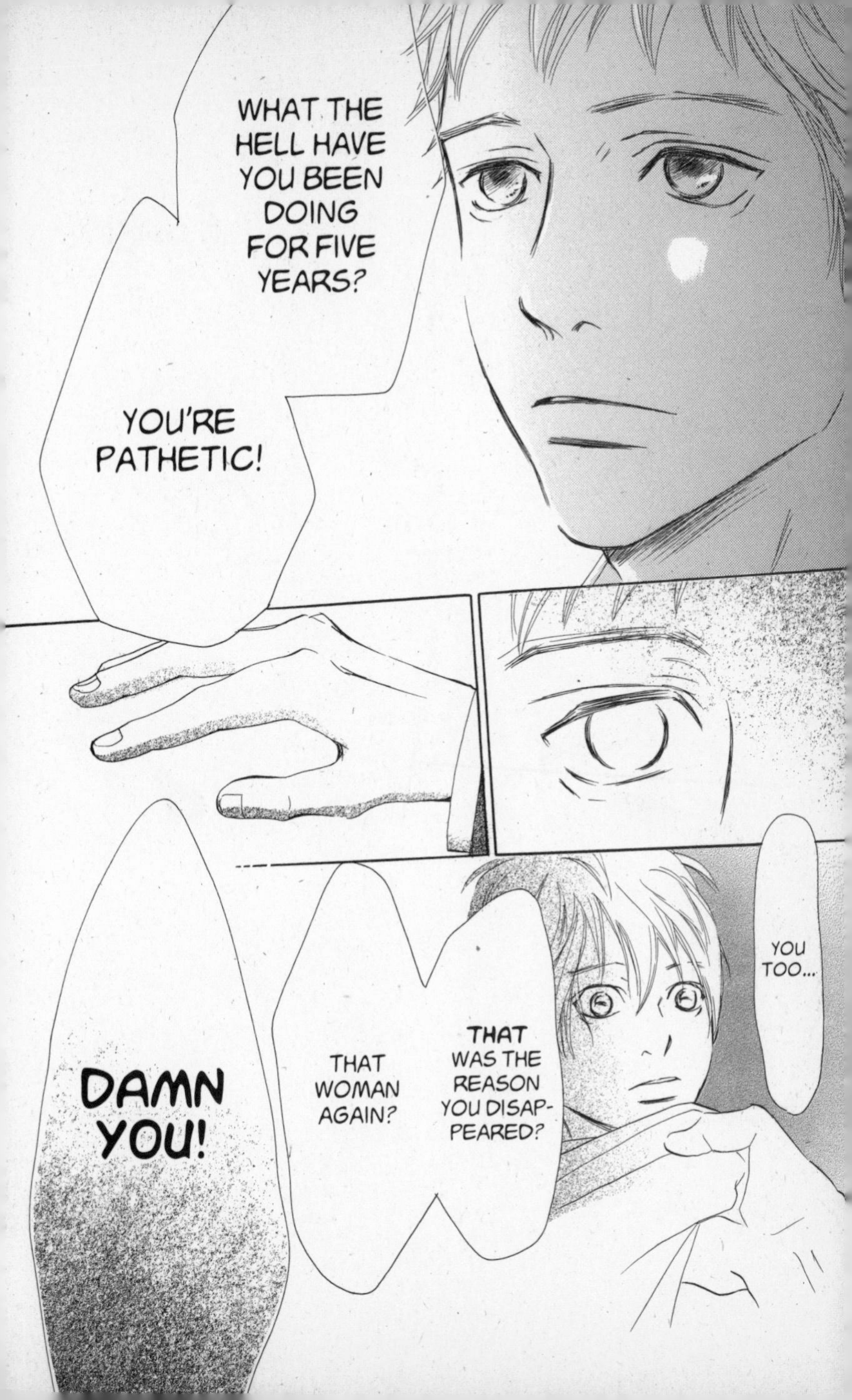
WHAT THE HELL HAVE YOU BEEN DOING FOR FIVE YEARS?
YOU'RE PATHETIC!
YOU TOO...
THAT WAS THE REASON YOU DISAPPEARED?
THAT WOMAN AGAIN?
DAMN YOU!

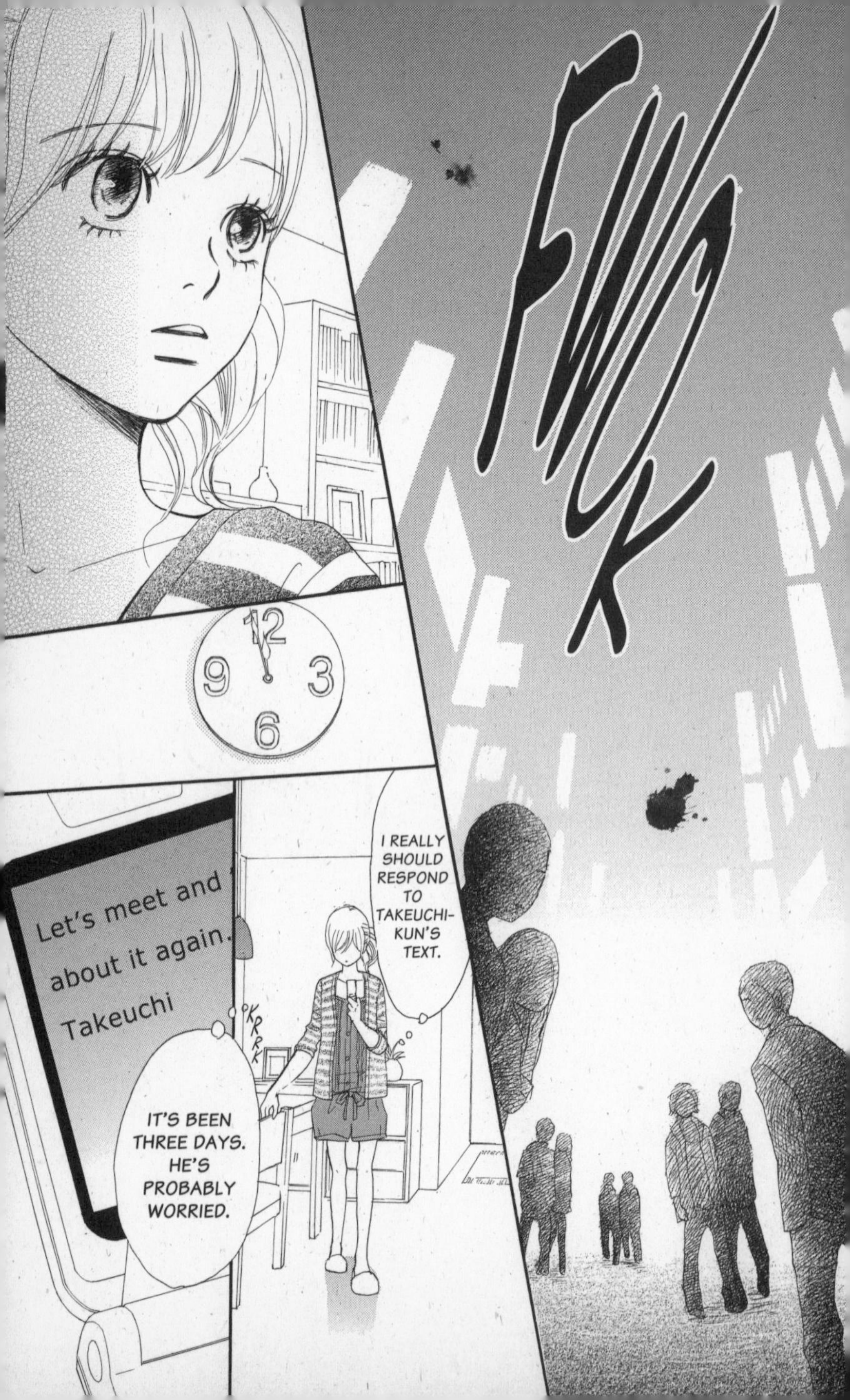

I REALLY SHOULD RESPOND TO TAKEUCHI-KUN'S TEXT.
Let's meet and
about it again.
Takeuchi
KRRK
IT'S BEEN THREE DAYS. HE'S PROBABLY WORRIED.

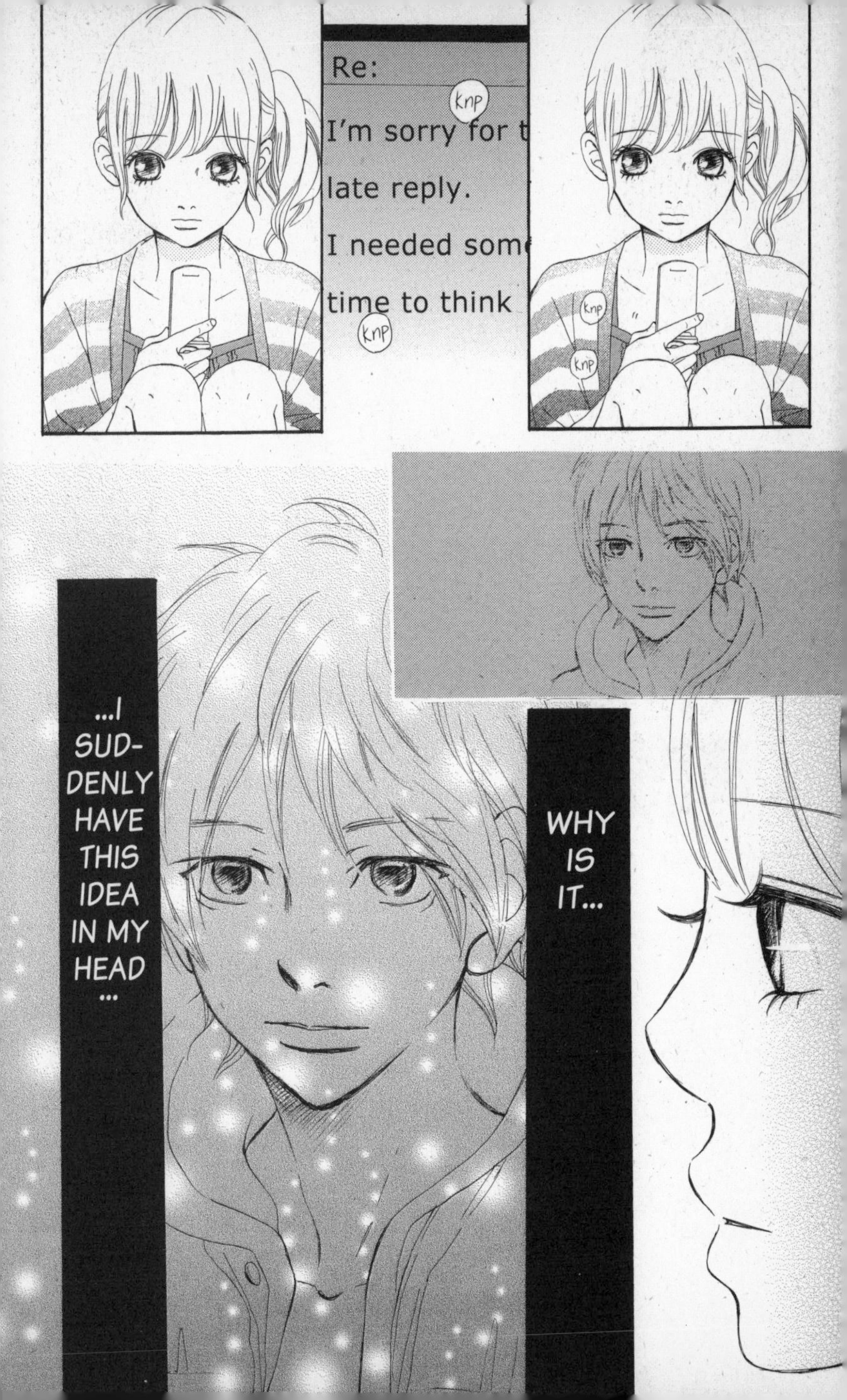
knp
knp
Re:
knp
I'm sorry for t
late reply.
I needed som
time to think
knp
WHY IS IT...
...I SUDDENLY HAVE THIS IDEA IN MY HEAD...

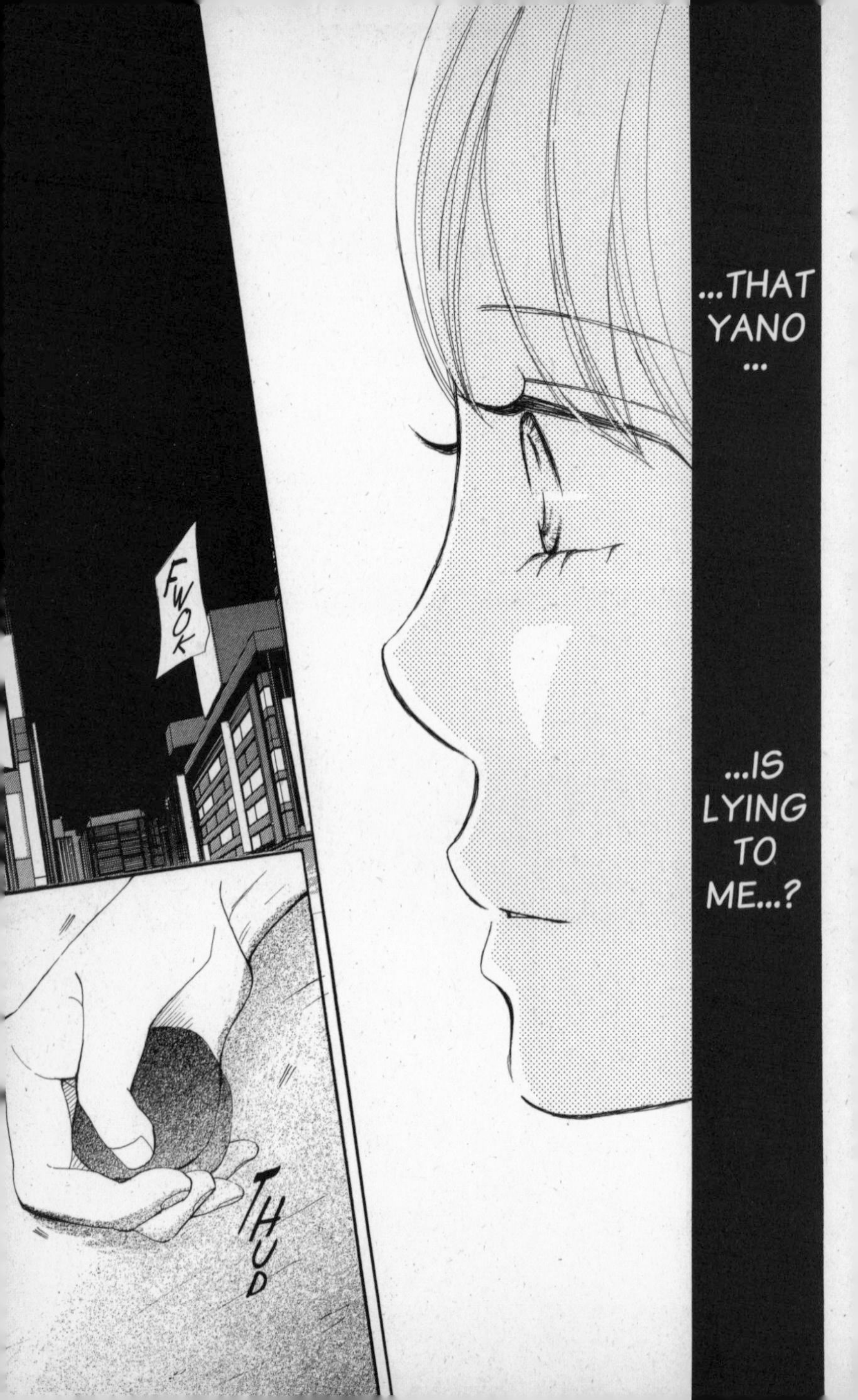
...THAT YANO ...
...IS LYING TO ME...?
FWOK
THUD

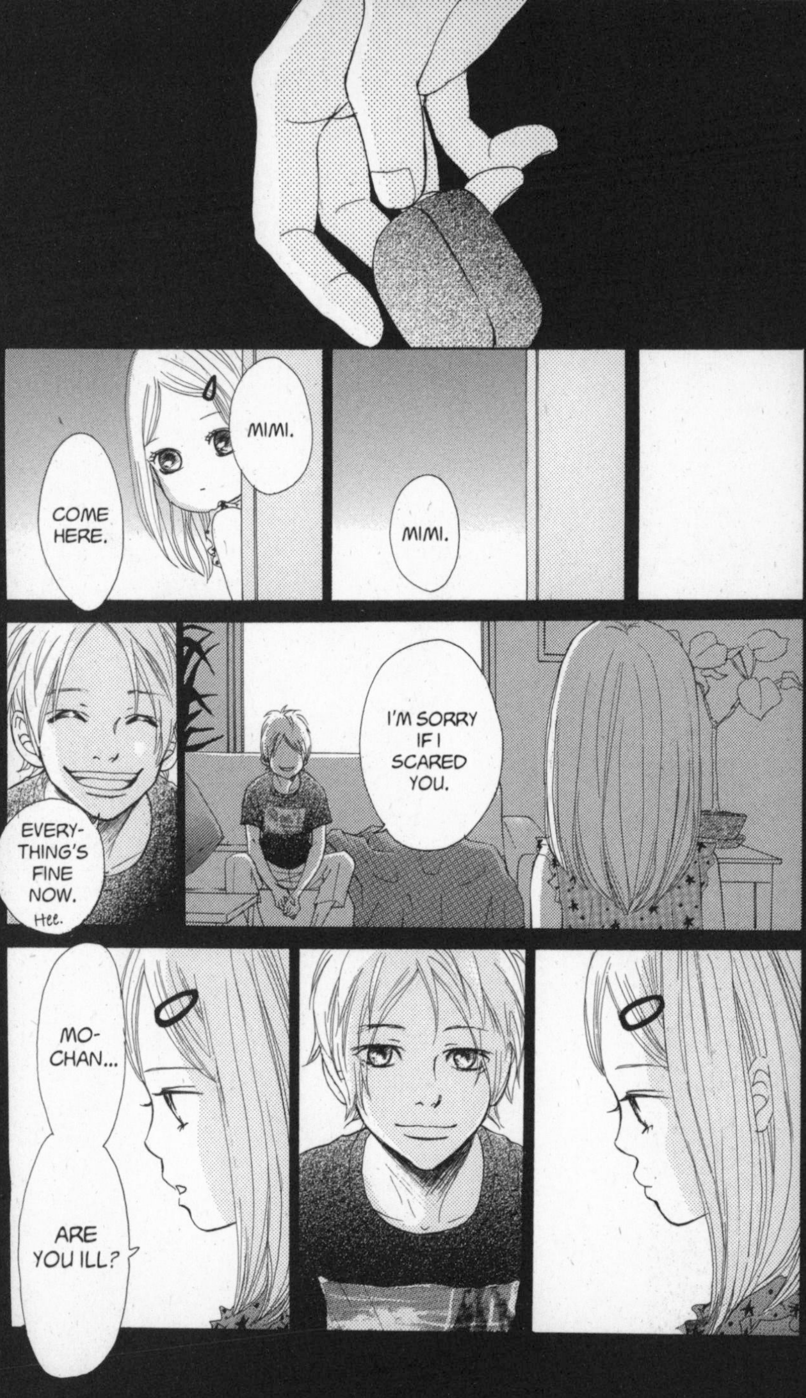
MIMI.
MIMI.
COME HERE.
I'M SORRY IF I SCARED YOU.
EVERYTHING'S FINE NOW.
Hee.
MO-CHAN...
ARE YOU ILL?

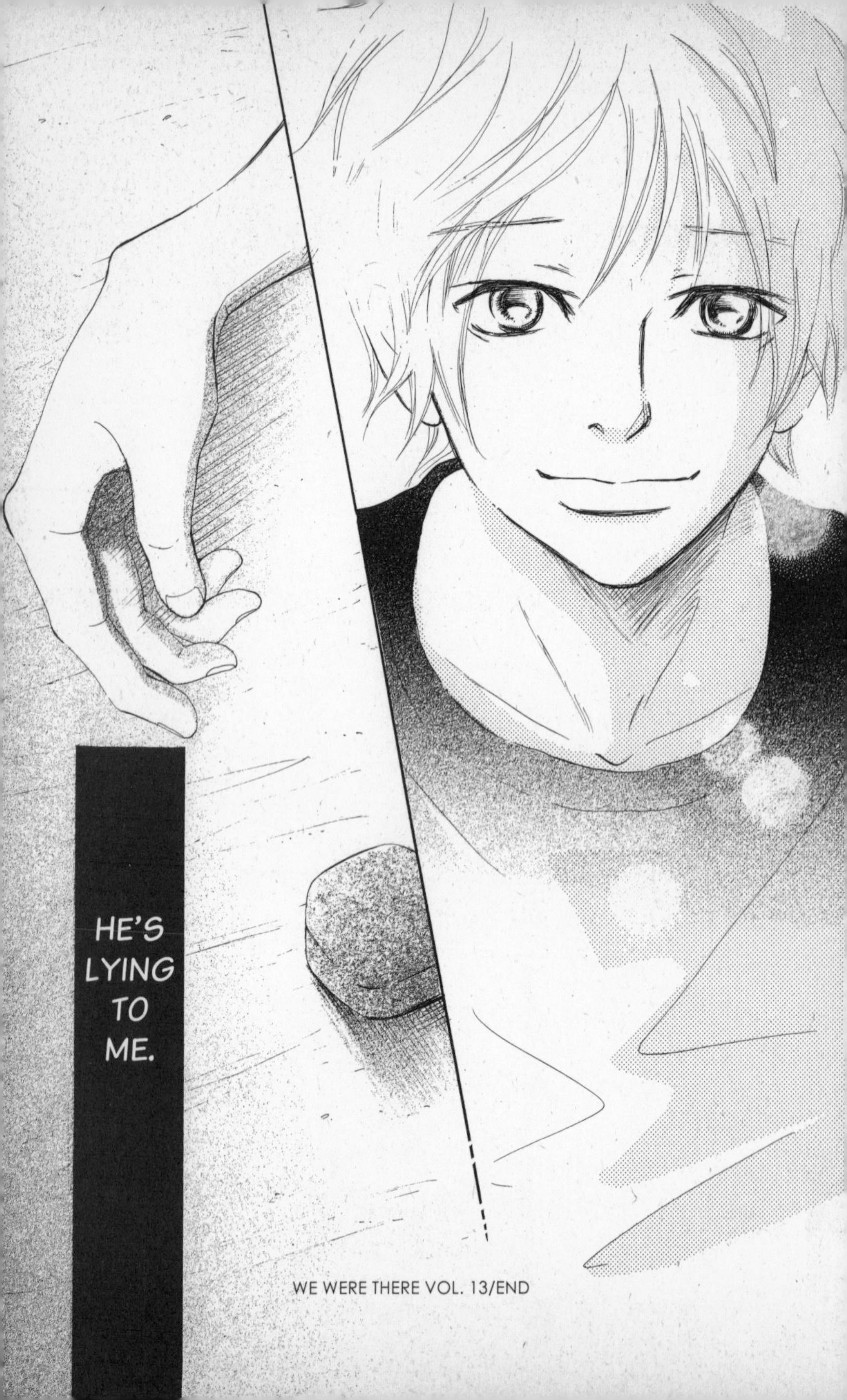
HE'S LYING TO ME.
WE WERE THERE VOL. 13/END

Notes

Honorifics

In Japan, people are usually addressed by their name followed by a suffix.
The suffix shows familiarity or respect, depending on the relationship.

Male (familiar): first or last name + kun
Female (familiar): first or last name + chan
Adult (polite): last name + san
Upperclassman (polite): last name + senpai
Teacher or professional: last name + sensei
Close friends or lovers: first name only, no suffix

Nana-chan vs. Nana-san

Nanami's nickname is "Nana-chan." Yano's ex-girlfriend
was a year older, so she was known as "Nana-san."

Terms

Lovers who are destined to be together are connected by an invisible
"red string of fate" according to Japanese and Chinese folklore.